BEST "NEW" AFRICAN POETS 2021 ANTHOLOGY/ ANTHOLOGIE DES MEILLEURS "NOUVEAUX" POÈTES AFRICAINS 2021/ ANTOLOGIA DOS MELHORES "NOVOS" AFRICANOS 2021

Edited and Compiled by:
Tendai Rinos Mwanaka
Lorna Telma Zita
Balddine Moussa

Mwanaka Media and Publishing Pvt Ltd,
Chitungwiza Zimbabwe
*
Creativity, Wisdom and Beauty

i

Publisher: *Mmap*
Mwanaka Media and Publishing Pvt Ltd
24 Svosve Road, Zengeza 1
Chitungwiza Zimbabwe
mwanaka@yahoo.com
mwanaka13@gmail.com
https://www.mmapublishing.org
www.africanbookscollective.com/publishers/mwanaka-media-and-publishing
https://facebook.com/MwanakaMediaAndPublishing/

Distributed in and outside N. America by African Books Collective
orders@africanbookscollective.com
www.africanbookscollective.com

ISBN: 978-1-77925-583-9
EAN: 9781779255839

© Tendai Rinos Mwanaka 2021

DISCLAIMER
All views expressed in this publication are those of the author and do
not necessarily reflect the views of *Mmap*.

Table of Contents

iii

v

About editors

Tendai Rinos Mwanaka is a Zimbabwean publisher, editor, mentor, thinker, literary artist, visual artist and musical artist with 21 individual books and 23 curated and edited anthologies published. He writes in English and Shona. His artwork has been nominated, shortlisted and won several prizes, and have also appeared in over 400 journals and anthologies from over 30 countries. He has translated 2 books into Shona and his poetry collection *Logbook Written by a Drifter* has been translated and published into Serbian, Albanian, Arabic and Spanish and his poetry pieces have also been translated and published into Shona, Serbian, Spanish, Arabic, Bengali, Tamil, Macedonian, Albanian, Hungarian, Russian, Romanian, French and German. His artwork has been exhibited in Sweden *Arna Gallery*, South Africa *Alice Gallery* and Canada by *Vancouver Book Art Exhibition*. He is currently working on two musical works, one album is composed of Mbira, Keyboards and lyrics and another album is composed of Marimba, Keyboards and Poetry which he hopes to release soon.

Balddine Moussa est un poète et artiste né dans les iles Comores. Actuellement éditeur des poèmes d'expression française dans BNAP, il a d'abord participé a l'édition 2018, 2019, 2020, ainsi que dans une anthologie intitulé « Les Cadavres de l'unité » 2019.

Lorna Zita também conhecida como BlackMelanin é orgulhosamente negra, é poeta e Slamer residente em Moçambique. Seus textos são uma verdadeira afronta para a classe opressora, luta contra injustiças e nos seus poemas procura dar voz ao que não conseguem ser ouvidos. Foi terceira classificada da primeira edição do Moz-Slam (campeonato de poesia falada). Foi campeã da quinta edição e vice-campeã do Slam Delas realizado em são Paulo em Brasil Foi campeã da 22 edição do Slam Pé Vermelho realizado em Maringá no interior de Paraná. É actual revisora e editora do Best New African Poets uma antologia destinada a poetas e escritores do continente africano.

Contributors' Bio Notes

Iloke, Chukwuemeka hails from Okaleru Umuezekoha, Ezza North, Ebonyi State, Nigeria. He attended Ebonyi State University and The University of Nigeria, Nsukka for his first and postgraduate degrees respectively. Mr Iloke has been published in several local and international anthologies including: *Best New African Poets: 2019 Anthology, For Ikeogu: For Poetry*, Peace and Love Inkers Poetry Society Anthology, Break The Silence: An Anthology of Poems Against Domestic Violence Vol.2, Quintessence: Aspects of the Soul;
and Rhythms in Honour of Gerry Agada among others. Mr Iloke is also a recipient of numerous poetry awards.

    Uche Uwadinachi is a broadcast journalist and spoken word poet, the author of poetry collection "SCAR in the HEART of pain" and " Songs to a Flowerbird". His poems has earned the 1st Prize winner at the ANA Poetry- LAPOFEST- 2006, 2nd Prize Poetry Ken Saro-Wiwa Winner USA- 2010, 2nd runner-up National Poetry Slam Winner Abuja – 2012, 1st prize Winner (March) of Poetry African Street Writer – 2013, Spoken word Poet of the Year Nigerian Writers Award – 2016, and in his journalism works, he has been recognized as the Humanitarian Reporter of the Year 2018 (For Peace and Conflict Resolution).

    Abu Bakarr Kamara (De Sierra Phoenix) hails from Kambia, Northern Region of Sierra Leone, where he spent his early childhood days and later moved to Freetown to pursue his academic studies in Physics and Mathematics at Fourah Bay College, University of Sierra Leone. Despite his pursuits in the pure sciences, his passion and commitment towards writing and raising a voice over the ills of society earned him a seat in the world of poetry. He is more of a satiric poet, a freelance writer, a story and song writer; who contributes regularly to various online weekly and monthly publications.

    Olaiya Alfred is an English and literary studies Student in Federal University,Oye, Nigeria. An avid reader, enthusiastic lover of African literature, a simple poet and gentle lad.

Amani Nsemwa is a farmer, a lazy one. Nevertheless, he likes making love as much as he does like coffee, the lords haven't yet blessed him with a kid nor a wife. It all started ten years back with letters to beautiful chicks at numerous schools, then to poetry, when there was no one to write to. He's tricked by good romance, and to a great deal when there's PlayStation. When he isn't reading or holding a smartphone, he's probably listening to the Ladysmith Black Mambazo, watching Coming to America, Playing Scrabble or dreaming of Keri Hilson. You can connect with him on Instagram @papaamojamoja.

Andile Nayika also known as Ecalpar is a 33-year old poet born and raised in Makhanda, in South Africa. The humble young creative has been writing for about two decades. He was actively involved in the formation of a number of poetry collectives in his hometown like Poetic Tuesdays, Writers' Movement and the Cycle of Knowledge. He is published in the New Coin, Badilisha Poetry Exchange and Ons Klyntji to name a few. He published his debut offering Akuwe The Poetry Collection in 2019. Andile has also written for media outlets such as Mail & Guardian and News24 as a reporter.

Jonas Zaithwa Chisi is a poet and English teacher. He writes on various topics such as love, politics, nature and absurdity of life. His other works have appeared in BNAP 19, Malawi News, Journal of African Youth Literature and Scribble Publications.

Gonapragasen Kathan Naicker AKA Danny says, "As a poet I am also exposed to the truth with no ambiguity. – all truths, even those leading to uncomfortable insights, which may be hard to face. That to me is the ethics of Poetry I am motivated to change my mind set through the power of observation and listening to other perspectives, also by sad and tragic depressing stories. Like people dying because of wars, poverty and disease and religious bigotry and political intrigue. Imagining what it's like to live in these places, plagued by wars, dictatorships and the suppression of freedom, I feel the distress… Knowing that it could have been me. I am determined to bring a more balanced experience of the revelations haunting my deeper inner thoughts through the exposure of the written word. The rate of change in our behaviour is simply not fast enough. We write about things, for which there are consequences that will follow from the things we write and we must not fear the consequences. Which becomes more severe each passing moment. No longer tomorrow, but today. Too much evidence calls for a total mind shift that guide me and will steer the poems I write.

Oscar Gwiriri is a Certified Forensic Investigations Professional (CFIP) who also holds a *Master of Science Degree in Strategic Management, Bachelor of Business Administration, Associate of Arts in Business Administration Degree, Diploma in Logistics and Transport (CILT, UK)* and a *Diploma in Workplace Safety and Health,* as well as other ten certificates in the fraternity of United Nations Peacekeeping. He was born on 15 June 1975 at Gwiriri Village, Chief Mutasa, Zimbabwe. He attended Manunure Primary School (Honde Valley) and Dangamvura High School (Mutare). He has more than 35 publications both in English and Shona languages. Oscar is both a creative writer and an academic. He was nominated twice in the National Arts Merits Awards (2019) categories for his books *Hatiponi* and *Chitima nditakure.* Oscar is contactable on email: oscar.gwiriri@gmail.com

Priscilla Arthur born by the shores of Tema and bread near a little tent is a budding Ghanaian writer and Haijin. Her literary works have appeared in Mamba; Journal of Africa Haiku Network, Haiku Universe, Wales Haiku Journal, South Wales evening post and elsewhere. She loves to bring to light what cannot be seen in mere sunshine. If she's not found swinging the tennis racket, or reading, she's carving words on a bone. Her works are forthcoming in the Ghana Poetry Festival Anthology and Ghana Writes International Poetry Anthology.

Nkaimbi Wan N'tieh is a Cameroonian political analyst agitating for the freedom and emancipation of the peoples of the former Southern Cameroons. When he is not busy adding flesh to his soon to be completed long story entitled 'Angry Nation', he roams the street with his camera and immortalizes the plight of his people in a country governed by geruntocrats.

My name is **Mohau Mohlope**, I am a 31 years old man. I reside in Ikageng (ext7), Potchefstroom, in the North West province of South Africa. I started my education in Boitirelo primary school and later went to Botoka Comprehensive School. My interests have to do with art and serving disadvantaged communities. I have found a way to express myself and project my thoughts through poetry and other different outlets of art.

Xolile Mabuza is a 24-year-old spoken word artist, cricket commentator and a designer from Msogwaba, a village outside Mbombela in South Africa. She started writing poetry at the age of 17 and she has not looked back. She writes mostly about things she couldn't talk about: the pain, the lessons and experiences that have brought her to where she is today. Xolile began speaking when she started performing and that is how she found her voice after so many years of been quiet. She has been profiled on different radio stations and newspapers, Xolile is an International Poet, she has performed on different stages around the world including Maseru and Morija art centre in Lesotho, 2019 Story-Fest in Sydney, Australia, Red Dirt Poetry Festival, Perth Poetry Festival, Satmas Awards Nominee Announcement and more. She has her short stories published with Naane Le Moya (where she was a resident writer). Xolile host poetry sessions and book readings in her city/village because she believes that words hold space and healing, she believes that there's always a way to write black people and their magic back to life.

Gideon Sagbo is a Nigerian student of the department of English and Literary Studies, Federal University Oye-Ekiti, Nigeria. He is a poet, prose-writer and essayist. His works are greatly inspired by happenings in the society and the burning zest for portraying the realities of life. His hobbies are, writing, drawing and singing along to good music.

Archie Swanson's first published poem appeared in 1973 in *English Alive,* an annual anthology of South African High School creative writing. The poem was also included in the 20 and 50-year *English Alive* commemorative anthologies. Poems have been published in Stanzas, *New Contrast,* the *Best New African Poetry Anthologies* (2015-2020), *Experimental Writing: Africa vs Latin America* (2017), *Vol. 1&2 of Africa vs North America* (2018; 2019) and *Writing Robotics: Africa vs Asia Vol 2* (2020). Two poems, translated into

Japanese, were included in *Experimental Writing: Africa vs Asia* (2018) and a poem was included in the anthology, *Love Notes Volume 1* (2021). Translated into Spanish by poet López-Vega, poems were published in the Spanish National Newspaper, *El Mundo* and Bolivian newspaper *Correo Del Sur* (2016). In 2017 his poems were listed for the Sol Plaatje Award and the UK Bridport Prize. His poetry has been included in the *Patricia Schonstein curated anthologies, Absolute Africa!* (2018), *Naturally Africa!* (2020) and the *McGregor Anthologies* (2014-2020). His poem 'déjà vu' was the inspiration for Grant McLachlan's composition for clarinet, violin, and piano, *from the direction it should depart*, performed at the Baxter Concert Hall (2019). He also wrote the words (translated into isiXhosa by Lungile Jacobs Ka-Nyamezela) for a choral piece composed by Grant McLachlan and entitled *Intombazana*, commissioned Margie Barry and the Herschel Chorale to be performed at the 2020 World Choir Games. Poems, translated into Spanish, were published in the South American literary journal *Libero America* (2020) and 'Afourer' was selected for *Clemengold Poetry Writing* (2020). His poem, 'my Guernica' placed second in the AVBOB Poetry Competition (English/2019). He has been a regular guest poet at Off the Wall Poetry, the Cape Town Central Library Poetry Circle, the McGregor Poetry Festival, and the Prince Albert Lees Fees. He has previously published two collections of poems — *the stretching of my sky* (2018) and *the shores of years* (2019). Archie serves on the Board of the SA Literary Journal which publishes *New Contrast*. www.instagram.com/poetarchie

Susan Gamuchirai Muchirahondo is a 23 year old, female writer who's been writing for over a decade since she discovered writing at eleven years old. Absolutely crazy about the arts and looking forward to expanding in the community. Published in the 2018 and 2019 BNAP anthologies and self published a short novel on Wattpad.

Jennifer Chinenye Obidinma is a playwright, poet and teacher. She teaches Diction – In – English and Spelling. She is an ambassador of *Teachers' Naija Reality TV Show Season 2* (a Teachers Reality Show in Nigeria). She is a graduate of English and Literary Studies, University of Nigeria, Nsukka, Enugu State. She is

Better Than Starbucks Vol. 3 Issue 3 (USA, 2018), *Tribute to Penny* (Zimbabwe, 2018) *Mupakwa weRwendo* (Zimbabwe, 2018)....

Fayssal Chafaki, also known as the Poet of the Kingdom of Morocco and the Great Sa'lok, is best described by his humble expression "I am a mere farmer, poet, and writer. His poems are composed in four main languages, Arabic, English, Spanish, and Russian, where each poetic composition is an independent entity, per se. English, Spanish, and Russian poems are by no means a translation of the Arabic ones. The poet gives each different culture a just share of the same poetic creativity. Fayssal Chafaki is a modern Arab poet who still keeps faithful to the Old Poetic Classical Line.

EGWUMA DEBORAH OJOCHENEMI, I am a graduate of Accounting from Kogi State University Anyigba,in 2012, proceeded for my professional program with the Association of National Accountants Of Nigeria (ANAN),in 2014. A young , vibrant lady with potentials.I am also a poet, spoken words artist,an MC, event planner and a brand Influencer

Glamour Adah is student of Covenant University, studying Mass Communication. She is a young poet, an aspiring author, screenwriter and film director. She is a talented poet and aspiring prose writer. She believes writing is an art and a voice. She writes because it has always been a part of her and is one of the few ways she enjoy airing my views. "Writing is my voice. I hope to be one of the best writers of my generation."

Adjei Agyei-Baah is a lecturer, translator, editor and a doctoral student at the University of Waikato, New Zealand. He is the co-founder of Africa Haiku Network, Poetry Foundation and *The Mamba*, Africa's first international haiku journal. Adjei is a worldwide-anthologized poet and winner of several international awards. His maiden haiku collection *Afriku* published by Red Moon Press (2016) has been commended by Professor Wole Soyinka, Africa's first Nobel Prize Literature laureate. His other poetry collections include *Ghana, 21 Haiku (2018)*, *Piece of My Fart (2018) and Finding The Other Door (2021).*

Musa mukelwa simelane is a swazi born poet, Born and raised on the Dusty streets of kashewula. He is a swazi but currently based in south Africa. He fell in love with words at a tender age (13) where he could write Letters with no meaning, later his life took a toil, where he became A street kid, where he spends most of his time writing poem's under dead bridge, The streets nurtured him into the poet he is today. With the grace of God, He went back to school and completed his high school, where the love of literature was fueled. Musa known by his stage name MUMU DA POET who is a versatile poet, he writes therapeutic poems, Most of his poems are love poems, he believes that if every one of us could drop a cube of love everyday onto anyone the world would-be better. He is an award winner from (apapa) best musical poet, he also holds an award from kwandebele poetry awards(kpa) best poet. He has many international features into anthologies, and national features. He has a Book entitled "tears of a broken wind". He had performed locally and internationally, winning prizes and awards. most of his poems are found on Google, from a variety of platforms. he weaves words with wisdom, currently he had the Nobel prize, and has a feature of poetry from a locally book which tackles the issues of corona, as one of top ten. he is a phenomenal poet, who paint pictures with words.

I , **Jabulani Mzinyathi** am a former teacher, former magistrate and currently a legal practitioner. I am a poet in particular and a writer in general. I have three published poetry collections namely: Under The Steel Yoke, Righteous Indignation and In The Steel Talons. My debut ChiShona novel Mumambure was recently accepted for publication. I am polishing a poetry collection entitled Along The Way and a novella and other short stories entitled Derailed And Other Stories. I am an avid reader, art enthusiast and deeply in love with reggae music especially from the late triumvirate- Peter Tosh, Bob Marley and Bunny Wailer.

Kirsten Miller is the author of four novels: *All is Fish* (Jacana 2007), shortlisted for the Jacana/EU Literary Award, *Sister Moon* (Umuzi 2014), *The Hum of the Sun* (Kwela 2018), which won the Wilbur and Niso Smith Foundation's Prize for Best Unpublished Manuscript, was long-listed for the Dublin Literary Award and translated into German under the title *Hörst du, wie der Himmel singt?* (Baobab Books) in 2021. Her non-fiction book, *Children on the Bridge* (Jacana 2006), about her early experiences working in the field of autism, was long-listed for the Alan Paton/Sunday Times Award. She lives in Durban, South Africa.

Lubabalo Tatase: I am final year Bachelor of Arts student, majoring in African Languages: IsiXhosa and Industrial Organisational Psychology. I am a BNAP poet published in 2019, my poems are; GQALANI UKWENZA KWENU MZ' ONTSUNDU, NDINQWENELA UKUBA YIMBONGI, NDITHUNYWA NGUMOYA. I write poetry, essays and short stories. I believe that readers are leaders. As an African Languages student at Rhodes University I learn under the guide of Professor Ncedile Saule who is not only a great custodian of IsiXhosa literature but a great teacher too, my teacher.

Musa B Jibril alias Aboo Hanifa is a graduate of Bayero University, Kano Nigeria. He obtained his Bachelor's degree in Geography in 2019. He lives in Kaduna State, Nigeria. You can get him on musabjibril18@gmail.com

Wilson Tinotenda Waison is a the author of Murder Me, poet from Chitungwiza, Zimbabwe. A human rights advocate, prose passage writer. Also a brave voice, the Chitungwiza poetry consul of Poets of the World a global platform based on contemporary writings poetasdelmundo.com Waison is the content curator of Deem.lit.org, interviewer of the Contemporary Poetry Online magazine as well as the editor of Whitepages Concept . He is currently doing Journalism at Harare polytechnic.
https://deemliteratureorganisation.wordpress.com

Jide Ajidahun is Professor of Comparative Literature, Department of English Studies, Adekunle Ajasin University, Akungba Akoko, Ondo State, Nigeria. Research Interests: Dramatic Literature, Comparative Literature and Creative Writing

Onoruoiza Mark ONUCHI is a creative wingman, wordsmith and poet with offerings across a wide array of anthologies. He is a Corporate Communications Consultant. He wrote the foreword to the highly acclaimed collection of poems titled 'Oracle' (AuthorHouse) by Dayo Ibitayo Phillips. He has his poetic offerings in 'Crossroads' (an anthology of poems in honour of Christopher Okigbo – 1932 – 1967). He has his elegies in 'Wreaths for a Wayfarer' an anthology of Poems (Daraja Press) in Honour of Pius Adesanmi Edited by Nduka Otiono & Uchechukwu Umezurike. He's also been featured in the Guardian and Thisday newspapers in Nigeria.

Mohammed U. Yusuf is a poet, writer and lover of real human stories who lives and writes from somewhere in Nigeria. His works have appeared or are forthcoming in *RoseyRavelston Books, Lunaris Review, Salamander Ink, Olongo Africa Journal, Literary Garland, The Shallow Tales Review and elsewhere*. He is a big fan of radio dramas and can be reached as @umypaper on Instagram.

Adiela Akoo is an award winning South African poet and author. She has been published in a range of anthologies including Best of Africa, Best Emerging Poets of 2019, The Penmen Review, Fidelities, etc. She was nominated as one of the Top 7 'Most Promising Literary Influencers' in the GBCAwards 2020, is a recipient of the prestigious DUX Award, a recipient of The Silver Star Award from the Global Literary Society for her 'excellent contribution to world literature', among others. Lost in a Quatrain is her soul stirring debut collection of relatable, inspiring and thought provoking poetry on a journey to becoming, a journey of hope and healing.

Dennis Brad Kunguru is a graduate of Makerere University and currently teaching English at Shah Lalji Nangpar Academy in Kenya. His passion for writing began during his studies in Uganda and he has never looked back ever since. He is also a part time actor and a script writer.

Obinna Chilekezi lives in Lagos Nigeria and is an insurance practitioner with background in librarianship. His poems and stories have appeared in newspapers, journals and anthologies. His published collections of poems are Songs of a stranger at the smiling coast (Kraft Books) and Calligramme (Emotion Books). One of his insurance textbook won the African Insurance Organisation Book Award in 2016. He has travelled intensively in his West African sub-region and dreams of travelling too to other parts of the world.

Dr Clement Chukwuka Idegwu lectures at the Department of Languages University of Delta , Agbor, Delta State, Nigeria. He is from Alihame in Ika South Local Government Area of Delta State. He is a season writer, a novelists, poet and scholar. He is published in international and national journals such as Criterion and Asian Academic Research Journal of Social Sciences and Humanities. *The Worst Devil on Stage and Other Stories* (1997) is his first published text. His other published work include *The Procrustean Creed and Other Poems* (1999), *Broken Dreams* (2000), *Lilies That Fester* (2000), *A Guide to Effective Essay and Letter Writing* (2001), *Just for Love* (2002), *The Vale of Tears and Other Stories* (2003), *Writing for Special Purpose* (2004), *My Precious Jewel and Other Stories,* (2009), *Mooning Our World* (2012), *Right to be Angry* (2016) and *Bath of Blood and Other Stories* (2017). He has been published in Five Hundred Nigerian Poets, volume one, edited by Jerry Agada. "Life is a Tempest" will soon be published.

Wisdom C. Nwoga is a dramatist and poet from Delta State, Nigeria. He also teaches English language and literature. His writing focuses on Futility of existence, political disillusionment and moments that have really moved him. He sees creative writing as tool for social change.

Dr T. O. Adesanmi lectures in the Department of English, Adeyemi College of Education Ondo, Ondo State Nigeria. His interest and researches focus on Applied Linguistics, Discourse Analysis, and Anthropological Linguistics. He is also a social commentator and motivational speaker. He has published articles and attended conferences within and outside Nigeria particularly US, UK, Lesotho, South Africa, and Germany. Much as he has no aversion for feminism and womanism, he is ideologically humanistic in most of his contributions.

RANDHEER PRITHIRAJ: I am a young, motivated and enthusiastic individual with a flair for poetry. I am 23 years old and an educator by profession. I have taken up poetry as a hobby, of recent, which has awakened my creativeness. I have a burning desire and passion for teaching and enriching the minds of the younger generation. I am proudly South African and live in the city of Durban. Purposeful in the pursuit of inspiring many individuals using poetry as a medium of expression and conveyance of deep

Dr Deena Padayachee is a medical doctor, a graduate of Natal university, who is the recipient of the Olive Schreiner and Nadine Gordimer prizes for prose. Some of his oeuvre has been translated into Xhosa, Zulu, Tamil, Hindi and Italian. His poems have been published in Australia, the United Kingdom, the USA, India and South Africa.

Sithembele Isaac Xhegwana was born on the 22nd of May 1972 at Grey Hospital in King William's town. He is qualified with a BSocSc (HONS) in sociology from the University of Cape Town and also a Master of Arts degree in Creative Writing from the same university. Through funding from the NRF Chair he is presently registered for a PhD degree in sociology (based at the Centre for Critical Studies in Sexuality and Reproduction) at Rhodes University. Between 2018 and 2019, through funding from the South African Reserve Bank Centre for Economic Journalism, he was registered for a Master of Arts degree in Journalism & Media Studies at Rhodes University. Land of Thorns (2021) is his third book. His debut novel, The Faint-Hearted Man was published by Buchu Books in 1991. His second book, Scatter the Shrilling Bones was published by Lovedale Press in 2003. He has also contributed to anthologies like the Sol Plaatjie Anthology of Poetry.

You will find **Zongezile Matshoba** in your township or village or school or town hall or open ground, and wherever there is a literary event for the young and old. His writings narrate the humour and hardships of township and rural life, and interrogates whether it is yet uhuru in people's livelihood. Matshoba writes in isiXhosa and English, and has published two books, *Izinto Zehlabathi* and *Intlambo Yokufel'amahashe*. He also produced a short wildlife film titled *2nd Life Thoughts* with the Wildlife Film Academy. He has written, produced and directed stage plays for the Border Youth Dance Theatre. His works have appeared in several journals and anthologies.

The poet, **Ogunleye Gbemisola** is a sixteen year old Nigerian poet who has just recently completed her secondary education. She graduated from Nigerian Navy Secondary School Okura, kogi state, Nigeria. She loves to read, write and learn new things everyday.

Joseph Daniel Sukali is a Mzuzu University graduate with multiple publications to his name. He is the author of *Dealing with a Heartbreak: Therapy for the Broken* and has co-authored a love poetry anthology, *Whispers of Beating Hearts*. Sukali has managed to get his works published in *Best "New" African Poets 2020 Anthology* and *An Anthology of African and Eastern European Languages*. The author is also a columnist and editor of a number of magazines including; Love Feast Magazine, Malawi Talents Magazine and Writers Global Movement just to mention a few. The 27 years old is an award winning spoken word poet with two albums to his name that's far.

Yugo Gabriel Egboluche is a Nigerian born multidisciplinary writer. His writing covers genres such as script-writing, copy-writing, fiction, and poetry. His poems have appeared in chapbooks and webzines including, The Kalahari Review, Praxis Magazine Online and Words, Rhyme & Rhythm. In 2017 and 2019 his poems featured in the 'Best New African Poets Anthology' and the 'Universal Oneness Anthology' respectively. He has his short stories published in: 'Experimental Writing, Africa vs Latin American Anthology' (2015) and 'Africa, UK, and Ireland: Writing Politics and Knowledge Production (2018). His debut poetry collection is set to be available in the spring of 2022.

Mohamed Fuad Kamara, known to most as Prince Hamlet, is a student of Public Administration and Management, a radio poetry show presenter, a stage poet. He was born in Mange Bureh and grew up in Port Loko, Northwest of Sierra Leone. He attended Bureh Catholic Secondary School in Mange Bureh, and Bullom Ahmadiyya Secondary School in Lungi respectively. He holds a Higher Teacher's Certificate (HTC) Secondary from Milton Margai Technical University, Sierra Leone. Fuad is a hungry writer with a deep soulful wording carrying the burden of societal vices.

Godwin Gabla is a published author and critically acclaimed poet cum copywriter with over 7 years of experience in storytelling and poetry. He has published more than 100 poems, over 3,000 articles, numerous short stories and a novel. He's the author of Doom's Dawn, a contributor to BNAP 2017 and a finalist at

Ghana Writers Award 2017. In 2018, He became the first Ghanaian to be published in Writers Space Africa's monthly journal.

Hopewell Amana is a Nigerian poet and writer. He is the co-founder of Hikmah House, a platform committed to literary excellence. Some of his works have appeared or are forthcoming in WRR, Verse-Virtual Journal, ANA Journal, Ofi Press and Shallow Tales Review. He is currently working on his debut collection of poems, *Broken Psalms* and a chapbook on romance poetry, *A Stir in a Vanilla Twilight*.

Precious Ifeoma Benjamin is a poet and novelist. She is a native of Eziobodo in Imo state, Nigeria. She went to Liberty college in Akwa Ibom State Nigeria, 2014-2017. A student of English language and Literature of Nnamdi Azikiwe University. She has worked as a secretary of God's Delight Company and also as an English and Literature teacher in Livingshore Secondary School. Ifeoma is one of the contributors of BNAP 2020. She is the writer of *Momma's Care, Power misuse* and *So is life*.

Lind Grant-Oyeye is an award winning poet of African descent, with work published in several literary magazines and anthologies.

Valentine Okolo is a poet, a filmmaker, a social activist and a spoken word artist. He is the author of the poetry book *I Will Be Silent* and the studio album *I Will Be Silent: Spoken Words*. His poetry has been published internationally in various literary magazines, including *Apogee Journal, Origins Journal, Shot Glass Journal, African Writer and Best New African Poets 2018 Anthology*. His work was also featured in a community based pandemic poem, along with the lines of 220 other poets, selected from sixteen countries from across the globe. This community poem was published by Muse-Pie Press, a literary establishment based in the United States, which has been publishing award-winning poetry since 1980. For his poetry and for his activism, he has been interviewed by the social advocate network T & Tie, Summation52, RaveTV and others.

Mr. Yemi Orasakin was born in Ilode quarters, in Ile-Ife, the Cradle of Yoruba race fifty-nine years ago. He attended University of Ife now Obafemi Awolowo University where he started his Education with B.A. Education in English Language and graduated in 1985. He later graduated in Masters in Public Administration and Literature in English respectively. He is currently a Principal in one of the Secondary Schools in Ile-Ife, Osun State, Nigeria. He is the Author of many poems which includes "New Generation Africa Poems, 'published in 2011, Ile-Ife, The Cradle of Civilization and other poems in 2012. The new poem, title "Societal Issue, Feminism and other poems is one of the fascinating poems that project the poet as a poet of all seasons. He is among the renowned poet in Africa and the commonwealth countries of the world. He is married with children.

Né un septembre à Porto-Novo (République du Bénin) d'une commerçante et d'un journaliste, **Sadlay Fiat-lux Hounyeme**, pour son amour de la langue anglaise a poursuivi ses études en littérature anglaise à l'Université où il se spécialise en Etudes Américaine. Brillant qu'il fut au cours de son parcours universitaire, il essayera de toucher à tout ce qui réclame de l'esthétique, à commencer par la peinture, avec un goût prononcé pour la musique et enfin la littérature. Sadlay empoigne la plume pour s'ériger en voix des sans-voix. Il s'y est bien tenu que les Prix n'ont pas tardé à le distinguer. En 2018, sa nouvelle La dame à Toyota qui constitue le fond de son premier roman reçoit le prix AfroYougAdult de Goethe Institut. En 2019, il reçoit successivement le Prix de l'écrivain en Herbe (PEH), le Prix des éditions Mémoire Héritage.

Arnold Mondo Kobi est un poète né en 1992 dans la ville de Kinshasa, capitale de la République Démocratique, d'une grande famille de 8 enfants dont 5 garçons et 3 filles. Il est donc le 5e de la famille, Fils de Monsieur Mukulu Mondo Roger et Madame Kazimbusa Kiulu Wivine. Il est licencié en Relations Internationales, à l'Université de Kinshasa.

Akpao Gninwo Armel est un poète béninois âge de 27ans. Il est technicien supérieur de laboratoire en service au centre de santé de N'dali République du Bénin.

Sanogo Ousmane est un jeune passionné de l'art sous toutes ses formes. Et il aimerait faire connaître ses textes au monde.

Diafouka Mabiala Presneil Aimerith est né le 27 juillet 1995 à Dolisie au Congo-Brazzaville, il étudie actuellement le droit des affaires à l'Université Catholique d'Afrique centrale de Yaoundé. Il écrit pour appeler le monde pour qu'il revienne au monde. Son essai sur : « De l'amour et de la Sagesse » extrait dans lequel est tiré ses kyrielles de poèmes est un appel pour revenir à nos vraies valeurs, à se connaître soi-même, à rechercher sa propre vérité, car la plus belle découverte du monde est celle que l'on fait sur soi-même pense-t-il. En effet, beaucoup de personnes n'arrivent pas à avancer dans la vie parce qu'elles ne savent pas qui elles sont réellement raison pour laquelle on doit toujours se poser la question de savoir : Qui sommes-nous ? Quelle est notre mission ici sur terre ? Une fois que nous arrivons à répondre à ces questions, nous pouvons alors vivre une vie sans complexe et en paix avec nous-mêmes et les autres.

Né le 4 mai 1981, à **Engondo, Boundji, CerafinItoua** dit ITOUA L'Okalé fait ses études à école d'Odikango, ses secondaires au CEG Sylvestre Tsamas et au lycée Jacques Opangault de Boundji où il obtient son baccalauréat en 2002. Il est enseignant d'anglais au lycée de la Révolution à Brazzaville, il est auteur de : - L'identification

- Les parasites de l'habitation, toutes deux publiées aux éditions Edilivre.

Il est aussi auteur de plusieurs œuvres encore inédites incluant romans, recueils de poèmes, chroniques et essais.

Née le 28 novembre 1998 à la maternité de Moroni, **NAIDA MOUSSA** est une jeune fille descendant d'une famille cuisinière de père MOUSSA MOHAMED et de mère SITINA TOIBIBOU. A l'âge de 13ans, elle a découvert son amour sur l'écriture. A 16ans, NAIDA MOUSSA a eu une attestation d'une formation d'écriture à l'alliance française de Moroni, qui a était organisé par Riama Moussa. En 2017-2018, elle s'intégrait dans les scènes libres à la CCAC MAVUNA de Moroni. NAIDA MOUSSA est une jeune fille dynamique à travers les différentes activités qu'elle mène dans les sociétés. Orpheline de père mais elle reste toujours sympa, social et ouvert avec les autres personnes par son bon cœur hérité par ces ancêtres. Elle a une bonté exceptionnelle, est optimiste et garde toujours ces bras ouvert pour accueillir les gens et les aider dans les pires et dans les bons moments. Naida MOUSSA une personnalité a part .

Né à Mindouli, dans le département du Pool, en République du Congo, **Alvie MOUZITA** est un écrivain qui évolue dans plusieurs genres littéraires, notamment la poésie à qui il a hâte de restituer les éloges qui lui sont dus, de ce qu'elle luiparaît le genre de prédilection favorable. Suivant les pas de Tchicaya U Tam'si, Léopold Sédar Senghor, Saint-John Perse, la poésie de ce poète congolais évoque plusieurs thématiques dont l'épicentre et l'éloge à la femme souvent émaillé de timbre mélancolique. Sa plume dite *négriplume,* s'attèle aussi à moucharder les tares qui corrodent le commun des mortels.

DJIKOLOUM BIENVENU est licencié en géographie - environnement à l'université de ngaoundéré. Il cherche à s'inscrire au cycle master en géomantique à l'université de Yaoundé 1. Coauteur du recueil de poèmes *" Que tes voisins admirent tes enfants "* paru aux éditions Toumaï en mars 2021, le fils de DINGAONAÏMOU NGANA et de MADENODJI DIMADOUNGAR est le promoteur du recueil de poèmes de l'Afrique d'espoir intitulé : *Afrique lumineuse, Afrique d'espoir* qui est en voie de parution. DJIKOLOUM est né le 26 octobre 1998 à baibokoum au Tchad. Il est de nationalité Tchadienne.

TSOKINI Emmanuelle âgée de 20ans est étudiante en 3e année de licence à l'Université Marien NGOUABI évoluant à la faculté des lettres. Amoureuse de la littérature depuis sa tendre enfance, c'est en 2018 qu'il a mis sur papier sa passion pour la poésie en écrivant son premier poème ! Ses deux poèmes ont été publiés dans l'anthologie « Les mots face aux maux » à l'air de covid 19 organisé par l'éditeur et écrivain Elvez NGABA NSILOU.

ELEMVA Sarai est une Étudiante camerounaise, qui est en licence de traduction, à l'école Normale de Zhejiang en Chine, dans la ville de Jinhua. Passionnée par l'écriture, elle écrit et partage avec ses proches sa plume. Ses poèmes sont publiés pour la première fois dans BNAP édition 2020. Outre le monde des mots, elle est aussi une artiste. Elle a créé et produit quelques tableaux d'art. Amoureuse de la nature et de l'art, elle croit que la spiritualité est le seul moyen de communication avec notre créativité

CHANDRELLE. N. MOUNTOULA est une jeune étudiante en troisième année de Droit à l'université Libre du Congo née en 2002 et amoureuse des lettres. Elle participe à plusieurs concours de poésie dont elle est lauréate deux fois et occupe des places d'honneur.

DJELASSEM Ghislain est né le 07 Mars 1998 à Doba dans la province du Logone oriental (Tchad). Il fit ses études primaires et secondaires à BEBEDJIA où il obtint son baccalauréat A4 en 2018. Nanti d'une licence en *géographie environnement naturel et aménagement du territoir*e à l'université de NGAOUNDERE au Cameroun, il est actuellement en Master 1. DJELASSEM Ghislain est membre actif du club littérature dénommé "Plume de verve" dans la dite université. Il est auteur de quelques tapuscrits en voies de parution.

Précieux GOMA est un poète congolais (Brazzaville) étudiant en 1ère année de philosophie à Yaoundé UCAC. Né en 2000 à Pointe-Noire, il y fait ses études primaires et secondaires. Il obtient son baccalauréat littéraire en 2018. Ayant fait ses études en sciences humaines à Marien-Ngouabi en 2018, il poursuit ses études en philosophie à l'UCAC.

Fils de DINGAONAÏMOU NGANA et MADENODJI DIMADOUNGAR, **DJEGUEDEM TRÉSOR,** est né le 05 octobre 1995 à Ndjamena/ Tchad. Il est coauteur de l'ouvrage poétique "Que tes voisins admirent tes enfants" paru aux éditions Toumaï en mars 2021. Il fait actuellement master professionnel en sciences de l'environnement deYaoundé1, option assainissement et restauration de l'environnement. DJEGUEDEM TRÉSOR est un poète engagé.

EL BASSE de son vrai nom BASSIROU MANSALY né en 1996 à kounayan dans la région de Sédhiou du Sénégal, est devenu amoureux de la poésie en Octobre 2019. Ainsi, il décide, par la magie des mots, de faire une carrière littéraire. Bassirou est un poète qui valorise la peau noir, la femme. Il s'adonne aux lettres pour intégrer le cénacle des plus brillants poètes du monde. Sa plume se baigne dans le royaume de ses ancêtres. Mansaly est un poète en quête du savoir. Il réside au royaume du Maroc à Casablanca et est chef de fil d'un groupe dénommé Temple littéraire qui regroupe plusieurs nationalités. Bassirou est deuxième du grand prix de poésie Francophone 2020 dans la catégorie SLAM-POÉSIE sur le thème de la paix. Il est aussi co-auteur de l'anthologie des meilleurs nouveaux poètes africains 2020.

Amoureux des lettres et des cultures diverses, **Abdou Rafiou BEREKOU** a une formation en Anthropologie et Études Africaines et en Management des projets culturels. Finaliste du concours Écrivains Humaniste édition 2019 ; Technophile et Social Media Manager, les lettres font partie intégrante de toutes ses activités et la poésie un genre qui lui permet d'aligner le copywriting et la vente à persuasion.

Lizete António Sitoe ou simplesmente; Lizete Sitoe é poetisa-declamadora moçambicana. Gestora de comunicação no movimento para mulheres *My safe space mz* o Meu espaço seguro, mapeadora voluntária do projecto MAKE & CRIAMOZ, Membro e coordenadora de eventos no *Movimento e Associação Fénix*. Participou do Livro de poeta e escritor brasileiro Edison Botelho *Um quarto de lua* (88 páginas, Editora Palavra Malagueta), participou na Antologia de poesia Moçambicana + *258 poemas* de Nélio Gemusse e Luís Nhazilo, participou também na antologia de *poemas em tautoindriso ou da auroda do manifesto* de de Kheron-Hapuch e Daúde Amade. Participou da oficina das escritas criativas patrocinadas pela Procultura na Fundação Fernando Leite Couto. É Administradora do projecto *Arte Demais* e actua como declamadora para eventos como serenatas juntamente com os artistas participantes do mesmo projecto que cantam e tocam instrumentos como violino e guitarra. Modera lives de poesias com poeta e escritor Álvaro dos Reis com titulo *Recital de poesia*, uma inteiração entre Brasil e Moçambique.

Maria Manuel Godinho Azancot de Menezes, descendente de S.Tomé e Príncipe e Portugal, é médica em Angola, onde reside. Escreveu "Lua Mágica"- (2017) e "Voo Colorido"- (2020). Participou nas Antologias: " Entre o Sono e o Sonho" (2017) (2019), "Tributo" Homenagem a Autores Marcantes da Literatura Universal (2019), "Cartas de Amor" (2019), "Natal em Palavras" (2019), "Quarentena" (2020), "Liberdade" (2021), "Alma de Mar" (2021). Participou no Best New African Poets (2017, 2018, 2019 e 2020), Participou na Antologia Portuguesa de Poesia

Contemporânea "Não Posso Adiar o Coração" (2018), no Libero América- África Jornal (2020).

Chamo-me Benedito Carlos Ngome, tenho 24 anos de idade, sou Moçambicano vivo concretamente na província de Maputo onde nasci. Já faz alguns anos que escrevo poemas no anonimato, escrevo por diversão. Meu nome artístico é Benedito Carlos.

Larson Da Piedade Bento Fernando, nasceu em Saurimo, província da Lunda-Sul (Angola) aos 23 de Fevereiro de 1999. Actualmente reside em Luanda, município de Talatona. É co-fundador e presidente da Associação Mentes da Literatura (AML), que se dedica a promoção da leitura e escrita criativa, também faz parte da PROFASA (projecto farol do saber) que se dedica a dar aulas ao domicílio. É estudante de engenharia electrotécnica, orador e amante de filosofia. Deu seus primeiros passos no ano de 2015, começando por escrever frases e poemas.

Osório Herno Feliciano Vilanculos Data de Nascimento 02 de Dezembro de 1985 é natural da Província de Nampula Nacionalidade Moçambicana, Filho de Feliciano Charles Vilanculos e de Carolina Aurélio Matavele residente actualmente na Cidade de Maputo-Moçambique

Dalton Alfândega, nascido aos 17 de Maio de 2001, natural de Moatize, província de Tete. Despertou a sua paixão pela poesia no ano de 2016, quando na altura frequentava a 10ªclasse do ensino secundário, declamou pela primeira vez a sua poesia em público quando esteve a frequentar o Instituto de Formação de Professores em Tete, na sua cerimónia de graduação. É Professor do ensino primário desde 2020. Já possui 6 livros escritos não publicados, cujos os seis livros há um Romance, dois conto, e três obras somente de poemas. Já participou no concurso de poesia (Antologia honrando o Eduardo Mondlane).

Niurka da Orla, nascida ao 5 de Julho de 1994, Nacionalidade Moçambicana, residente em Moçambique, província de Inhambane, distrito de Inhambane, 27 anos de idade, solteira, formada no nível superior, História com habilitações em Geografia, na Universidade Pedagógica da Maxixe – Inhambane.

Gerónimo Daniel Mabote, Moçambicano de 26 anos de idade, nascido aos 16 de Fevereiro de 1995, é licenciado em ensino de História com habilitações em ensino de Geografia pela Universidade Pedagógica de Moçambique. Escreve e declama poesia desde os 11 anos de idade. Trabalhou como coordenador do projecto English Network da Smile Mozambique entre 2020 e princípios de 2021. Actualmente presta serviços freelancer no mercado de IT

Leide Tila, nascida e criada em Moçambique, concretamente na província e cidade de Maputo, actualmente moradora do bairro Machava social km 15. Poeta de 19 anos, amante da literatura pintura e apreciadora da arte. Tendo dado início na sua trilha como poeta aos 10 anos descobrindo a paixão pela poesia e desde então não tem parado, a fim de expressar e fazer conhecer a arte da escrita a todos quanto poder alcançar.

João Chico António Santos: Pseudónimo: literatura JC, escreve poesia como forma de dar vida aos seus pensamentos. Mora em Tete – Moçambique

Hilton_Fortuna_Daniel nasceu em Angola, na província do Cuanza Sul, na Gabela. Escreve poesia desde os 17/18 anos. A sua literatura inclui conto, crónica, ensaio e tem publicadas algumas recensões literárias, colectâneas e antologias pelos países lusofalantes. Participou, em 2017da Colectânea de Poetas Africanos.

Fernando Paciencia Luteiro Palaia, de 26 anos de idade, natural de Luanda, Municipio de Viana, estado civil casado, licenciado em engenharia Informática. Actualmente professor de Informática. Poeta escritor com participações em mais de duas edições de antologias "BEST NEW AFRICAN POETS".

Introduction Note

Best New African Poets 2021 Anthology is the 7th volume of the yearly Africa-wide poetry anthologies we started in 2015, making this series the largest archive of African contemporary poetry in several African languages including among others English, Portuguese, French, Arabic, Shona, Yoruba, Tswana, Zulu etc....This anthology series has published over 800 African poets from almost all African countries.

In *Best New African Poets 2021 Anthology* we have 18 French speaking African poets, making it the strongest French entry section ever with poets from DRC, Congo Brazzaville, Cameroun, Ivory Coast, Benin, Togo, Chad, Senegal, Comoros etc...

In the Portuguese section we have 14 Portuguese speaking poets from Angola, Sao Tome and Principe, Mozambique etc....

63 English speaking African poets from among other countries, South Africa, Nigeria, Zimbabwe, Kenya, Uganda, Malawi, Swaziland, Lesotho, Zambia, Tanzania, Ghana, Gambia, Sierra Leone etc...make up the English Poetry section, with South Africa and Nigeria dominating the entries. As usual there is a full gamut of issues dissected from love, marriage, relationships, spirituality, politics, culture, tradition, environmentalism, interstellar etc....

In this anthology we also carry our yearly collaboration of African poets, and this year we have two collaborations, the first deals with marriage, i.e., Monogamy vs Polygamy thereby delving into long held African marriage traditions, and juxtaposing them with the 21th century lived experience. The second imagines humanity living as intergalactic beings. This year saw the rich billionaires like Bezos, Branson etc... going to outer space, and SpaceX, a company owned by Elon Musk has the intent of colonizing Mars in a few decades, creating cities out of earth into space, thus most likely humanity is heading towards living as intergalactic beings, spread all over the vast universes. We asked the poets to be imaginative (to be fictional poets) and try to create and imagine human agency in this interstellar civilization approaching.

Another section has 5 group interviews we did with 5 previous contributors of this series. These interviews were interactive and collaborative, whereby as a group we would interview a poet, critically engage with their work, discuss literary and social aspects we thought the poetry and poet addressed.

The last section of *Best New African Poets 2021 Anthology* carries 4 reviews of African poetry, the first one is a review of our previous offering *Best New African Poets 2017 Anthology* reviewed by Andrew Nyongesa, the second is a review of Archie Swanson's collection *Beyond a distant Edge* by South African emeritus professor Geoffrey Haresnape, and Archie Swanson has been contributing to this series since we started in 2015. the third is a review of Jabulani Mzinyathi's debut poetry collection *Under The Steal Yoke* by Lind-Grant Oyeye, and the last is a review of South African poetry award *Oliver Shreiner poetry award* which was won by Best New African Poets contributor Allan Horwitz, this review was done by *Prof Rosemary Gray; Prof Ivan Rabinowitz and Ms Claudia Fratini* who were the judges of this important South African Poetry Award.

The language of the poet is never simple, whatever it may seem. He has the power to express in everyone's words, everything that not everyone else can express. Poets can say the same thing but differently. They are apt to use words; paint any kind of situation with words, through simple and complicated things. The poet sees beauty in ugliness, or ugliness in beauty. He creates what does not exist, and makes what exists disappear. Through words, worlds are created and disappeared. It is the strength of the poet. What seems simple is not necessarily so.

You will understand this through the writings of these young African poets. They are all from Africa; learn or forge on poetry. Their emotions have given away to writing, have taken hold of the words, mistreating them, in a sauce where different themes in the form of ingredients leave readers to delight in the flavor of a text that cannot satiate them by simple reading.

****

Le langage du poète n'est jamais simple, quoique cela puisse paraître. Il a le pouvoir d'exprimer avec les mots de tout le monde, tout ce que tout le monde ne peut pas exprimer. Les poètes peuvent dire la même chose mais différemment. Ils sont susceptibles de manier les mots; peindre toute forme de situation avec les mots, à travers des choses simples et compliquées. Le poète voit la beauté dans la laideur, ou la laideur dans la beauté. Il crée ce qui n'existe pas, et fait disparaître ce qui existe. À travers les mots, des mondes se créent et disparaissent. C'est la force du poète. Ce qui paraît simple ne l'est pas forcément.

Vous comprendrez cela à travers les écrits de ces jeunes poètes africains. Ils viennent tous de l'Afrique; s'initient ou se forgent sur la poésie. Leurs émotions ont laissé place à l'écriture, se sont emparées des mots, les malmènent, dans une sauce où différents thèmes sous forme d'ingrédients laissent délecter aux lecteurs la saveur d'un texte qui ne saurait les rassasier par simple lecture.

******

O Best New African Poets é sem dúvidas um encontro de poetas apaixonados pela literatura, e cada ano que passa conhecemos novos e talentosos autores que ousam transcrever as suas dores e alegrias no papel.

Antologia BNAP 2021 a nível da lusofonia conta com a participação de poetas de Moçambique, Portugal e Angola. Os poemas abordam diferentes temáticas tais como solidão, injustiça, vida, isolamento, morte, revolução, revolta, miséria, natureza, amor, ódio, paixão, política, resistência, crenças, vitória, paz, decepção e nacionalismo.

A temática isolamento foi também um dos tópicos explorados pelos poetas tomando diferentes facetas de solidão, medo e questionamento da existência humana. E foi gratificante ver que a maior parte tinham como objectivo trazer uma luz em meio ao caos. O que deixa claro que a escrita neste período tenebroso de isolamento surge como um meio para difundir mensagem de esperança e amor pelo próximo.

As restantes temáticas mostram as tentativas que os poetas usam para expor as suas dores, alegrias, desamores, reafirmação de identidade doando-se um pouco de si para os amantes das letras.

Best New African Poets continuará sendo essa ponte que liga poetas da mesma mãe África que se encontram espalhados pelo mundo e estamos felizes com percurso que esta tomando: unido e conectando novos autores na mesma esfera literária.

English poems

REVOLT IN THE FOREST
Iloke, Chukwuemeka

Now that the birds witnessed a century siege
 In the forest that housed their eggs,
Let them revolt to claim the nest.

Now that the forest is a land of Egypt
Where Pharaoh opposes the call of Moses,
Let the birds revolt to overthrow the reign of Pharaoh

Now that the birds are up for their right
Long clutched in the hands of old hawks,
Let them revolt and take the lead.

Now that the birds are eager to build
A new tower of hope with unity of heart,
Let them revolt and lay claim of their resource.

Now that the birds are aware
Of their stolen eggs,
Let them revolt and chase away the thief.

Your Music
Uche Uwadinachi

I'm 'dangerously' in love
with your ringtone

Please, tell me
was it patterned from an 1840 mouth organ
or plucked from the vocal cord
of a sleeping goddess?

How come no classic violin string
can play your awesome notes?

Wait, is it a self-made vocal gift
you found while trying not to sing?

I've turned up all sound speakers
yet your soft tune rises from an old chorister's voice

Some gossip neighbours have gathered
like sound technicians waiting to learn

While I'm here with all your music
and wine pouring on my keyboard....
Sing, sing and moan
Distract me from campaign jingles
Of these political parties
Sing on to me!

Omalishanwa
Uche Uwadinachi

Let me photograph
your face daily
In its shades of laughter
to show
My unborn daughter
How to grace
Front cover magazines
Without a naked butt

Let me stand here
All moments
and stare at you
till scientists gather
On your timeline
Only to tell gossips
Of your awesome
Beauty

Let me switch off
The sunlight
The moon, stars
For just two hours to prove
The sufficient
Megawatt
Lush in your radiance.
You are Oma!
The beauty
Whose skin
Is the 3D version

3

Of the early morning Sun.

Good morning Nwanyi Oma !

HER PAINS ON A PORTRAIT
Abu Bakarr Kamara

I saw her paralyzed portrait,
Hung on grieving galleries
Of ladened hearts,
Benumbed by brokenness.

Tears of her forlornness,
Mildewed the portrait of her brokenness,
With epitaphs engraved;
By glaring grief.

I saw her bereft heart,
Tempered by tribulations,
And aurified into stone and steel
To ravage reavers of her riches.

In seeming calmness,
Her pale portrait puffed,
Like pregnant clouds
And rumbled with rage.

In weariness; she portrayed
Her bundle of burden,
Tied round her neck like hairband;

4

With backwardness carried on her back.

To her rights being raped,
Her identity being mutilated,
And her growth being subjugated;
I saw her portrait soaked in tears.

She dragged her limbs helpless,
While she staggered with feeble hands,
To fight the horror,
That had statued her in a standstill.

THE PORTRAIT OF PIETERSON

Abu Bakarr Kamara

(In Commemorating the Heroes, who died in the June 16 Soweto Uprising)

In the portrait of Pieterson,
Glimmer the graves of unsung heroes,
Echoing the ululations of school children,
Who heed to the voice of Tietsi Mashini
And stood together in unity
To fight for their right.

In that sulky portrait,
Of tears of prejudice,
Reflect the screams and sounds,
The cries of faces without races
In the streets of Soweto; flooded
By students who faced sheer brutality;
Amplified by the apartheid regime.

This portrait reflects the retaliatory-
Anger of angered school children,
Stimulated by the senseless killings,
Orchestrated by the police,
For fists raised in their face.

It mourns the massacre,
Of school children, all over Soweto;
Who shared the same problems,
Same sorrows and same causes of resentments;
Fighting for a just cause.

In the vicinity of Regina Mhundi Church in Orlando
And the heart of Esso garage in Chiawelo,
Stands the portrait of Pieterson;

No more in fury and frustration,
For the burning hostility against 20,000 students;
Who slipped from the hands of oppressors,
To lift the rocks against their muzzled voices.

Fate
Olaiya Alfred

For once or twice, when darkness thicken
I set my fears ablaze ---
A ritual of peace to my sacred mind.
My soul trembles on cold fragments
Which has been my strings of hope
But now fiery linens around my loins.

With my Gold at my bosom,
I've felt the warmth of love
But with no Mirror to see the
Reflection of my charred face,
I've indulged in perfection of my shadow.

 Dawn of revelation
Dated Twin twos in the tenth moon

And with the beams of the sun at dusk,
I've seen the flaws in the being;
A projected shade of body
That buries the scars in darkness
And mould a flawless clone.

When life gives an empty cup
Filled with bars of dreams

And fate plays its strings on fragile fingerboard
The sinking sun is the anchor of hope
Which carries my wishes away.

The Question
Olaiya Alfred

Let's come together, comrades
And reminisce the golden days
When the soil, wet with our sudor,
Chants on our heaps of guts
And the Intruders from the grey land
Swam in through the tide
And brought the dreams of new vision.
We were confined in yokes by our brothers
Bloodshot with nails of strangers,
Sickling our fields of grains.

Then a full moon came,
Splashing its rays on fighters' swords
And surged the revolt.
The night went by
And took some fighters along.
But the dawn came
With yokes broken by the seashore
With the strangers voyaging away.

Comrades, these days are gone;
When vultures licked the fifth finger on our heads
And out wrists were strained with chains.
We are now with beads on necks and wrists,
Happily greasing our remains of grains.
But the question bangs on our ears now and then
As we fight our fellow brothers on the field:
"Are we truly free?"

YET TO SEE THE DIVINE
Amani Nsemwa

I have been in the battlefields
where soldiers engaged in cannibalism.
I have been in the Hip Hop concerts
where rappers engaged in Poetry.
This is no controversy
But I've been in churches
where padres practice witchcraft
And us kids cant do arts and crafts
Because they seem to be like the devils pie
A church boy who raps
For the church thats a wrap
They prolly think we on crack
Ive seen couples so hot
That they burned down and crushed
Love killed by lust
A foundation of marriage filled with cracks
I've seen it all yet to see the divine.

A Ghost's Reflection Post-Depression
Andile Ecalpar Nayika

It's slippery where blood is spilled by shivery;
Colours clash as red drips from the silvery.
Birth is the afterlife, holding death in delivery.

Children cry for father's feathered limbs,
Building skies for shattered dreams.
The core of life is hard for the man, it seems.
The planet eats half of the hand that gives.
While a neck is clinched on a deadly string,
Tears fall down digging deep beneath where granite lives.

Pass the stone is theft,
So what hope is left?
A sigh of breathing for the ropeless necks?
Or finding meaning from the souless text?
Akuwe falling on homeless tracks,
Izibele follows next;
A daughter wrecks her boat on the story's facts.
Children lost on stolen maps.
Man, exhume your grave with no regrets,
Swallow the blood the soldiers spat,
Stomp & step on a starving poet's pen.

It's slippery where blood is spilled by shivery;
Colours clash as red drips from the silvery.

Birth is the afterlife, holding death in delivery.

Be your father's will & his brother's zeal,
Fight 'til none is nil.
A pensioner's gold was a gardner's meal not how it feels.
Whether the heavy sun was still,
An hour's wheel was a harmless drill.

A body swims in a sea of stones,
Maggots hunting flesh, fishing bones.
The land crumbles on a plant which it grows.
Seedling nodes reading notes
Written in cryptic codes.
This ghostwriter's ink is known for linking roads between dawn &
evening modes.
Death waits for no man digging holes,
Spilling his own blood, cursing life-giving oaths.

It's slippery where blood is spilled by shivery;
Colours clash as red drips from the silvery.
Birth is the afterlife, holding death in delivery.

Remember the path paved when your breath is scew.
Follow the light pass the noon,
For the sunset is due.
Peace to the rested tombs & respect unto the present few.
Pour a simple breath of life for the fallen dessert dunes.
A family stands & stood
From a mother's domestic residues,
Squeezing her last drops of effort through, With a cancer she never
knew.
My essence, my previous jewel
Thanks for the message & lesson of gratitude.

She said: The strength in you asks for the answers to the quest in queue.
But some words can't say what your actions do,
Only you can narrate your own tale in two.

I said: But it's slippery where blood is spilled by shivery;
Colours clash as red drips from the silvery.
Birth is the afterlife, holding death in delivery.

Corners of Constriction

Andile Ecalpar Nayika

A box of matches
Is a humble abode,
Even sticks and stones
That trouble the bone -
Lash skin-deep
But pardon the soul.

At the heart of the informal
Where sentiments are checked -
Pride outshines the zinc bling,
Breaking shackles in a shack.
A sharp metal in a wreck,
Cutting edges travelling aback.

Rhythm penetrates a spare ear.
A Black fist mystified
Punches the air clear.
A movement caught in a rare snare.
Beware of the watchdog
Where nothing is declared fair.

In the folded edges of the metro -
Pass the city's bridging rails,
Time is ticking, picking pace.
A writer converts thinking
Where ink is placed.
Thoughts capture the essence,
Building bars with bricks and brains.

Corners of constriction

Lying in the dark,
Annoyed and jealous
Of the fire in the spark.
Much like the hill
With which society obstructs.
Indeed all fortune
Is an irony of luck.

Marechera's House of Hunger
Reads strongly below the dust -
As solid air blocks the nose and trunk.
Bones sneeze
At a broken past.
Passing streets with no names
Injecting faith with hope and trust.

A Dream of the Southern Shores

Andile Ecalpar Nayika

A child is proud to scroll
Its feet masked with soul -
On the sheets of the southern shores.
Every step prints out a form
Of peace the fountain pours.
No dust peaks the seals of the grounded pores.
The ink;
Nectar from a flower draws one colour,
Moulds skins into a thousand-fold.
Flagged in peace,
Holding hands -
Reaching for mother earth's mouth to sow.
Our seeds have found a home,
Indeed tomorrow's sun is ploughing hope.

From the Greater Kruger National Park's grazing fauna
To the icey rocks and waving waters of the Cape Agulhas.

From Thohoyandou's sun-bathing borders,
Mapungubwe's unveiling orders
To the holy hills of Qamata named in honour.

From the Drankensberg's caving shoulders,
Down the arms of the Kalahari's naked bowers -
To Dora Nginza Hospital's labour warders,
Nurses, baby mothers braking waters.

From every province's local radio station sources
And air-waving prowess,
To mainstream's tape recorders;
Famed reporters

And front-paging authors.

From jailing corners -
Cuffing culprits of a blazing forest,
Chained for braking orders,
Police, agents, watchers -
Uniformed in their safety office,
To our nation's soldiers,
Defensive, brave and cautious,
Our sons with great and conscious
Gun-aiming daughters.

From street-vendors paving offers,
Clarred in aprons, floral,
Wives, retailing shoppers,
Husbands hand-scraping walls,
Some taming forests,
Groundbreaking forces
With spades and shovels,
To railing croppers
And trading farmers
Praying for harder rains in August,
Aided bosses taking orders,
Graduates of the nation's education quarters -
Counting their daily numbers,
Checking pockets,
Making profit.

From edu-taining hawkers,
Vagrant dancers,
Painters, sculptors,
To theatre staging artists,
Actors playing others,
Cameramen and women

With zooming, framing powers

On soil cracked, divided and beat,
A dream basks under African heat.
Ours is reploughing the footsteps,
Where the African soil and wood stand.
Pick up a piece of that shattered dream,
Add another and others as a team.

We are Flowers

Jonas Zaithwa Chisi

We are seeds
That break into bud in the wee of the day
And blossom, and grow and glow
We are petals
Bright and beautiful in noonday
Petaling fresh air to leaves around us
Giving nectar from the heart of our souls
We are flowers
In unison singing about brevity of existence
And with sunset
So we close our petals, fun the last air
And break the final cord in an amen of life

My Africa
Gonapragasen Kathan Naicker AKA Danny

my mother Africa
In her eternal womb
I have been nourished and nurtured
I have suckled the rich nectar
from her supple breast
her blood flows through my veins
and feeds my life, my body and spirit
she replenishes and uplifts my being
I am one with her, joined forever to her soul
by that sacred imperishable umbilical thread
that can never be severed by mortal hands
death will not separate my immortal soul
from her being
distance will not be a void between us
I am her child no matter
wherever I sojourn

her landscape textured tapestry
interwoven in bold geometric symmetry
defines the vast unfathomable
panorama of her soul
man and beast sharing the equilibrium
flowing, flowing from
the depths of her noble being

her majestic beauty, her serenity
her stark fearful austerity
testimony to her ancient distant
prehistoric birth
wild raging desert storms,
sweeping flood waters forging chaos

devouring with wanton recklessness
all that stands in her path
her personality, hostile yet in harmony
with the rhythms of the universe

her passive serene demure
and her untamed moods, erratic
since the creation of the universe
her dual nature, monolithic giants
standing side by side defiant and volatile
mortal man can only stand
in awe in her awesome presence
and marvel at her rugged beauty
and her scathing hostility

on her colossal strong body
ancient mountains stand
in elegant foreboding splendor
their beings forged and molded
from molten rock, and fire
spewed from the deep
volcanic furnaces, of her being
her rifts and valleys
sculptured by flood waters
and drifting mountains of ice

I stand diminutive on her tranquil shores
and watch her oceans boundless vitality
it betrays her power and magnitude
and reminds me of man's certain death
and how mortals like you and I
diminish before her primordial presence
but still she sooths and feeds
my fragile, solitary soul

I am beholden to her
she is my mother
this ancient land Africa

A long letter to my trustees
Oscar Gwiriri

This secret letter should be secretly passed onto
Grand generations of my superior race.
Oh children, acknowledge our cunning wit
Of external investment for your generations too
We colonised and terrorised Africa for you.
We are done; we subjugated them to the bone,
Stirred and distracted their traditional strength,
Transplanted our god into their bone marrow.
We engraved our superiority in their souls,
Inseminated their poor brains with self-loathe.
Their grand grandchildren shall bow unto you.
We granted quasi-independence and pseudo-rights,
But held onto what we exploited and explored.
We pretentiously preached for their democracy,
Which can and should never be, come what may,
Since we pro-lobby and distract it secretly,
Through blinkered activists fulfilling our agenda.
We go looting their precious resources and brains,
Amidst their demonstrations, chaos and mutiny.
Get to know that every one of their governments,
Should be clandestinely opposed with a plastic smile.
Empower and mobilise politico deviants for mass revolt.
As they tassel, wrestle and pestle for their revolution,
Take no chance, loot and loot and loot, more and more.
Perchance, extinguish them with extreme poverty,
Impose sanctions; hold them at ransom for assistance.
Blind them with paltry donations and supply slave codes.
Never ever feel pity for Africa, neither their kin nor kith.
Give them abundant freedom just on paper for a glance,
Yet yoking them on your supreme oppressing stance.
Suppress the socio-ecopolitico and culture systems.

23

Hold on fast, be firm and keep holding on their resources,
Stir wars and invent diseases to appease your superiority.
Sow seeds of greed, divide and corruption in their leaders
Pretend! Pretend! Pretend! Pretend to befriend them,
Covertly mastering their strengths and strategies.
Be strategic to weaken their naturalistic intelligence.
Invite the leaders and kin to extravagant state banquets,
But their citizenry should cater for every single cent spent.
Drench them with whiskey, meaningless toast and all sorts
Malted from their hopeless peasant farmers' valley barley.
Hypnotise them with diplomatic gifts from their minerals,
And mastermind coups as they esoterically dine and wine.
Gather and stab them left, right, centre and backwards
With compulsory religion, health, sports, food and education,
Even rights to abortion, polyandry and socio-cultural misnomers.
Destroy their royal empires no matter how small they may be,
Let no other tongue be international, but ours.
Tantalise them with our culture, but push them asunder.
As they enrol at your institutions, relocate your to St Beyond,
Start elsewhere at whatever cost, for our pride and culture's sake.
Force their schools to put their vernacular languages at stake,
And insist for our education and belief to be the standard core.
Maintain our systems in all systems, even in their breathe,
Root it in legislature, and their constitutions will be vanity.
What rights do slave descendants need, yet we are the masters?
It will take me many scrolls to guide you, my ink is washed up.
Briefly, ride on Africa like a donkey, stick and carrot strategy.
Never ever release our hard fought legacy on a silver plate.
Fight tooth and nail using native soldiers against other natives.
Identify intelligent bastards; lure them and brain drain Africa.
Blackmail and bait them with modernity and universality.
Extract or extinguish their spiritual revolting blood, but be careful.
Degenerate Africa's freedom dispensation, and pseudo-democracy,
Make their children shun their statues and pay homage to ours,

Maintain the sacredness of our legends statues and history.
Colonisation, exploitation, domination and isms are our Trust.

Yours sincerely
Lord Anonymous

Haiku
Priscilla Arthur

mid-spring
at the porch
a crocus' first blossom

summer solstice
a Scrub-wren sunbathing
on the cattail

sirocco
the chrysanthemums toss their heads
in no direction

late winter
the early sprout of the chamomile
spring

Relics (Senbun)
Priscilla Arthur

Joy is a pet called bird; we don't get to hold on to it for long. It flies home at dusk and barely leaves anything concrete behind for remembrance. Mum said, as we got to the event. She wipes chocolate from her upper lip. My cousin completed tertiary school this year. With pleasure, she invited the family to the graduation. In the whirl of busy hours, I sought permission from school to attend the graduation. For present there were cakes, champagne, cookies, bracelets, long hugs for memory, fat envelopes, a parcel of things that can be eaten & things to be kept as relics. It was all fun at the party. From her fading yellow bag she brought out a feather, for cousin; that she can hold on to happiness and never let it go.

behind mother's exhilaration
dancing ribbons

It Shall Blossom Again
Nkaimbi Wan N'tieh

Police batons lash against bare skulls
Blood oozes and flows into tiny red rivulets
Agony spirals from voices suppressed
Water cannon run down rioters with sewage
Stones crisscross tear gas canisters mid air
The boulevard is soaked in a thick cloud of teary gas
It's a deafening silence broken momentarily by howls
And the rallying song has bravely defied the order to vacate

Tic tac! Tic tac! Adrenaline gushes
Tic tac! Tic tac! Fear switches camps
As astonished silent onlookers observe with impartiality
A voice from amongst the rioters intones the anthem anew
Protesters tighten ranks with human chains
Military boots intimidatingly boot against the tarmac
And from a window in Geneva's five star 'The Intercontinental'
An old enfeebled geruntocrat observes unperturbed

How Many More shall they kill?
Nkaimbi Wan N'tieh

Today a child went to sleep
She was hushed by the cum of the earth
A barren rascal who will never know
What it takes to be a parent

Today a child went to sleep
Her tiny princess shoes never left her feet
But they blanketed her with her blood
And fragmented her brains into tiny bits

Today a child went to sleep
And the oppressed paraded her remains
To show the world
How angels sleep in their part of Cameroon

Today a child went to sleep
Leaving a mother to sleep in tears
And a people to wonder
"Who is next in line?"

Binging Wind
Mohau Mohlope

But usually, I hang in there quietly.
Before slipping away with kindness
And huffily raid dirt piling in the township streets

I 'am a binging wind, steering wings where it pleads,
raging dusty rumbles and arrogantly exhaust queefs
In its wilderness as it creeps

I toss my body around, like possessed initiated jinn
alone, I twist and turn
wrestle waste in country yards and succumb flowers
Picking myself grossly and embed contagions in humans
And still binging

Across the god's land
I grovel with my gut; I taste and tease bitter of seasons
I trot whistler's secret in the mist
quest along wavering wanders
And surge dominance in the eagerness

For I am binging wind soothing in existence
Un-topping mounting heaps
Prowling power fronts from coiled atoms
Disfiguring rusty rooftops
And I'm still binging winds.

COLOURING SEQUENCE
Mohau Mohlope

Perhaps, pride arrays a dispatch
to the struck route.
I hold onto finding things,
not missing but just left further.
'And assemble moves in the
Depth of city plight.
'And Wither deep in neighbouring asylums
saying hunger sees no grave,
as long tries are content.
When a hawker's handcart
spawn sweat,

I'm self-imposed to myself,
But conscience creeps
'And sweeps beneath lingering moons.
hanging lengthy in the guise of creeds.
Like a richness's shenanigan with
desired tunes.
Walks tell, I'm a starved misfortune,
not fearful to pass on.
My Forged silence is from where gullible boys
of age are tamed on,
punted with vulnerable hymns to a boneyard.
In a reality there is too much to lose.

Perhaps, I'm finding things never lost,
I got a gallant stranger in me.
Wiping tears in a brothel housing ripped men,

than sacred scripture.
If faraway world has haven to converse about,
I would just need a second stare in the eyes
of a stranger,
But treachery amount no cure.

Lifeforce
Mohau Mohlope

Spiritual seer, accentuator of the hiddenness
That causes omits of distractions
In the wields of a blasphemous holocaust

Formidable fumes of chattered chants
reigning spiritual realms of thunderous vanity
Caster of briskly burps yet not appeased with modernity

Glows of fire plumes nulled from origin
When initiator's roar roast riverside shadows
Spirit yearns, menacing flakes of its medicine

Resonates as gallons shrills seashores.
numbing of revelations reverting omens
Spirit yearns its own, yet not appeased with modernity

Dreams gauges souls and accede bodies
See, calling is not in ruptures and amends of world
Is the aggression of forces shivering modernists?

Spiritual seer, accentuator of the hiddenness
Row sower of sworn to the humorous
Humble seed root for its wondrous nurture
Spirit yearns its own, yet not appeased with modernity comfort.

BOWLER
Xolile Mabuza

For: Kagiso Rabada

It's been years since the sun started running into the hands of the night
Looking for a place to hide its face
Forgetting that the rest of its body will somehow show in the half moon, in the hands of a fielder
It's been 25-years since stars started falling off the night skies chest,
Building your strength, skill and talent so you can be seen
in grounds that are not used to black people being beautiful

Like Moses who stretched his hand over the sea, called water to stand still
and led the Israelites through the red sea.
You stretch your hand to lead a congregation of cricketers between overs
You call the sea of runs to stand still.
All the batsmen who try to cross over your deliveries drown on the crease;
their lungs are always left searching for air in the hands of a fielder.
CAUGHT! OUT!
Every ball you bowl holds a hungry face of batsman walking back to the change room with nothing to offer his team but an empty stomach that was starved runs on the crease

You wrap fire on your wrist like a bracelet
The flames you hold have a language that batsmen can't understand
They speak in smoke; they can't hold a conversation without putting a pause on lungs

A cricket ball leaves your hand, lands on the spine of a popping crease, play hide and seek with the batsman as it sweeps all his breathe off his lungs
Bowled!
Smoke grows weight and pushes past the stumps
It leaves bails searching for a home they once knew
Again a wicket falls
A run out is also a wicket

You are a holy cricketer
A church of bowling, scriptures are read on your deliveries
8 Overs, 3 maidens, 6 wickets and 16 runs lost is a holy scripture
God wrote magic at the palm of your right hand
He gave your fingers a voice to read spells to red and white balls
On the field you are a prayer waiting for the clock to tick you back to the alter
where you will take a catch and be holy again.
You are a worship song rolling out of tongues of cricket fans, and hanging like an earring on Gods ear
God himself can't speak about light without calling you to the bowling crease
"Let there be light" sounds like a right hand fast bowler,
It sounds like you.

AROUND THE SUN
Xolile Mabuza

God wrote our life on the sun.
We know we are alive when the sun rises.
He told the moon to tuck our future in its belly,
A half moon is sign that we've reached our destination.
No one really knows what a full moon stands for
but it definitely doesn't mean we die here.
Tonight the moon will be full again;
our lungs are already tied on our graves, we struggle to breathe.
A cough seems to be a line in our obituary.
Maybe the fever they warned us about is the way life chose to life our bodies,
but this is not where our story end.

Because of you social distancing is now a new way to stay alive.
Safety means lonely.
Responsible means depression growing two inches tall,
And being a responsible citizen means locking yourself and feeding your anxiety.
You are a child made out of hate.
Clearly your parent's hearts are oceans apart,
Hence your presence requires washing hands every two minutes.
You think washing our hands in water will bring your parents together?
You think locking ourselves and breaking down will help put back the missing pieces your fathers stole from your mother's heart?
This is not how humanity will rewrite love stories for viruses.
This is not how we choose to die.

You will leave us.
We will go back to our beloveds.
We will write our love stories on clouds,

And post pictures on the ocean weave.
Our hearts will beat twice what it used to beat,
sweep the white beach sand as we hold hands with the ocean again.
Depression will kiss us goodbye
as we return to the hands of our lovers.

DEATH
Xolile Mabuza

Tomorrow means time hiding from the sun, there's no such thing as the right time because the sun is still searching, and it is searching for itself in all the wrong places.

LOVERITHM
Gideon Sagbo

The tempo of her heaving chest
Calls every Adam's head to rest.
Àshàké , the fairest of eve,
Charming even the haunted.

Your presence makes my
Heart betray my head.
These two were two good
Friends yet until now.

White eyes like crystal balls
Of dew on the coco leaf.
Her brown beads beat rhythmically
As she whirls her waist.

She romances the soil with
Her calculated dance steps.
Calling the best of drummers
To hard labour.

The wind gives way as she
Bisects it with energetic arms.
Àshàké, the finest, best and
Masterpiece of all pottery works.

Your beauty stirs nature to
Its wake, and stalks hunters
For the take. Unlke the sun
Yours lives to shine at night.

Her smile like fresh palmwine,

Intoxicates even lords of repute.
And she glamours at their dispute.
She with a royal touch.

Akpón bekpo remi,
Will you take my hands,
Let us explore the nook and
Cranny of the land of love?

Let's surround its high walls and
Besige it, bring down it fortress,
And leave its spoils to ourselves.

*Àshàké (Yoruba) - Born to be cherished .
*Akpón bekpo remi (Yoruba) - One who is as fair as palm oil.

inner sanctum
Archie Swanson

to build this hall
choose your words well
place them row on row — just so
and let the cadence fall

hand mix the bricks from latticed clay
and bake them in your special way
then mortar in with measured trowel
each consonant—each rhyme—each vowel

to clothe the core of your basilica
make plaster from the elements
of mineral quartz and iron ore
and lime and chalk

and sand and shells
and shale and slate
and marble dust and silica
and rain

render lucid frescoes
onto wetted walls
apply your powder pigments
then allow to dry

build door of ancient Baobab
inscribed with circling years
that speak of pain and hope and tears
and every other thing

now enter through the open gate

onto the inner sanctum floor
and join the table of debate
below a wheeling lilt of stars

Victim
Susan Gamuchirai Muchirahondo

This isn't the first time someone has had more authority over my body
than I do
My body is a visitor who rests in my care from time to time
Somehow every time I say no
It seems like an invite to try harder and more aggressively

I fall out of love by deciding to protect myself from the men I'd have
given my safety to.

You fall victim involuntarily
And before you know it
Victim is who you are
Victim is embarrassing
Victim is something you can't tell anyone
Victim is putting on facades to the world
Victim is dying inside and blaming herself for giving all the wrong
signs
Next time victim will say no with a knife to a throat
Next time victim will twist an arm to get the point across
That no means absolutely no
Get your hands off my body you do not own a single part of me shock
you as that may

DEAR IVORA
Obidinma Jennifer Chinenye

Dear Ivora,
How are you?
I heard some men talking about you.
They said things that involved you being loose and wild
They said you were deceptive even though you looked like a child.
Oh! Those men! Such vile things they said!
One said, on one stormy night, he left you and fled.
The other said you were extremely sweet
Every time you met in his hotel suite.
Another licked his lips and let out a scream
While narrating how you were smooth like cream.
The others had wet dreams in their eyes
Dreams wherein you were their awaited prize.
They clinked their bottles,
Their laughter not subtle,
They laughed and laughed and laughed.
Oh! How I flamed with anger!
Such slander!
Against a friend so loving and tender!
Here I am at your front door
Askance at why it is slightly ajar
Strange noises greet my ears all the way from the floor
Noises of you and my man in a realm quite afar.

THE PHOENIX
Ojonugwa John Attah

I stand in the middle of fallen bodies,
There are cries that sting my ears
There are shouts that I hear before they stop
For many decades we have stayed indoors
We have been swept away by the tide of dictatorship
Our fathers and mothers have their own tales
We refuse to bear the same tales as theirs
We will speak before we die
We know that death is never far away
But we also know that life is never sure
From the ashes like the phoenix we will rise
We will rise into the promise we want for our children
That land flowing with milk and honey
That land which bears all things possible

SIGHTS AND SIGHTS

Ojonugwa John Attah

Warm air

Young men pulling the lighted cigarettes in the dark
Young boys wrapping the latest brand of weed
Teenagers salivating at the sight they behold,
Waiting for anything that would be handed down to them.
Girls swinging their large hips carelessly,
Their breasts hanging on the embankment made by the loose tank tops
Like a river about to overflow its banks.
The young men whistle and call out to them.
The response is more swinging of the hips
And the breasts struggle for attention unconsciously.
Elderly men sending out the latest bandits,
To steal from the thief and survive
The ones who will be greater than Anini
The brave ones who will keep up the flow of the street hustle
Elderly women urging the young ladies
To travel to Holland, Belgium and Italy
And join the trade of bodies for the paper
The only way to survive is there or here.

Hot air

Exotic cars in convoy visit this area
In the daytime, it is an abomination to be seen here
At night, it is acceptable and goes with a blessing
Young girls in miniskirts and short tops
With cleavages showing twin partings like the red sea
And faces made up and lipsticks on their lips
They jump into the waiting cars and off they go
The young men around take their tip
Off the number of girls they supply to the untouchables

The area which is in perpetual darkness
Settles for the flickering light from the bush lamp of a mai suya
And the candle of Mama Ngozi's buka

Cold air
The prodigals of last night return to roost
The convoy of cars repeating the earlier rituals
An exchange of smiles between the givers and the takers
More cigarettes in the pocket to smoke
More weed and tramadol for the cold day
A new day to think about a lot
To think about survival and existence
To think about living for today without the future

Open air
What do the teenagers seek to learn here?
Ruins here and there
The stench from urine mapping the walls
Rabid dogs struggling for a piece of bone
Caked soil refusing to be tilled
Bad roads leading to nowhere safe
The struggle for survival is written in the eyes of everyone
The untouchables, the same who promise heaven in the daytime
And bring down hell at night continue to speak the colonial language
"Not every promise must be fulfilled," is what they say on the TV
Bags of unfulfilled promises stacked in the area
All there for us to see
While parties and merriment remain a norm in Abuja
The untouchables await the next election
To show how much they love the area
But the smoke and the drugs have made the people wiser
They will not be fooled any longer.

THE BROKEN POT
Emmanuel Tumwesige

I went to the well
To fetch water
on reaching the well
I slid.
I broke the pot
I broke the pot

I walked home
In shame and fear
With no water
I had gone to fetch
Because I slid
And broke the pot
I broke the pot.

She came near me
And asked why
I had no way to begin
I bent my head
The pot was broken
I broke the pot.

But I burst the balloon
Pitifully she stooped
Patted my shoulder
Told me not to ponder
The pot was broken
The pot was already broken.

My impropriety

Broke her heart
But she stood firm
To fortify the matrimony.
My infidelity
Broke my prestige
But she looked at my heart
Told me not to regret
For the broken pot
Shall be remoulded.

TO MY SON...

Ntensibe Joseph

Pass me that red pen,
I want my son to read when I am long gone,
Pass me quick
It is burning...

I want my son to read
Why we pass by our land
And rent where we live.
To know of the bullet hole in that wall
To read of the scars on my wrists
To know how shackles tattoo scars.
Why his sister never talks of who fathers her child
Why his brother's arms are rotting off because his fingers flashed some
signs
Why his other sister was stripped naked and her skin burnt off because
she wore the colour
And why I see this and cry no more!

I want to write in red
Pass me my pen
For my son to read why we didn't bury his grandfather
And why we don't know where he is!
To know why I talk of many prison walls
To read why I can't pronounce patriotism
To know how they hold guns like guitars and play
the music...

Remember Me in December

Litsitso Cooper

Remember me in December, when the trees grow again,
As the flower blooms from the once barren ground.
Remember me in December, when my soul is at ease,
and the summer rain touches the grave.
Your eyes will no longer have sadness,
and your thoughts of me will no longer be tragic.
Hold out your hand as the summer rain pours
and let the happy memories take over.
Be at peace that I am no longer in pain,
watching over you as you move on.
I will be your strength, your courage, and your guide.
Remember me in December, forever in your hearts.

RISING
Emman Usman Shehu

    i
on the surface
of consciousness
a poem takes
shape

like a mansion
like a ship
like a spaceship

like a limousine
like a train
like a plane

like anything
the mind
wants it to be

rising
with the dough
of being

coated
with the plaster
of meaning

    ii

a poem takes us

on an elevator

of the mind
until we find

the floor numbered conclusion
and step out

into the light
enrichment bright

      iii

a poem takes us
without a ticket
without a visa
without a passport
without biometrics

a poem
takes us
there

LEKKI LIE
Emman Usman Shehu

At Lekki
gestating playground
of underhand deals
and sprouting castles
of nouveau riche

the so-called dead
at the rally alley

have no names
have no next-of-kin
have no DNA

alive only
in the imagination
of mischief
and tollgate
wizardry.

NO WHISPER
Emman Usman Shehu

Six trillion
not million
not billion

down that Delta drain
of festering creeks
not a whimper
not a whisper
only a train

of shamefaced silence.
Self-styled knights
of citizens' rights
swamped in sullied armour.

before the month is over
Goodenough Mashego

before february is over
we have not yet said 'amen' but his will is already being done
we sit paranoid asking whose number is next
we can't look each in the eyes
for we scared our fears will show
our weaknesses exposed like a limp penis of an emperor

before february is over
whose grave are we digging next
whose pal are we bearing next
whose epitaph are we inscribing next
are we eulogising you or are you singing me praises
we refuse to cry
refuse to be afraid
avoid hospitals like a plague
flee from medics
like they are the pandemic
last we had a date with 'em we returned eyes sealed facing north
god bless the dead they died behind oxygen masks
george floyd incarnates our last breath is 'we can't breathe'
he martyred for a cause we die for the cost of a pill
shepherded toward a jab became a flock of sheep
like our lives depend on syringes on our veins
big pharma plays us like a record with its needle on our vinyls

before february is over they run to cash the cheque
while us lab rats queue for their placebo jabs
food replaced by millilitres of life in a vial
live today die tomorrow from hunger they yet to unleash

before february is over we scared to talk to our kindred

can no longer stomach our loss
we drown our sadness in beer
choke our lungs with purple haze
before february is over we scared to ask 'who's next?'

As we march on
(Re Batho le Mmino)
Goodenough Mashego

Beware the Ides of march
Careful of scissors that nip our buds
Remember death comes in pairs in our faith we trust
Before March is over we wanna live forever
Resurrect fallen souljahs we couldn't bid farewell
Matete Motsoaledi lives eternal in our hearts
We ain't letting Mokone go he's the reason we hoping
That death is a wart a mere mild irritation
Before March is over we shall gather stones
Build a shrine to befit the forty years of your life
Build a shrine to retrace the forty steps you took

Forty days in the desert we lost like Israelites
They say before March is over we'll be vaccinated
So we can fly like condor
Travel distant places
Spread the message of a revolution aborted at birth
They say it won't be televised
No wonder our stone-throwing is nothing but a commercial break
Re Batho le Mmino Matabane our new national anthem

We remember love unparalleled before the Ides of March
Acoustic guitar strings strummed in the name of love

53

Melodious singing eulogies in the name of art
How will you remember me?
Am I worth your memory?
Am I worth your tears when time comes I can't cry for self?
Are we so distant we can't feel when one's heart is beating?
See when one's heart is bleeding
Through the nose blood is seeping

Beware the Ides of March
Beware the March of the demons
For they burn everything on the path they walking

before the month is over
(take two)
Goodenough Mashego

before july is over
we once again gather in the name of pain
hold hands clasp palms
in vain attempts to squeeze the hurt
the sword has fallen
we came to count corpses
commit some to the ground others we turn to ashes
to later mix with colombian marching powder overdose and
reincarnate as ghosts
for those who die by pandemic
return to mete revenge on the surviving
we are corroded
like ice we melt
our feet made of clay we stand ready to dissolve
before july is over some of us will fall
the rest of us will fail
we'll fade pointing fingers to those we trusted
'you killed us with your greed
unquenched thirst for millions
your quest to live like peasants but be buried like kings
you dropped the buck when it mattered
and now we dying like buck
i wonder where you'll get votes when balloting comes
graveyards filled with bones of those you drowned
when you refused to steady the ship
when you were drunk on the wheel'

before july is over we sing the nation's anthem
leave the Boer version aside for it rhymes like your version
omit your version for its sounds hypocritical as their version

we know we've been lied to
have grown immune to truth
believe not our own dreams
for they are deferred like Mbeki's
we die calling for Nkosi Johnson
oblivious to the hand of puppeteer Gail Johnson
Nkosi died for a cause we scared to die like Johnson
for they'll say we were puppeteered by Johnson & Johnson

before july is over they say
they say half of ya will be jabbed
from leftovers they missed when they stole the batch
leftovers from their last supper
crumbs of unleavened bread that survived the feast
plus unfermented wine that's the blood of Gates
we shall sip and ululate
say our *au revior* 'fore it is too late

The Artist

Daisy May

There is a fine line between
the artist and the art
at one point the artist becomes the art
and at another the art is the artist
perhaps it is in the meeting
of the chaos and the calm
that the art is born
perhaps the magic lies
in the moments
that we wish we could change
perhaps it is your dance with life
that mirrors across the canvas
that brings us alive
the unexplainable emotion and connection
that whispers in our souls
and makes us see life
a little differently
a little brighter
maybe that is the purpose of the artist
for it is in the light
that we can see the complexity of rainbow colours
the tragedy and the joy
all that is and can be
and somehow
you immortalise living
into brushstrokes on canvas
as though it were easy.

Lighthouse or the storm
Daisy May

You must chase the light in you
you are both a lighthouse and the storm
sometimes you just need a reminder
that it's okay
to take up space
to hold your own
for beginnings and ends
are both starts and endings
it's all about perspective
and even with that
there can be more than one.

Still Alive
Chenjerai Mhondera

In the middle of the night,
When all love is trapped in you,
But network on a vacation
Or on some sort of a sabbatical break,
Dejection rises in you
Like bile,
And you never know
what your love is thinking this time

That abandonment forced on them,
When you are absent from them

That animosity, that anxiety,
that uncertainty, that discomfort,
that insecurity,
you never know what feeling
takes on them

But like a sacrifice, you keep burning,
burning and burning -
hoping, your smoke
'll spread faster than a whipping and stubborn signal
and reach your love,
Before they die

The queen bed, like an altar
And you are consuming in hell and fire,
Shut in your bones

You crack to think,

You lay by the edges of your bed, to move
Messages piling in you, like ice falling
To a cold feel of you

The transmitter in a
terrible show off, of power,
Basking in its bastard lot,
Sending only cold shoulders
And firing blank anger
And corking disappointments

And as bars, keep barred,
One is a victim if ever they don't want to forgive
For whatever time, may name inconveniences caused.

#&+/-
Chenjerai Mhondera

You Used To Greet Me At Eight
Of dawn and yawn
But Then That Was That,

> For Since Then You Got
> Used To Break Me Every Now
> and Again.

Perhaps, It's Because,
**You'd Come To Realize You've Got Nothing Else To Do With
Me**

The Lost Kingdoms
Fayssal Chafaki

Modor o' Lands, part o' Heaven
Grant o' the Lard o' High Seven
The place o' birth, the early sparkle,
Lighten the way ye al' darkle!
Ane Continent tha' gives 'nd na tak
Bestolen her riches sack afte' sack
Frea North t' South, frea West t' East
Be safe the ground fo' the Hungry Beast,
The thousand-headed greedy Monster
Tha' feeds on ev'ry eald 'nd youngster
But now Africa awakes
Enough she suffers 'nd she aches
Respect ye must show t' yer roots
Away yer bloody hands 'nd dirty boots!
Recall tha' fury only brings fury
Ond 'tis now time t' change History.
Less beknown o' Lost Kingdoms
(Whilst today mo' o' ye blow into condoms)
Enjoy, play, 'nd hae fun
Sin as mu' as ye can
Hwaet ye seest, if ye seest, lak empty ruins,
Hwaet collapsed, o' becovered by dunes,
Wert grete cities 'nd splendid palaces,
Ond mo' beautiful maiden faces
Alas! They be eal gone
Truth 'gainst which na 'thing can be done
Yer blindness leads ye t' yer fate

Fo' the Previous disappeared, 'nd so the Late
'Tis time, 'gain, I must explain
Before the Oppressor begins t' complain:
Record the lost fame o' Axum,
The Defeat, the Signs, the Doom,
The Wealth, the Arc, the hidden treasures,
The spiritual liquor, the Huri who pleasures,
Blink, die, 'nd resurrect
'Tis earthly life hae n'v'r been perfect!
The Link be in the Kingdom o' Ethiopia
Eternity ye seekest, na Utopia
Saints sought refuge in Lalibela,
Sat 'round ane pond wi' few wolffiella,
The day they pleaded the High Lard
By the guidance o' Jesus 'nd the Sacred Ward
Remember I am ane Muslim Bard
Dost ye na turn Faith int' ane playin' card!
The Saints escaped oppressors
Hwaet be the sins o' early confessors?

African Unity

Fayssal Chafaki

African beings! African poor
I still see tha' diamonds lure
Ur' Hame-continent, detinue,
T' decorate ane certain Avenue!
African poor! Suffering brothers
Will you keep worshipping others?
What if ane day we unite
Ond declare tha' decisive fight
The bloody pond is dried,
The black infant eal night cried,
The land is divided, shared wi' blood,
Misery, famine, calamity, 'nd flood
So' titles in bold; so' faces are sold
So' stories, untold; so' corpses, cold
Who cares! It is only Africa
Na England, na France, na America
It is, on earth, the largest laboratory,
The Greatest Slavery & Fear Factory.
Civilized beings are mean
Too mu' suckin', time to wean
Africa must feel free,
Completely independent, prae!
Be deaf, 'nd turn blind
Fo' humans are 'nother kind
Be safe! We do na bite
We strongly claim what is ur' right
We owe respect, we n'v'r harm
Is na liberty meant to be ane charm?
Thinkin' eal Africans are fools,
Creation o' the Almighty, na tools
Being hated, too, na longer endured

O' murdered, poisoned, 'nd na cured
Cure hearts tha' are dark lak tar
Clean brains whose sole aim is t' mar!
African unity is na hard t' achieve
If African learned solemnly believe.
Stop enfeeblin' ur' mother-continent
It has na 'v'r been fo' sell o' rent
Plundered, looted, stolen by force
Who refuses will scream, of course!
Na now! Na to-day! Na 'tis moment
We are na made fo' ye t' torment
Leave us in peace! Eal tha' we want
Sacrificing humans, racists are wont
Hate, ane day, will cease
Africa will na mo' fall on her knees.

THE PEOPLE CALLED AFRICANS
EGWUMA DEBORAH OJOCHENEMI

We are many, a people with skin that glow like the stars at dusk and like light rays that seep through window blinds at dawn

We are the ones whose paths have led through seasons of woes, wars and darkness

We've fallen hard, like the phoenix, we rise

We won't forget the warriors who subdued kingdoms and etched their names on the sands of time:
Mansa Musa, Haile Selassie, Queen Amina, Jaja of Opobo, Yaa Asantewaa

We are the people called Africans,
a people intricately woven together by love,
endowed greatly with minerals, diverse in culture

We are Africans, civilization's first kiss,
With a history, vibrant and rich,
We are builders, artists, warriors, farmers and thinkers,
our mind, a deep well that never runs dry,

We are a people once chained to the gory sights of yesterday,
Our eyes, blinded by phobias of Father's past,

Today, like the phoenix, we rise

We are Africans
Bold, gallant, like a soldier battle ready, we march

Our voices raised,
echoing the songs of our heroes past, we march

The future sings of a long awaited redemption
They are a forgotten race, they say.
They are a race with no identity, they jeer

They failed to see us for who we had grown to be,
an army whose time has come.

The wake of a new dawn

Flavia Waighala

The miles we have moved to get to the side of truth! Can never be compared to the giants we have faced, Across valleys, hills oceans and seas, Our feet have often felt the stony and soft ground, Yet even as we have trod on we have not stopped, Even as we have run, we have not fainted, Yet we lost our breathe countless times, And have learnt to inhale deeper, I know that Our reckoning is here, Time has triggered change in the norms, One day on a full moon,

We will go out there and swing our hips to a podium, And tell of the tales of freedom, The ones we told on cold floors, the only kind of tales that end in more love, For peace and justice, The kind you can only see in the looking back. We will forever look back and see, How we changed. How we rose. As a nation

MOTHER NATURES BOWL IS EMPTY

Glamour Adah

Mother Nature's bowl is empty,
Another night to sleep hungry,
No water to wet her dry tongue,
Or food to fill her growling stomach,
Her bosoms are dried out so her children have nothing to suckle,
And her skin has grown dull from wariness,
For this was not a good season for crops to grow,
Because the rain will never came,
Thus, her dry bosoms,
Thus, her growling stomach,
Because you see, when she checked the cupboards,
When she rummaged through the fridge,
There were filled with snakes,
Big green eyed slithering snakes,
As fat as pigs
And mouths that left no crumbs behind,
So there she sat to await her fate,
To waste away all through the day,
Because mother nature's bowl is empty,
Another night to sleep hungry.

WHEN THE RIVER RUNS DRY
Glamour Adah

When the river runs dry,
Where will we fetch from?
Dry mouth of thirsty children will cry oh-so-bitterly,
Will they drink their tears?
It is already shallow and brown,
Dirt from centuries washed into it,
Polluting our once blistering river,
So now that it is almost gone,
From greedy mouths drinking it up with mouths like elephant trunks
And filthy handed criminals washing their muddy hands and feet into
it,
Where will we fetch from?

When the famine finally comes,
Where will we eat from?
Hungry stomachs of the young will growl like bears,
Will they then eat one another?
The crops are already dwindling,
Wilting on the ground,
The dried up ground,
That was once nourished and pregnant with nutrients,
So now that is almost gone,
From weevils and locusts destroying our crops,
And the soil now impotent,
Where will we farm?

When the market place is empty,
Where we gather resources?

The market square once full of life, now a ghost town,
Will traders sit idle?
Empty hands of once eager traders now source for other means to
feed mouths,
Even if it means getting their hands dirty,
So now that it is almost gone,
From scheming thieves robbing us blind,
And stingy eyes hoarding what belongs to all,
Where then will we gather resources?

Leaders, fellow people of this land,
We are the ones who will make the children's dry mouths cry,
And their empty stomachs to growl,
Because the traders will be idle,
For you and I are the dirty mouths like elephant trunks,
We are the filthy hands and feel that turn the river muddy,
By washing our dirt into it,
We are the weevil and locusts that destroy the crops,
And the ones who make the land impotent,
We are the ones who subject the traders to filthy hands,
By robbing one another blind,
And our stingy eyes will never let us see the truth.

So what then will we do,
Once our great kingdom falls apart,
We no longer sell our people into slavery,
Instead they sell themselves free of charge,
Do we subject ourselves to this suffering?
Will we trek miles to find another river to drink from?
Will we force ourselves to travel afar just to find potent land?
And hawk from mountain to mountain just to make a living?
What will be left for our children?
What will be left when it's their turn?
For our fathers told us, "Be careful , children" ,

But our ears turned deaf to their warnings,
So when the market place is empty,
And the famine comes,
And the river runs dry,
What then will we do?

THE TALKING DRUM THAT HAS NO BEAT
Glamour Adah

In an orchestra,
The Guitar cried out melodies as its strings are plucked,
The moans of pleasure that arouse men,
Then the Shekere sways to the beat,
Her mesmerizing beaded waist is hypnotic,
And then sings a tune that is forever sweet,
That no man can resist,
But you see that one over there?
Yes, that Talking drum over there,
It is empty,
Even the giant Bata mocks it,
How can the King of Rhythm,
Be as mute as the air?
How come you have no tune?
You were the most beautiful of them all,
What happened?
Who defiled you?
Who took your voice?
Ah! It is over for you,
Oya go! You have no place here,
We have no use for an empty drum,
One a talking drum,

Now a side stool,
Go! We don't need you,
No one wants a talking drum that has no beat,
We have slapped and slapped,
With pankere and owo,
The empty talking drum is useless,
Go! And never return.

{:. **Pankere- cane;** :.**Owo- hand;** :.**Bata- drum,** :. **Shekere- beaded instrument**}

Me To Wo Nkabom Ho Nwom
Adjei Agyei-Baah na ɔtwerɛ

Afrika tie me,
adɛn na wo nkabom anamɔntuo
ayɛ nyaa sɛ nwa a n'akyiri nyɛ ahomeka yi?

wo da so dwodwo woho wɔ baobab nwunu mu
da na hɔɔ wɔ wo agudeɛ aboɔ so
wɔ berɛ a woahafoɔ boro wo nnadeɛ brom sɛ bogya
dwen sɛ sɛbi wo yɛ kwadwofoɔ bi a wo kuta kora
de nom nsa, sane de srɛsrɛ adeɛ

sɔre waka kabom ɛnɛ, Afrika!
na ntatea mmienu kabom a ɔtumi fa abɛbɛ soa

I Sing of Your Unity
Adjei Agyei-Baah

hear me Africa,
why this snail walk to unity
without a silver trail of hope?

you still bask in your baobab shade
sleep dead on your rock bed of riches
while others strike your metals into glow of fireflies
and think you, a lazy person who has the calabash
for drinking and begging

Arise to your unity today, Africa!
for two ants do not fail to pull a grasshopper

74

Pentsiwa

Mede ma medɔ, me yere, ne me nkwa
Adjei Agyei-Baah na ɔtwerɛɛ

Ɔsɔɔno a wo nante ma woahwenɛɛ to nnwom
Aaah yaa na ebi se ɔkoteterɛ bɔ nitiri nko kwa
Me Nubia hemaa a wo honam te sɛ sinamon dua, wɔ honam sɛ ɔdadeɛ dua
Woanim te sɛ ɔsram apaeɛ ama nsoroma ahweteɛ
sisie a ɛfrɛfrɛ anadwo nkɔmɔ, atentenhuo ɛnam ɔpɛ mframa soɔ!
pentsiwa, w'ano nkawa te sɛ sare so afurum, a ɛdɔ kɔn sɛ abibirem nsafufuo
pentsiwa, n'ani nkosua te sɛ ɔsebɔ tuntum, a ɛrebɔ osum ahweteɛ

Aa.. na woho hyew
Na me kɔn adɔ anadwoberɛ yi onwunu reposa me yi
Menya sɛ me nsa nam wo tiri nwi mpɛsɛmpɛsɛ mu
Na mɛyi me nkwammoa agu woadukromu hɔ

Na m'akyini wiase afa ɛnan ahunu ɔtan a adasa wɔ de ma nipa tuntum
Me tuntum wedeɛ a wode nkuto sra so daadaa
Ayɛ wedeɛ denden sɛ bɛnkoro, na wo Akyenfo nsuo na bɛtumi ama n'ayɛ mmerɛ
Na ɛmere tenten na wɔn aboto me kra, twe no wɔ wɔn nsutam ani wɔ berɛ a wɔn nnim sɛ me yɛ ɔdehye kɛseɛ
Ɔhene ba barima a metu mpasa wɔ me hyeɛ mu a esie ne nnowa ahyɛ mu ma
Nsebɔ bruwaa a wɔ bɔɔ bena wɔ me pea ano

Nanso wo nsutadeɛ ano na mesan reba, fa Elimina pono a ɛgye abrɛfoɔ
Wo sereɛ mu na mehunu menkyi

75

Na wo kube nsuo na ɛkum me nsukɔm
Na wo mframa nwunu mu na me nsa ka nea mahwere nyinaa

Pentsiwa
For my love, wife & life
Adjei Agyei-Baah

The goddess who struts in rocking beads
Ah! So you think the lizard nods for nothing
My Nubian queen of cinnamon skin, fleshy as a baobab
Face of a blossom moon, dispersing stars to an early sleep
Hips of sinuous gestures, floating kapok in the Harmattan Winds!
Pentsiwa, with her lips of zebra stripes, inviting like the froth
of African palm wine
Pentsiwa, her eyes are of the panther's, pushing darkness
into a broad daylight

Ah…but for your warmth
I have missed in these wilder nights of lashing coldness
Run my fingers through your fronds of jet black dreads
And have my sorrows drown in the grove of your shrine

I've sailed the seven seas, and felt its turbulence against my skin
This blackness which you nourished with your soothing hands of shea-
butter
Are now tough like the rhino's that only your Saltpond waters can
dissolve
So long my soul has been tramped, muddied in the waters
of lords who never knew me a Negus
A prince who once surveyed my savannahs of anthills and darting
impalas
Of crouching leopards who felt the sharpness of the warrior's spear

But into your coastal arms I return, through Elmina's *gate of yes return*
Your radiant smile, my bearing found
Your coconut water, my thirstiness quenched
And in your gentle breeze a moment restored!

POEM 2
Musa Mukelwa Simelane

From the molecule of time,
To its atomic steps,
I traveled the world from all rites of passages,
To baby steps and stammering syllables,
Where deafening silence made the songs of ants to be heard.
Where snakes travelled longer distances than their bodies,
Where my age and theirs were kissed younger by the pimples of love.
Life emerged from cradles of a poetic mind,
We the creation,
We are just lines and stanzas in his beautiful sonnet.
Our trials and tribulations are just metaphors
And similes to him,
One day,
back,where it all began,
Life will shrink its meaning back to the hole it crept out from.

POISONED FRUIT

Jabulani Mzinyathi

There's need to dig deep
Not just scratching the surface
The fruit does not usually fall
Fall far from the tree
So learn these lessons well

When you walk down the streets
Keep your mind's eye wide opened
Many wolves in sheep skins
The false piety is there displayed
And you fall into the deep pits

Look beneath the bland smiles
There lurks death and destruction
There lies the snares of deception
Dig deep not scratching the surface
That you may find boundless joy

MELODY
Jabulani Mzinyathi

That was her name
There was no melody
Sang far off key
In that discordant voice

Perhaps it was that stud
Embedded on her sharp tongue
Spewing all kinds of expletives
That nauseating verbal diarrhea

Rued the day I was trapped
That day the hunter was hunted
The impala trying to devour the lion
That was how it turned out to be

She was there at that bar
Laughing where no joke was
Bob Marley termed her pimper's paradise
Leaving nothing to imagination
She paraded her flaccid wares

The copious amounts of alcohol
She became not wise but otherwise
Till she vomited her way to shame
That could be her way to fame

There was no trace of melody
In her insipid and drunken slur
The highest bidder had his way
For her privacy had turned public

THE QUEEN
Jabulani Mzinyathi

She is a slave driver
Feeding on their desperation
She bites off chunks of flesh
From the carrion of their ways

She retired from active service
She was a soldier of fortune
That house she built long ago
From the fruits of her nocturnal activities

Now in the twilight of her life
She gets the pound of flesh
She also gets the drops of blood
Chewing time white bones like a hyena

She collects the sordid coins and notes
She is the queen among slaves
She drives them to exhaustion
Her eagle eyes scan the bar for suitors
And the slavery continues with no end in sight

Hindsight

Kirsten Miller

I remember hindsight,
the way she curled
around my brain,
twisting like rope
to tell me what it was
I had done wrong.
I recall the staircase
of backward glances,
her wit ascending
away from you;
an afterthought
that might have me triumph
and you turn and decide
to take it all back,

and me;

me over years, waiting for dreams
in which you'd appear,
stepping softly over lives
as though they were only
stones on a river crossing that,
like hindsight, might lead me back
over time's broken river;
a return to the forest
of you.

Mornings
Kirsten Miller

Sometimes
just to write in the sun
is enough.
The clink of your spoon
against the cereal bowl,
a vervet watching
from a tree
waiting
for what we both can eat
sharing
the view of this green valley.
Below there is green,
a world we both have known
trees
between the branches
green
and the sound of distant tractors,
machines coming closer
clearing away any possibility
of there being any more butterflies
in the sun.

River crossing
Kirsten Miller

Open, my hands,
the shadows of my fingers
still entwined with yours.
Love flows,
the river offers us
fluidity and motion,
unexpected depths and
unforgiving time.
Cool your hands
in this water, watch
the stones unfold
the mosaic of a time-worn path.
I am waiting at the end
of the river for you,
unfurling fronds, my
aching green overshadowing
sound, and birds dipping
their beaks, tasting bubbles
and motion and fluid air,
bringing home to the sky
what was not.

Konke endikwaziyo...
Lubabalo Tatase

Khange kuhlale kunje kum, andizalwanga
Ndingumkreqi nto nje ndasuka ndaziva ndindedwa.
Ndaziva ndisoyika, ndiyakhubeka unjalo nje ndinqwenela
Ukuba umntu ebendixelele ukuba ubomi sisilwane esimazinyo
azizixengeba.

Ebendixelele ukuba obu bomi bobethu ukuba sibukhethe.
Akukho mntu uyakukunika iizitshixo okanye incwadi
Enemithetho yonke, mincinci endiyaziyo ndiyakuxelela
Inene sihlobo sam. Xa bekunxibisa ubuxoki,

Ude ushiyeke uze, uze nenyaniso uyishiyele ilize.
Masifuduke ke esihogweni, siqiqe engqondweni,
Xa kanye isaqhwithi sivuthuza, sele uhlawule
Ixabiso elipheleleyo ngemapazamo nganye.

Uyakutyekeza umhlaba, ithemba lixel'ithamsanqa.
Ziye ngokufiphala iinkwenkwezi ezikukhomb'indlela.
Konke endikwaziyo ozokuthi ga ngoku ithemba liyaphilisa,
Xa lingakudanisanga. Xa lingekathi ndithenge.

Qubula intshuntshe yakho ubinze uqengq'ugodo,
Kaloku kwesisihlandlo kuzokwenziwa umntu omtsha.
Yiba ligwiba nekhaka ke kwisizwe sakowenu,
Kumaxesha onke ezaqhwithi. Tshini ndiyaqala ubona umntu!

Nanku umntu efika mamkeleni! Kakade lent' umbona
Imnandi ngochubelana. Kakade ebanj'íbele imazi iyehlisa.
Akho mveku iyawulala ngephango kwisizwe sakowenu.
Tshini wanceda uMdali wadala xa kuhlala kuhlale kuhluthe
Nembacu efana kanye nam lo!

85

Intliziyo yam...

Intliziyo yam iyaxhuma
xa ndibona umnyama esibhakabhakeni;
Kwakunjalo ke ukuqala kwam ubomi;
 Kunjalo na ngoku ndiyindoda;
 Makube njalo xa ndaluphala,
 kungenjalo mandife!
Umntwana nguyise woMntu;
 Kunjalo nje ndinqwenela ukuba
 iintsuku zam zibophane nganye
nganye oku kukuhlonela kwendalo.

These are the things
Lubabalo Tatase

These are the things
That come to me
In my sleep at night.
When last did you allow
Spirit to sink into,
Self, take in the not
So pretty parts.
Be attentive to the
Silent corners, listen in on
The chatter of your inner
Walls, when last?
A voice inside my head,
Reverberated and echoed,
Into thousand several thoughts.
Now these are the
Things that come to me in my sleep.
Which tongue does your
Mind wander to, for
Colourful thoughts?
Not those with time lags.
I mean extended moments of,
Searching for words to,
Describe the simplest,
Of things.
But those which,
Mind finds with ease.
These are the things,
That find me in my sleep.
They come with whispers,
And metaphors. Are you really

Good or have you gotten
Tired of giving elaborate
Answers to fickle souls
That lose sense of your
Reality after they give
Their hollow "sorry"?
Now there are the
Things that came
To me in my sleep
At night.

Make Me
Emmanuel Mwenye

Make me green
like the trees before the 90's
make me blue
like the skies of Nyasaland

make me a seed
of peace and joy
love and courage
make me a seed
of faith and hope

make me resilient
from fear and doubt
make me strong
against the anger of mother nature

make me recyclable
that we may meet after life
make me blind
that I may see no colour

make me your own
educate me for potential
make me warm
like the heart of Africa
make me nothing
but a new Nyasaland

The Gemini of lovers

Musa B Jibril

Shall you bring forth thy tropical breasts?
Sun sights them glittering, swelled down
Like a bucket of water in a deep well
Which swelled by the liquid in it

Extinct is the death before you
Black forest foretells living without you
You are the climber of prayer within me
We are the Gemini of lovers within stars

Dormant is the pain before you
Shall I call you the breeze of dawn?
A daring man lulled by your winy voice
As the birds of pain pecked at his health

My last wish
Musa B Jibril

Guns girt on our chest.
Helmets, like a bridle of a horse.
Blotting camouflage with blood,
like crimson sundown in the tropics
Before the night folds his wings

.

Crawling on the bog.
Battlefield today we hug,
on the blind night of hyenas.
Then I freet the memories of dear
A pregnant wife on the bed of pain

.

May the she cradle her child
With the green white flag
When my dog chain locate her palms

.

Rough life
Musa B Jibril

Solace is to nocturnal rain
A blanket of thieves and frogs.
Sizzle is to diurnal rain
That drops from the lids of clouds
.

The eyelids opened for her eyes
Ruby like an ember in the night
And the rain on her laps
Disappeared like mizzles on a dune
.

Then, she leveed the tears with palms
As she heard the arriving patter
Does this depicts the life of Khadeejah
Before the appearance of her Maharaja?
.

Or she even added some pain lines
In between the between the love lines
On her palms, with a sharp knife
In trying to cut a sorrow and bliss

LACERATED GLOMERULUS

Wilson Waison

A nephron impulse,
I have befriended dialysis for cleansing
All the glomerulus clotted
I pass irons, thick urea corroded
the duct and borrowed me impotence
Devoid a seed to bury in her fertile womb.

Yes I drank too much anything of everything
Kissed like a French man from every bottle
And you broke me with no remorse
Gradually we became bonded
Yet you ate me deep within
The irony of I devouring you when ice cold
You lacerated my flesh.

Now she bares the blame,
Stereotypes from the family name
And you coincided with her jolly
Ceased the laughter in our matrimony
Yet I can't confess to your Judas kisses
Conform to that bitter truth
You bored in me...
 Poetics

ON THE WAY . . .

ALLAN KOLSKI HORWITZ

At the intersection of acorn lane and
louis botha
I give two rand to a stained woman with a hole
for a mouth
At the intersection of walker road and
bertha
I give one rand seventy to a smirking man with
a crippled swagger
At the intersection of albertina sisulu
street and main
I give fifty cents to a burnt-out child with a
burning hand
At the intersection of joe slovo drive and
abel
I give one rand twenty to an old woman who
carried a bundle of snot
on her blanketed back
At the intersection of jan smuts avenue
and empire
I give five rand to a vacant glue sniffer who
pawed the heavens
and drooled on my window

Home?

How can I reach

H O M E?

Ja hey
ALLAN KOLSKI HORWITZ

she gets mugged for her
cellphone
work was draining
figures
calculations

on her way

home

passing in half-light   *two*

guys in track suits

knives
push her into a park
push her down into a deep

triangle

of trees
she breathes very quickly   this is an old

story
she doesn't know whether to scream or   not to scream   and
the more she thinks about

it

the less likely she is to   scream
as they push her
DOWN

95

on her way home

on her back   going back to her kids and

her man

and

this?

SO WHAT IF SHE WAS ON HER
WAY HOME
ISN'T EVERYONE ALWAYS looking for a warm hole?

this is an old story
adam has never forgotten
the dog moves alone or in packs but has never
forgiven
why did the bitch have to eat the fucking apple and make us
ashamed?

This is an old story
A very   old   story
They push her face into the mud   spread her
legs with their sticks

Then they take turns

they *take turns*

they take turns *take turns*

This way and **that**   dogs

Dogs making

turns

This is an old story

96

STATE OF THE DOMINANT SPECIES

ALLAN KOLSKI HORWITZ

One point two billion crammed on the
polluted banks of a caste-ridden Hindu
ethno-nationalist river
Another one point three billion
<u>squatting under the glare</u> of a Fong
Kong Communist Confucian <u>robot</u>
Over six hundred million in the Cradle of
Humankind crushed under the sagging belly of

the Big Man and his sadistic
cohorts
Over four hundred million ▮▮▮▮ on
the patios of sunglassed colonials and
Bolivarian generalissimos
Another three hundred and forty
million dangling at the ends of
kryptonite <u>missile heads</u>
emblazoned with the stars and *stripes*
of puritanical slavers

And close by another two hundred odd million bored by Bruxelle, strangled with the toxic tape of snarling lily-white borders

Rivalled only by the one hundred million licking the *KGB's*

lips with their frozen sweat

Beside the seventy-four hundred million women forced to robe the rape fantasies of bearded children
And the five hundred and twenty-nine million <u>depressives</u> devoted to gurus who ride pope mobiles over canonical cliffs

And the thirteen million paedophiles porning their hormones, <u>chanting the bitch</u> names of their heavenly Mothers

Slowly   the godless garden   roasts under a withering
   sun

Sunset at Lekki

Jide Ajidahun

SARS, the murderous hunters on the road
The instruments of cruelty
The messengers of death
Like the herdsmen
SARS, the malady on our roads
The licensed robbers
Swathed in the flags of our nation
The authorized agents of darkness
The devouring lions
Nosing and sniffing into our bedrooms
Cockroaching the streets
Extorting our hard-earned currencies
Impounding our valuables
Slaying our future
Raping our women
Dragging us as goats to the slaughter
Their stations, our abattoirs.
Shooting the harmless
Our blood flows on the streets
Our youths always their suspects
As criminals who should always be shot
Without any trial or conviction
But the baboons in the parliament
The czars that slice our throats
Their gods and heroes
But Haribu is not listening
And his idiot blind guide
 Adamu is snoring

Chain these rabid dogs!
The terrorists on our roads

These wild and weird men
Disband them and let us breathe

We have no jobs
We have no hope
And we have no freedom
In our own land
Jobs cannot go round
Food cannot go round
Scholarships cannot go round
Funds cannot go round
But bullets can go round
To silence our youths
And they are not listening to us

SARS recycled as SWAT
Sill the same leopards
Demons in uniforms
Cast them out of our lives
After all, these signs shall follow them that believe
Yes, I believe!
And let us live

Now the SARS exchanged batons
With the soldiers
In the darkness that they created
The soldiers who shiver before the terrorists
And shit inside their pants
Now roared before the unarmed protesters
Romancing with armed thugs
Hobnobbing with hired hoodlums
And then the Lekki massacre
Soaking the toll gates with the blood of our children
The survivors now under fire

Mothers cry and grieve
They pine away
Without any consolation
Without any compensation
And usually without any justice
And fathers sigh in endless agonies
Oh! The beauty of our nation
Is slain upon Lekki
With the national flags in their hands
Our future died before manifestation
We have eaten our seeds
And chewed their cods
The calabash is broken
And the water has spilled
Our *akuro* is flooded
And yams become the kings of the heaps
Our only ember has been quenched

But the Emperor said nothing
And his messengers exchange lies as usual
Butimun and Oluwosan
Passing the buck
And paying homage to the Tsar
To keep their empires.
But as Tiwa asked
"Who gave the order?"

The Ashes of Beauty.

Jide Ajidahun

Tradition gave me clothes
But civilization gave me nakedness
Nature gave me long black hair for beauty
But modernity gave me baldness and shame.
I was born in glory
But I grew up as Ichabod.
I was born with comeliness
With tenderness
And honour
But civilization turned me to a mulatto.
I walk in veils
And in rags in the name of beauty,
I parade myself with the attires of a harlot
And I call that civilization.
My nails grow wild like a predator.
My hairs are fried
To give assorted colours
Now a citizen of no nation
When sewn with the hairs of the dead
And the long hairs of Red Indians
I become a caricature of myself.
My eye lashes are fixed
Tummy Tuck to be fitted
And lips painted
My head with crazy cuts.
Boobs enlarged
Penis engorged
And buttocks ballooned
In the name of civilization
And clothes tight fitted
Showcasing the body curves

And contours
My fingers loaded with rings
And nose with jewels
My feet with twinkling ornaments.
To become fashionable.
My trousers are sagged like a prisoner
And my skirt slit
Flowing like the mask of a masquerade.
And my dignity is advertised without shame.
Nature taught me morals
But civilization taught me concupiscence.
Father taught me to prostrate when I greet.
But modernity taught me to hug when I greet
Mother taught me to kneel when I greet
But civilization taught me kissing
And hugging
And pecking
And handshake
When I greet.
Nature gave me shepherds
But modernity gave me wolves.
Nature gave me purity
But civilization gave me lewdness.
Born with naturalness
Bred with artificialities
Mine is a loose and wild generation

KING YOU
(Dedicated to my late father)
Onuchi Mark Onoruoiza

The fathering might
of your kingly clout
across ageless moons
and ceaseless dusks
across oceans
climes and coasts
remain an affirmation
of your unflinching commitment
to fatherhood.
From primordial times
to modern seasons
your courageous guide
continue to inspire all!
The cupid culture
of your warm arms
remain solace
for communal communion
a duke of unwavering pledge!
From your aristocratic gestures
to your democratic embrace
life's untarnished warmth rings through…
Your prophetic and priestly canons -
a reflection of your noble grace
and your shinning knighthood in blazing armour
stirred our hearts with adorable zeal
and timeless imprints on our fragile minds!
And now…
May we fathers
and fathers in waiting
with fresh mantles

ignite sparks of redemption
and continue to hack fresh paths of hope
forge new routes to better life
as we strive to be more!

RESTORATION

Onuchi Mark Onoruoiza

The greying mantis
unfurls dawn
with the optics of the sun -
radiating the blooming gale
of a chameleon
in search of its prey...
With the outcry of the phoenix
at the verge of rebirth
a new season births!!
The plume ignites
fireworks beyond the lair
and the slumbering dusk
to a bout of fistful rage
we are on an impossible sail...
As we engage hope forlorn
you flutter!
The awry spill
of a wobbling snare
snarls hard
as we seek restoration
from the shackles
of greedy cabals
whose light obliterating schemes
shall be mangled to restore

unflinching hope
to a battered orb!

BANKABLE SUPERWOMEN
(Dedicated to African corporate women on the rise)
Onuchi Mark Onoruoiza

The genteel warmth
of poignant bloom
beyond blurry clouds
and hazy snowstorms
inspire your rankling core
as meticulous high-heeled paragons
disambiguate your riddled sheets!
They are the duchess of the domes
a star cast of stellar nobles
exemplary beacons
who now run the vaults
with impeccable brawn.
The whirlwind merchants
dare not dare the crypt
for their venal whims
and well mastered gambits
have since been demystified
with penal codes
and undercover machinery!

We salute
our legend of the ledgers
incorruptible dames at the helms,
as you continue to crash ceilings
crush longstanding dogmas
and crack age-long myths

we cannot wait to have you
take on the reins of power
across corporate borders!
To attain new heights
at the nation's corridors of clout
the very apex
of the nation's throne...
Through the ballot!

Omoerio Bwebikoroto e'Bitigire

Bonface Nyamweya

Ekerero ekenene nkeroo
Igoro ya omoerio o mama Afrika
Amariogi yokorwanerera abande aakwagura ase emieya yaito
Na ebitongo
Amang'ana amange agoiteka
Korwa ase ebikoba bia Abaafrika bogwancha okuya
Na abarai baito nabang'aini
Gotwara ebigancha chinse chia isiko
Na gotiga Abaafrika bamwabo
Bakoria obotioku bwenchara bwoka
Chiganga chiabo
Ne'chikura
Emeremo ya oboagachi bwa ebinyoro
Ne'muma bariete batakore
Onye bagokora, bono teri ase amagania aito
Amakabeso amanoru nigo atunyete chinse chiaito
Oborimo oboyia banyora
Buna ayaigoro agotacha bosio
Twabeka emerindo yo'orogendo, goanchera okobuneka
Kwegesaku kiabagisangio ba bono
Ase igo twasimisia omoyio ime ye'riote
Eritaragwena
Tiga oborabu bobe
Erio eganga ye'bikoroto ebitigire buna ebiechisokoro chiaito buna Nyerere
Bibwatigwe erio Africa enyore amatunda ya amagenderero
Aburukanirie na amariga aito yo'omogoko

The Fate of the Abandoned Shoes
Translation by Bonface Nyamweya

There is a raucous cry
On the fate of mother Africa
Voices of activism tumble upon our plains
And valleys
Waterfalls of words cascade
From the lips of Africans of goodwill
And our leaders are wise
To own abroad banks
To leave fellow Africans
Eating only the foul taste of their hungry breath
Their makeshift goals
Is general election
The homework of development
Is a crime they vowed never to commit
If they dare, then not for our interests
Fatty loans dog our nations
Newfound discovery of lies
As history marches on
We set in motion waves; paving real breaking
Of our own generation
Thus timely twisting a sword in a wound
Hardly healed
Let there be light
That the fate of the abandoned shoes of our forefathers like Nyerere
May be traced for Africa to get the fruits of development
Mingled with Africa's tears of happiness

Ona Ule Duwu
Mohammed U. Yusuf

Uma di ami ufane kuli majan,
di ami ugbalu talu ka ro ti nyon

ami eje kuma jen— ami ogwu
ukejuno mi, ma she tabale

ugbola tane'un du,
ma do olomi duwu

ododa emi, uneke gwu
lefi odu
todu kuwe ji igbe'un

afu kiya ju'i
ya nukola ebor gbere mi,
ya kami kudago pkaka

ona ule duwu mu bi
kpai alu'n kibi te—

ohi ene meji
kuma tene ohi ogesha.

Exit Door

Translation by Mohammed U. Yusuf

I shouldn't have shelved the clues,
shot down the rumours

my denials— depressants
for suspicion, became overdose

every tactless defence
of his, gives away a lie

out here, I could sit
through the night
to evade his punches

this restless wind
serves me soft rhythms,
nudging my resolve

an exit door was flung open
with his mouth agape—

a reflex for twin questions
craving honest answers.

Ononojo
Mohammed U. Yusuf

Amoma mi & omi attah ye,
oko ye efu Tony ebguwa medor

okolo'un eyidordor no buwate,
mi ojima olopu konyi wa.

Ubi odo me gwa, iliya dagemi—
attah ki ra buwate— kpai omi aku

iko ki eun shane nyo
efu olayewa

kani todu keneke murida banema.

Stranger

Translation by Mohammed U. Yusuf

My children & I found a father,
a husband in Tony's full embrace

his crib offered warmth,
wore us the garb of family.

Ten years on, he called here—
absentee father— tearing

when meaning had smiled
upon our lives

may be just to flip it over.

Pledged
Adiela Akoo

Long, long ago
you pledged your heart
etched your eternal love
causing you to constantly
keep washing up at my feet
like a half forgotten
mystical message
in a bottle, cast into the sea
of souls, centuries ago!

Our paths constantly, curiously crossing
in a predetermined puzzle of perplexities
leaving us pondering, on the part played
by Providence - and the most loving hand
on a heart, etched with initials
carved into an ancient, magical tree
that still stands somewhere, bearing witness
long after the bodies, bearing initials
became fodder for its roots!

Lifetime after lifetime
we're magically, momentarily
drawn together, to decipher
soul memories, we vaguely recall...

COUPLING

(Sonnet)

Adiela Akoo

Tossing and turning, words won't let me sleep,
rhyming and coupling, emotions running deep!
I contemplate waking, to write it all down,
but don't want to disturb you, don't want you to frown!

I try very hard to remember each word,
over and over, silently, unheard!
I plan by the morning to record it afresh,
but duty takes precedence, so it remains just a wish!

When I finally find time to ink it all in,
my mind has already recycled the thing!
So I stare at the paper trying hard to recall,
that great wonder that would've impressed you all!

But the words refuse to come like they did in my bed,
so it may very well be said that my very best work, remained in my
head!

There was a time
Dennis Brad Kunguru

There was a time
When true love would chime
In the winds like the Elizabethan rhymes.
There was a time
When love was so much
And dreams seemed to match
As our souls shone bright like the heavenly torch.
There was a time indeed.

There was a time
When we felt that there was nothing
That could drift us apart
A time that we no longer seem to have.
Today's time seems to be pulling us
In different ways.
Our sweet conversations are no more,
For they have turned into heated arguments
If not nights of sorrowful silence and regrets.
True love is now being fed
On unwarranted hate and spite.
 "You are a liar!"
"You're a narcist!"
Have become our kind of talk.
Love is now turned to hate
And shown clearly in our eyes.

There was a time
A time when sweet admiration was felt inside,
A time when we sang songs of love
And not hate,
A time when the truth wasn't so hard to see in our eyes.

Today, we no longer can hug
Nor even play the tug.
Our morning goodbyes are dry
And our evening welcome backs are but neighs.
The truth ain't hard to see;
We are but thinking about the last goodbye
But afraid to say.

Could it be because there was that time?

I AM
DANIELS NANNA

I,
I am the pendulous breast
milked without rest,
sucked and chewed by the very best:
the fleas and bees from the West

I,
I am the open mouth cooking pot
After which the greedy political vultures lust
A pinch of salt in every pot
Enjoyed cold or steaming hot.

I,
I am the child that feed the father
A destitute without a mother
With state cares upon my slender shoulders
I can only grow shorter.

I,
I am the proverbial beast of burden
On whom the village depends
Whom the fleas and flies incessantly offend
And the gods will not defend.

I,
I am the heavenly finger
That feed your thankless mouths
That finger that is badly/wantonly bitten
Left to rot away
I, I am the Niger Delta.

I!
 I am the big heart
The nation's heart beat
The path no one must depart
If the national cake you want some part
Like the greedy political vultures

I! I am the scavenger's paradise
Manna from above!
The heavenly finger that feeds the land
The finger that is badly bitten
And left to rot away
I! I am the Niger Delta

Early year rains
Obinna Chilekezi

The heat had had its way
During the long time of drought
Agreed, in hot season, we are
Never had it this hot

The cloud darkens
Hiding the face of the sun
And gentle winds sail across
Leaving a gentle touch on the face

It began to rain …

You cannot imagine
This smile on the faces
Of leaves, under the showers
Of this mighty fall of rain

See the little bird nwanza*
Soaring and dancing in the rain, not alone
The fowls, insects and others all
Taking their first bath of the year.

*Is the smallest bird in Igboland where the poet comes from

Dimly and unwillingly, I had to leave
Obinna Chilekezi

"And then she thought, looking about the kitchen: 'Lord, wouldn't it be a blessing if he didn't never come back no more.' The Lord had given her what she said she wanted, as was often, she had found, His bewildering method of answering prayer. Frank never did come back".

- James Baldwin's Go Tell It On The Mountain

Eerie cries everywhere everyday
As gray clouds over shade the sun everyday
But looking outside beyond the shade are his
Invisible tears, hidden but walking about his day
And who will hear his own stories, no need today to tell

Adulterous, yes!
Scorn, tears filled the heart, not his dream
Not what he had dreamt along the moonlight dance
He left, stepping out on mists that covered the ground
With bagfilled regrets and betrayal full too, to unknown

Unlike Lot's wife, no looking back
He move, dimly and unwillingly, leaving behind
Both tears and joy walking out of that hateful room
He left. Never to revisit my vomit!

Night rain
Obinna Chilekezi

Night falls in rain
As night became darker than usual
Minutes later it rained, bucketful, everywhere, and
The stars ran too into their homes, for fear
Of flashing lightning, with no control
Across the dark face of night

The thunders too at war, roaring and rolling,
This night, unsafe, of moonlight steps
The moon calls of its shine, we call off our dance
For the ground slippery with mist and fear
The rain 'd taken off the moonshine, taken off our moonlaughters
Night has fallen in rain, fall in pains.

Men for Worms
Clement Chukwuka Idegwu

Pondered endlessly on the essence of this ill-fated
Why are we here?
One, fated to fail before its' commencement
A journey we never asked for
One, our opinions were never sought
That which we know next to nothing about
One, we will never know anything about
Not even what will befall us in the next second
One that profits nothing
Why indeed are we here?
Yet, men in their ignorance
Considering the powers they acquired mischievously
Could tap their chest severally
Boasting of what they will do to others.
Though they could kill and maim
And repeatedly do this
None raises an eyebrow for fear of being a victim.

No sooner had the killed gone, the killers
Become special delicacies for worms
Worms that even the killers could tramp upon
Grow fat on them
Their blood and that of the innocent victims.

Cross –Examine
Clement Chukwuka Idegwu

Ours is a club
We mean and do no harm to anyone
We are mere singles interested in coupled men
People in their ignorance call us male poachers
We don't snatch
We only need an attachment that do no harm
We don't need this scoop or dipper that stirs our thing full time
We want to be as free as birds in the air
We value our desired breathing space
Not to be accountable to any man
They come around, stir our thing
And what more, when we are full
Allow them to go back from whence they came
Be it mid night, they go back to their keepers
To cork their bottles
Even for life, apart from the seconds opening for a drop of wine
The permanent keepers of our coupled men get crazy
Get crazier and call us names
When we decouple them for a while
They see us prettier and more desirable than they
And that indeed we are
For what else could make their husbands
Go searching for the goods they carry and display
Like a butcher in New Benin market endlessly driving flies away
Leaving these meat for flies, their husbands come for ours
The same goods
We are proud we are what we are
No 'akara' seller at a road junction
Whether in the cities or villages
Feel ashamed when buyers queue up
Either in scorching sun or heavy downpour

To spend a life earning just for a ball of her juicy 'akara'
Our juicy 'akara' is irresistible
She whose cock strays
Should cross-examine
Indeed cross –examine herself
For why will one complain for one's errors.

Life is a Tempest
Clement Chukwuka Idegwu

Each second of our lives sees us set on the
boisterous wind
Tossing us to the cardinals like sulphur darting in a
glass of water.
A ball set in motion
Bouncing violently at the four walls of a room
Can never escape being scathed
And that is man
For no man goes to his rest intact
He goes home either maimed physically
Or with a battered and fragmented soul
For what is a man but a toddler set against
tornadoes
Life is indeed a tempest
And man billed to swim in it unto death.

LONELY EMBERS
Wisdom C. Nwoga

Here I am
before your smoky cave.
I have ran too far
than legs could carry.
By my ignorance,
I have left the flames of this ancestral
cave to a bunch of lonely embers
seeking heaven in western breasts
where even my shadow rejected me.

Before you mother of light,
I return, kneeling wearily,
broken like Chinaware
ready to pour libations
at your long-dejected feet
& turn this smoky cave
into a home of burning flames.

AMBUSH

Wisdom C. Nwoga

Dawn, in this black home of ours,
We SMILED in unison...
In the back of yesteryears
And its unfruitful fronts,
Things have happened
Which break us apart at noon
In fury of whirlwind;
Then nurtured hope, swept away.

Hunger, war, sorrow, and our big brothers haven.
Budding leaves shred off branches,
Unriped fruits fall unyieldinly
And hopes buried in tender graves.

Night, and brothers come,
Draining the oil in the lamp.
Like 'suppliant snake', they coil
On trodden parts expecting 'the killing cry'.

Ambush,
Our brothers strike with smith's red metal,
Puncture the womb of expectations and
Trod ruthlessly on planted hopes.

NGOZI OKONJO-IWEALA
T. O. Adesanmi

A human not a woman!
Her vision very clear
With a long periscope
the long distance she saw
The receivements achieved
The celebrations here focused!
A human not a woman!
Well prepared she was
For the long journey foreseen
Sandals buckled, reticules prepared
And the bubbles of gum along the way
'Cos it was a long journey!

A human not a woman!
No room to laze around
No humming of complaints
Only with hymns of readiness and carefulness
The books she hooked
The hills she climbed
Shoulder to shoulder with men
Yet not tired, neither dismayed!

A human not a woman!
With the mind made
With the price paid
With the fears caged
And the trophies claimed
All maids bade her Champion
And feminine voices sing her accolades!

A human not a woman!

Clear mind I have here!
To my mind she's a true model
For all she's a quintessence
Not a womanist to some
Nor a feminist to others
Ngozi is a model
Okonjo is an epitome
Iweala wears the crown
But for all trailbazing!

A human not a woman!
She's a moral book for all
A must read a piece
Borrow a leaf not a sheaf
The way up isn't to look down
The road to success not gendered!

3 A.M.
RANDHEER PRITHIRAJ

Subtle sounds of early earth,
Evokes our mind with delightful mirth.
Treading the trails of guidance,
Unlit sparks gain its brightness,
Nightfall awakens in the hours of silence.

Submerged in thoughtful splendour –
The night-time high calls for surrender.
Creative abstractions begin to thrive,
In the early hours of the morning –
Our imagination comes alive.

The nightly pathway becomes lightened –
Inventive uniqueness is heightened.
We indulge in the corners of historia –
Feelings, words, unrealistic scenarios,
Carry us through the realms of euphoria.

We seek refuge in remoteness,
Seclusion, solitude and aloneness.
Our mind tends to drift away –
The tracks of fascination and curiosity,
Precedes the start of a new day.

A Prayer for Peace

Deena Padayachee

If I could turn the sands of the Sahara to sugar cane
and give some of it to the senseless
so fewer people might want to wage war.

If I could melt the ice of Siberia and help the earth hum with life,
And award some of it to the landless,
If I could make a little of the Kalahari,
green,
and grant it to the neo nazi denizens
so thieves might be less free with our enterprises.

If I could make a little of the Atlantic,
land,
and gift some of it to the greedy
so bombs might not dismember children
and people will not be paralysed.

If I could transform a little of the Pacific ocean into soil
And bequeath it to the wealthy to fight in among themselves
so that they might stay away from other people's countries...

If I could teach the people that there is enough land on our planet,
that they have no need to invade other people's lands.

If I could convince soldiers that invading another's country
Is criminal,
That destroying families, homes, hospitals, schools, and people
Is criminal.
If I could teach the smug to be satisfied with God's bounty,
That there's no need to steal.
If I could teach people that there is

no happiness in another person's unhappiness
or life in another's death.

If I could teach people not to strangle this beautiful Earth
with their progeny and annihilate other species.
If I could teach people that religion cannot mean hate,
that arrogance is merely a symptom of decay and doom.
If only,
O Lord!
If only!

QUESTIONS OF IDENTITY
Sithembele Isaac Xhegwana

Below me, a picturesque
valley, dotted, with undulating
hills. This valley, wanting to nestle
on the hills that I, dumbfounded,
wish to confide in.

Deep in these hills, I,
having rounded other heights,
more abstract than the guilt-inducing
panorama below my feet, I sense
inabilities, far beyond those of sight,

in defining this scenery. I saw
them sink, these grass thatched
domes, these corrugated iron
roofs. Upon the swift impact of this
view, I seem to trudge to an even higher

peak. Alone, shivering, I struggle
to locate any pathfinders.
Having confided all, in the secrecy
of these desolate hills – trusting
that no one would ever hear

my dark secrets – I walk down
to face more of my humiliation:
in this place, that only a higher
force knows why, I have decided
to call home. No matter how

sharp the contradictions that this
vulnerability confronts me with,
it is now – and only now –
that I absorb, with an even
sharper precision,
that what has been, has been –

the past almost shuts out
in the present. And even more,
that perhaps my presence
here is for other things, other
than those that seem to lodge
their claims.

RITES OF PASSAGE
Sithembele Isaac Xhegwana

Why should you always leave
us, unannounced? By the river's
bank, we could not see the stone
sinking, the fort from where
you spoke with the spirits. Only

the brim of your hair sailed
above the river's face. Shining,
the spirit world fused with
the waters –

we would not deliver you. And now
the timeless drums wish to lure
you back. Even the pigeons,
flocking upon these acacias, they
plead, relinquish yourself from
the river people.

The vigil dance, *intlomble*,
seems to be the only meeting
ground. The offerings we have
brought, the transigents song
we murmur, as you fluently sing –
all melt into the seamless tune
of your doom: half-human,
half-spirit.

Upon your return,
we do not wish to see you
divine the end of our courses
in life, and perhaps foretell

a new beginning –
along shores foreign
to our memory.

We are much happy to be
who we are and the tides
that billow encroach
our enclosures in such
a merciless mode.

HINTSA'S PORTRAIT

Sithembele Isaac Xhegwana

Through English picturesque, here
he stands. Overburdened with colonial
lexion, he still stands, an intransigent
opponent of colonial advance –
narrative of the war.

Possession of land through
nineteenth century Romantic
imagination – ceded territory.

Here he stands, as a figure
of Xhosa Royality. That only
through political maneuvering,
Smith could be the true meaning
of a traitor.

Yet, this portrait cannot reflect
the realities of the many voices
still crying for a ceded throne,
Of which the climax was
the burning of Hintsa's kraal
and the mutilation of his body.

And even more, the exportation
of the king's head to the colonial
masters.

Class
Zongezile Matshoba

We were told to attend school
To be taught in English
And be enlightened

We were in different classes
You will recall
Class A, B, C and sometimes D and E

The results came varying
Positions were the thing
First class was king

We looked for work
We got different jobs in different sectors
Skaftins reflected varied positions and salaries

We lived in backyards of our parents
Renovations differed according to the pocket
The better ones bought *standeni*

The class ruled
With some renting rooms in the townships
Flats for the better ones in suburbs

The *skoro-skoros* we drove tell
Many still walking and riding in taxis
Others with flashy bling-bling

Nowadays we live class
The clothes, food, drinks and places we go to
Class of the haves and have-nots

A class that equates privileges to rights
A class that boldly marvels *Animal Farm*
A class that sickens a big head with PHD syndrome

Class acts is the theatre for some
Promised by leadership
Leaving voters fighting for and about a class

*** *Standeni* – big house stands
*** *Skaftins* – lunch boxes
*** *Skoro-skoro* – old car
*** *PHD* – Pull Him Down

Angry
Zongezile Matshoba

The child was angry
And bitter
The other child denied everything
Claiming not to have been there

The child had nothing
A wonderer of soul and land
The other was living large life
Enjoying the fruits of inheritance

The motherland is angry too
Its tanned skin bare for our livestock
The others even have swimming pools
Silently thanking their forefathers for the largess

Elections
Zongezile Matshoba

Imagine a writer contesting elections
Using writer would be a disadvantage
Lagging at the bottom of the ballot
Author would be preferred
Possibly at the very top of the paper

Imagine the author canvassing
Giving each potential voter
Flyers with quotes from books
Hanging on the street poles
Posters of published books covers

Imagine the rally of a writer
Looking more of a literary festival
Sharing with the voters writing process
The manifesto taken from a manuscript
Supporters chanting poems and extracts

Imagine the opponents
Strangely the far right would be artists
Musicians, visual artists, actors
Blasting drums, beats, orchestra
Cartooning and sculpturing one of their own

Imagine the author winning
The office wall will have longlists and shortlists
SALA, Booker and Noble Prize on top
Reshuffling cabinet to favour artists
The SONA focusing more on reading and writing

It's only good to be a writer (than a persuader)
Wording these happenings
Being the voice of the voiceless
The eyes for the fooled
The ears that hear the whispers

*** SALA – South African Literary Awards
*** SONA – State of the Nation Address

MELANIN GODDESS

Ogunleye Gbemisola

'Your skin was made of sunlight
Dripping with honey and gold'
Earth goddess
With eyes the colour of night
Silky soft darkness crowns your head,
Thick and stubborn like the soul of your people
Your blood is thick with dreams and potential
It flows in sync, supporting heavy heartbeats that echo the strength of
your ancestors

Goddess stepped in earth and ashes
Moulded with earth that accepted the blood of your people
The tears of your people mixed the dark earth that formed you
Your sweat drops gingerly into your bowl as you work
Turning badness to strength

Goddess come to earth
With fury like hell and eyes like the heavens
Hold my face with callused hands
Redeem me with eyes that know pain
Gift me a smile like the moon on a dark night
So that I will say to your ancestors- I saw beauty before I died.

Black Boy
Ogunleye Gbemisola

Such things as these,
I do not understand
Such mysteries like you,
Refuse to unfold
Happy boy,
Your long, dark, beautiful fingers,
Nimble and happy in flight
Tremble in work
How long will you hold?

We are Gods

Joseph Daniel Sukali

"You should enjoy your life while it lasts", so we say
Without grasping the essence our souls mean by that
We get so naïve in these bodies every incarnation
As the soul gets caged in a body that withers
Immortality is married to mortality once again
We walk around just to die so that we live forever
Every birth is the birth of our inevitable death
We truly born again at our every last breath
That's why I close my eyes in this haze to see clearly
I listen to the noise of silence to understand deeply
It's the meaninglessness of our lives that makes sense
We are old spirits that have lived since the lie of time
We are just eternals bored of immortality
We migrate from one body to another
We play human just to taste how death feels
It's just a break from the loop of infinite hovering
For if souls don't really know the taste of death
We are as old as the beginning and the end
How many times should I tell you we are gods?

Spectators
Yugo Gabriel Egboluche

Why our roosters fight
I don't know

what prize they wrestle for
I don't know

who put them in rings?
I don't know

but what I know is…

we watch
we wait
we wail
our shillings go up in trade
our lands quietly decimate
and the roosters cry not in pain

we watch
we wait
we wail
till their beaks bleed crimson
till ants scamper from shelter
and the arbiter decides a truce

leaving us with roosters readied for the wild!

Now gods
Yugo Gabriel Egboluche

ours is a land
of rare species,
thriving daily on
the remnant mercies
of now gods

gods who in their hands,
hold our extinction plug
like the sun, rain and earth -
gods who dot cowries as robe,
accepting but sacrifices to bless

we let them seat on thrones
made from our finest trees -
awaiting chants of servitude
from corners of their reign
to intoxicate self with pride

ours is a land of sycophants,
who rather gabble till dawn
than seek redemption from
futile gods whose reign speaks
nothing, but euphonic heresy

Soliloquies of an African Poet
Yugo Gabriel Egboluche

we've muted our drums to the lure
of alien rhythm and bewitched dance,
we've sullied our pride to a dusk
of ferried carnival and spandex gears

we've run our kings amok with lust,
made them unable to know virgins,
unable to guise their lewd schemes
from dusks into daylights of perfidy

we've let our children loose on vogue
styled them become an extension
of our wishful future, blindly running
from an unknown past laden with bias

we've come to prefer the sultry voice
of foreigners to the sullen expression
of sisters and brothers, blindly slogging
to improve the validation of foreigners

we've began to un-know our proverbs
our stories and folklore, letting elders
fall asleep with them, while we meddle
with nuggets of profound dissimilarity

THE BELIEF
Mohamed Fuad Kamara

Like an implant in father's spinal cord
left in safe locket by origin
a belief hurled across his coral mind
perfectly responding to his circulatory system
Passed down to us, his soul's seeds
that his brother is our father too
and his children are our siblings too.
I burdened its tribal mark
since a name was murmured in my ear
But the mark washed away
in the waves of my broadening mind:
When my otherfather embraced my othersibling
polished his cheeks with kisses
for a reasonable performance
and my excellent card collected
the remnant of his smiles
When I longed for the close door chat
he chatted with my othersibling
and time's benevolence denied me
When I gazed him apportioned
the bail shipped in for the family
and not even the blue jean I yearned for got to me
When the ABC in my head split my eyelids
to see 'I have no bearing with extended family'
broke out of the dark tongue of my othersibling
spilling like kolanut fluid on white lankonor gown
sink beneath the heals of my ocean heart
When the dagger-verse in my flesh woke
my memories to the blushes she brushes my name
each time I bow with a broom at dawns.

Then I realised the West man's definition
My teacher's miserly mind became visible
His illustration did not score out
a branch from the family

The Night Worker
Gabla Godwin

Yet another moonshine
a glimpse through her open windows
arouses the fear of another night shift
Her customers are unknown...

Yet another moonshine
a glimpse at her golden phone
recalls names of pending clients
2, 3, 4 or zero?

Yet another moonshine
and Sitso's muliebrity stands
in how many hungry manhoods she feeds.
Big, small, medium or sick?

Her tears are a joy to her customers
'Oh I'm hitting it right' a skinny one said.
'Yea. She loves this one'. another fat one moaned.
But who knows the true pain of a night worker?

The governor beckons her sweetness as of candies
The minister rates her orals over his Betrothed
Even the president's foreign trips end in her private suite
But who cares what a night worker's pains are?

Her voice is only as good as forcing a man's climax
Her body is a man's temple
So long as he tithes, he shall worship
So be her mother's words, not?

The Sound of Things Bold to Speak
(—for Pius Adesanmi)
Hopewell Amana

A poem is such befitting grave
To stuff anthologies of all the worlds you live—
Even as a faxed star; headstone
Of scented flowers from every paged memory!
   (~Hopewell Amana)

From these row & intercontinental cries
   (You won't be back from your last trip)
As your mother hoped you'll wipe your shoes
On the doormat & plod to the kitchen
To sing a song of her magical hands

She has stopped to eat from the grief of her scathed heart
   (How you fared with the ashes of the jet-plane in Addis
& wrote your poem into darkness without a tombstone)

Her amethyst eyes bode among the stars

Under the shoulder of night she builds a sarcophagus
   (From a thousand books in the study)
To fill your lost pages in place of your frigid bed

Birds sing your name & the rooms shrink their size
   (Cars honk at the fringes from the mindfulness
 Of the street, whirring past the parking meter)
Tears nip from the flowers fraying in the sun,
Losing their bright, bright petals...

You must be the footsteps at the frontage,

(The doors banging shut!)
Inside, she sings with the dresses in the wardrobe
& pats the ghosts of things too bold in their whispers

Meditation
Hopewell Amana

The trouble with memory is it is easily broken
Thunderclaps nip swollen clouds
Beneath grandpa's eyes
—hung pouches in the sky—
With every punctuation of grief

Lymph & bloodstream sate parching guts
Of ghosts stretching over breasts of night
To suckle yoke from the abscesses

It comes with the remembering…

The sun mocking tears when it falls asleep
For lightning to thrust his ribs
U'N'I are silver pellets of rain
(Whenever the pain cannot withhold his sides)

Mankind was the story God spat
In the sand that formed my eyes

Vials of red ink in my veins,
Writing drapes
Drawn into the black mood of years

There are windows in these benign eyes
Probing you & secrets of trees,
What we fuck to replicate selves
Multipliers /probing hearts /
One kiss sooty as sin / binaries /
I LOVE YOUs
—antibodies & civilisation…

Little doors in my sleep probe the oceans,
MURKY WOMBS grey & murderous.
The moon, her harem of wailing stars
Press for the waters
As WE pellets of rain dot
The rippling surface like fur
Rubbed the wrong way

It has been a thousand years in memoriam;
Hope left & lost to attend
The sun's scalding embrace,
Lying bedded in a carnivorous water-land;

1) Uneasy lies a head

2) I don't eat the breasts of mermaids!

3) In my country houses grow like trees

Who holds the tears that lie with fossils?
Touching the ground
& dirt with molecules from sharp dentitions:
Fragments / Fins / Lilies / Planktons
When fingerlings care for leftovers

Here, I see the shadows
In the age-long eyes foreboding—
Love is grey in dilated pupils, grey here
& where the dead converge to mock earth,
Jarring like the witches of Mt. Olympus,
Grey in sleep that is half the way
To that eternal place

Heaven's Colonies
Hopewell Amana

There're colonies in heaven
Through pocket doors in my dreams:
Hydra of wailing flakes spread
In a crimson sea of heads the first night
   My father walked into
The side pouch of my pyjamas—dying by way
Of cats eating bowels from his trunk
   I see zombie faces & no grain
Of love in purgatory nor flowers & petty niceties

 One symphony of pain tug in the air—spraying
The putrefaction of Satan's armpit
   Clinging rebelliously to nostrils
The sun leans in the northern skies atop a giant crown
   Waiting to wear her sackcloth
Far from the nimbus on this gracious throne;
 Blinding white from the south of the zodiac
There're tribes orchestrated by stars
Harps / Cymbals / Golden crucibles
Incense smokes & flying wings in veneration
Seven seals & seven horses in spectrum worship
Seven trumpets, seven plagues
 All things of seven, threes & fours
Twenty-four & a thousand years of captivity
Rainbows arch like hungry boas waiting to strike

Twelve thousand generations of twelve tribes
Throng twelve gates of long-suffering
Souls dead and *un*-dead in a livid swamp,
Trenches of slaves
My father howls on the labouring queue

For the life he didn't wash his robe
In the blood stream that gushed from Golgotha

Everest no match for the banquet table
(Stuffed with martyrs beneath),
Feasting their butchered souls to grace
  The legions in the skyline,
The harlot that wooed my earth
Those subverted cities: Iraq / Palestine /
America—the woman of my dreams

I don't tell my mother of the love she has lost
I don't tell her of the lips that is blooming in my ribs.

Bans (fourth reading)
Austin Kaluba

For the fourth time we publish the bans
of marriage for John
Khumalo, a native of Marabastad,
who wants to marry
Anje Van der Merwe
in the Dutch Reformed Church.
Please inform the minister
If you know any reason why this couple
May be lawfully joined in marriage.

Not yet Uhuru
Austin Kaluba

When will I sit under my own fig tree?
To eat the sweat of my brow
When will my lord Kumbaya?
To wipe my black tears.
Who will debeak the bald eagle?
clip its claws and paint its head black.
When will that old bell chime for me?
To drown the cries from the Zong ship.

Who will unblock my voice?
to sing Nkosi Sikelele Afrika.
When will I walk freely in Orania?
The city of dark memories.
When our black mannequins learn to talk?
and shed off foreign garbs.
When will my calves suckle?
before they are weaned by the cleaver.
When will the drinking gourd guide me to the cotton tree?
To find rest with my Good Lord.

I am Afrika
Austin Kaluba

I am Afrika,
Fashioned in a clay pot
Hopeless and yet hopeful
I am Afrika
Deep as the Congo River
That flows and flows.
I am Afrika
Ancient, formless and dark.
I am Afrika,
Sodomised perennially
by countless rapists.
I am Afrika,
The oldest, yet the youngest
Wise but still a novice.
I am Afrika,
conjured in John Dee's cauldron.

FATE
Precious Ifeoma Benjamin

I craved for one which I love
That which I dreamed to examen for future
To be in an immaculatte-white shirt, black skirt, wig on head and black
rope
And stand to appeal for the vulnerable
In a room justice at times interred

My soul, spirit and body
Ready to ride that Precious dream
But fate so hard-hearted
Rode me to another. As if hurled I
By a whirl wind blowing mightily
Into a dream never I'd craved for.

What do I do?
Just be in it. Recreate it
I tell fate
I can fit in to you!

This is not Poetry
Valentine Okolo

This is not poetry. They are my words handcuffed and carried away in black Marias by men who play gods with guns. And wearing the official uniforms given to them by those who rule, in order to protect the people. Yet, they choose not to protect the people. Instead, they extort money from them and have them locked up on trumped up charges, written on statements of air.

This is not poetry. It is the rage of wasted years. Of youths, considered useless by a system which murders their visions. And buries them in a graveyard of lost dreams. A system which leaves the youths to wander in the wilderness of uncertainty, unsure of tomorrow. Because for many of them, tomorrow might never come.

This is not poetry. It is the cry of the molested and the raped. The detained, and the sold. And the forgotten faces of those killed in regional genocides, without names and buried in anonymous tombs. Those whose names might never ring a tune. Because they are poor. And the poor are the first to be forgotten in conflicts. Because they have no money and no fame attached to their names.

This is not poetry. It is a memorial. For those murdered at the Gates of Blood. For those who came before us. And those who would come this way again. It is a memorial for all of us. For the living as well as the fallen. It is a collection of all our rage, hopes and fears. It is a memorial of what we are and what we choose not to be.

These are not pretty words. They are the truth. Unadulterated by years of fermented lies and deceit. These are the words whispered in married couples bedrooms. And shouted in bars by men who drown their troubles in bottles of drink. These are the words raised up in protests by those who refuse to be intimidated by bullets. And whose voices cannot be silenced.

You Remind Me
Valentine Okolo

You remind me of sun rays
after much rain
like the sunshine of today
following yesterday's
unending shower
of chips and sawdust,
falling from the iroko in the sky,
cut by a mighty axe.

Your eyes remind me
of the ocean with a dozen dolphins
shooting out of the bathtub
of the deep like rockets
sent into orbit,
and turning somersaults
in the stratosphere
of a watery circus,
but with none to witness.

Your laughter makes me remember
the dropping of leaves
in the dry season
like reptiles shedding their skins,
or the striking scent of hemp,
as each leaf leaves the parent tree
and parachutes to the grass below.

Storm

Valentine Okolo

My love
I will not ask you
to be a pigeon or a dove
cooing your pleasures away
in our liquid moments of love.
I will not ask you to be tender
or to be a timid voice,
suspended in song.
If you must be anything, my Eve
please be thunder,
and shake the foundation of our union
with the audacity of your desire.
Unleash a cry from within
with a purity that vibrates glass.

Do not let your touch become ordinary
like words uttered without meaning or intent.
Do not be
a sapphire sky filled with birds in flight.
If you choose to be anything, my love,
let it be lightning.
Yes, be lightning,
and write your name across my chest
in fluorescent text.
Show me what it means
to be electrocuted by your nails.

HOPE FOR BETTER FUTURE

Yemi Orasakin

The house is embittered
like a pile, difficult
to urinate in the
defecating social life.

Oppression, destruction
Suppression, depression
Totalitarianism, egalitarianism
Chauvinism, Rightist, Leftist.

In the sense of doomed life
Become unending social disorder
social disability of social order
what causes this social disorder?

Someone beckon at the back
It is engineered by people
at the corridor of power
Friend enemy of peace

Bayonet of tribulations,
Giant kobold have enter
the market place in the noon.
The owl enter the town
It is an Omnious sign.

Beware soul brothers.
The aborted hopes
The aborted dreams
The aborted aspirations

Shattering and scattered
About in the capital.

Commentary: It is a poem of 6 stanzas of unequal length,
It has the message, which captured the mental picture of oppression of
the masses by people at the corridor of power using divide and rule
policy of disorganized the masses, not to know their hidden agenda.
The themes of social inequalities, political problems, oppressiveness,
unfulfilled expectations, subtle resistance, and caution optimist has
rendered the masses impotent to fight for their right.

Repetition: of oppression runs throughout the poem, to show the
degree of how the masses feels in the period of economics recession.
The tone of the poem is oppression.
The mood is that of social disorder, governance is disturbed, and
leading to destruction.

Simile: The house is embittered like a pile shows the hardship of
people who are being tormented in one way or the other everyday.
"The owl enter the town in the Noon" is a bad sign that something
evil is going to happen.
The poet is given a sound of warning for different people concern to
be careful and change their attitude towards the caring of the aborted
hopes, aspirations, dreams shows the general problems of the society,
of leadership followership relationship not cordial again. The two
group should allow peace to reign by each performing his roles in the
societies as expected of them.

THE UNCONDITIONAL ORDER
Yemi Orasakin

In the Naked thorn,
The naked soles of shoes,
By shoes mender has given
the unconditional order
which makes the less privilege
grudge and not at ease.

The hammer has been put
in the nail, to heal my shoes
But it does not heal, for
it refuse healing in the hospital.
They put the surgical blades
to heal the patient womb
But all to no avail.

He could not be healed.
They put thorn in the
gorgeous cloth to be wear
by him to the market
in order to buy and sell.

Blood gush out from
his legs, and he could not move
again to his place of work.
Leg Nail, to the cross of
no hope now turn hopeless.

The jigger has hit the
two legs, movement is difficult,
to go back, to move forward
is an herculean task now.

You must remain on the same spot
forward you cannot go
backward you cannot go
stagnant water you remain
on the same spot, life is like that
take it like that.

Commentary: The poem is divided into six (6) stanzas, of unequal length with rhyme and run-on line, with one line run successfully to the other. The theme of maltreatment of the masses dominate the whole poem. The naked soles of shoes has been nailed by the people at the corridor of power. Movement, progress is now the unconditional order in the society.

Before you do anything, you will be giving an unconditional order, if you satisfy it, you then move forward to the next level. If not your remain on the same spot like stagnant water.

The themes of oppression, maltreatment of the masses has affect the physiognomy and psycho-analytical structure of the masses is being affected. The masses cannot co-ordinate again, for mental problems has set in.

Image-of jigger in the leg, "Naked Sole" leg nailed to the cross" symbolizes the image of oppression of the masses.

Forward you cannot go
Backward you cannot go"
Remain in one spot
Symbolizes spot like stagnant water.

The tone of the poem is remaining on the same spot, no development at all for the masses who is hopeless. The mood of the poem is the precarious situation of the masses in a disorganize society of no hope now hopeless. To move forward or backwards, is now a debate by the unconditional order.

THE OBNOXIOUS POLICIES
Yemi Orasakin

The obnoxious policies
I am weary of it
So says one man in the theatre

Are you tired of life?
Yes of course
suicide is the last option
when everything is turning upside down
we are at the crossroad then

What do we do now?
The boy ask his mother
is life like this in your
own days or what?

I cannot tell, reply mother
that is how we met it.
but life is not like this
during our time, we
valued ourselves,
we do not kill
each other.

The down trodden are
facing an endless wars.
When one war ends
another war often resurface
when are we going to
escape from all wars?

The whole world is full

of wars and tribulations
which you must fight
at the battle field at
all times, in the garden

It is only those who
fought it to the end
and escape of societal
problems is saved.

Commentary: it is a poem of seven (7) stanzas, with unequal lines and length, having enjambment, with one line run successfully to the other. The personae is tired of life with introduction of several obnoxious policies that makes life hard for the masses. No food, no basic amenities, no money no security of lives, those to protect all these are the themes of social disorder, oppression of the masses, social stratification, cummed societal issues is now the other of the day. The tone of the poem is harmful, danger, disorderliness.
The mood is hardship through the introduction of the obnoxious policies.

French poetry

La Sphinge

Sadlay Fiat-lux Hounyeme

A la génération du Corona virus

Alors qu'ils s'enivraient de toute débauche,
Et s'offraient le bain des plus grasses noces,
Les fanfares tempêtant à péter leur tympan,
Rires violents, pleure de joie, de toute part fusant,
J'ai prié ma douleur d'adoucir ma frayeur.

Alors qu'ils hurlaient d'euphorie à en friser la folie,
Les éclats opulents des dents pouffant de bonne vie,
Sous le fouet de l'oisiveté et la fièvre de l'aisance,
A ma peur et mon aigreur, j'ai dit : allons-nous--en.
Allons en hâte apprendre au désespoir

Que le futur par ce jour sinistre écœure.
Allons conjurer au divin d'ôter nos déboires
Avant que sa colère ne tonne sur la terre.
Alors qu'ils assoyaient la perversité à leur face
Et la voyait rayonnante de tout attrait,

Les colombes, œuvres de leur main agile,
Pavanant par millier la quiétude des océans
Avec le Pérou, la richesse à leur flanc,
La sphinge surgit. Elle surgit à la lisière de la nuit.
Alors qu'ils s'assoupirent dans un rêve qui charmait leur envie,

Alors qu'ils rêvaient d'une somptueuse vie à venir,
Elle vint tel l'émissaire du faiseur de vie.

171

Alors qu'ils exagéraient dans leurs profanations
Et ne retombaient point leurs pattes
Tant qu'ils parvenaient à broyer tout obstacle,

La sphinge vint claironner la halte de leur audace
Et sonner le terme de leur insolence qui outrepasse.
Alors qu'ils s'égosillaient le gosier éclaté,
Voici que se lève la sphinge d'au-delà de la bleuté.
Elle se lève, le pas sectaire, la corne au rare.

Pour désavouer la mégalomanie humaine.
Elle se dresse sous d'assourdissant cor au nard
Pour mutiler le rêve et abréger l'espoir.
Elle surgit pour perdurer l'effroi et trôner la foi
Au milieu des êtres qui de rien aux yeux n'ont froid.

Vivre selon Lui
Sadlay Fiat-lux Hounyeme

A tous les démunis d'Afrique.

Des flancs d'une voie veuve de paix,
Tinte une indolente voix veule de vigueur.
C'est le cri d'une folie repentie
Qui avec force et au son d'un sobre cor retentit.

Je suis l'amer fruit d'un regret.
L'espérance d'une mère
Que la douleur supplicie,
La promesse d'un père
Que la ferveur ternit.

Je suis un sans-abri.
Et si vous me demandez ce qu'est la vie,
Je vous répondrai de mon accablée voix:
C'est naître pour, tout froid, périr sans toit.
Je mène la vie des *malgré-soi.*

Mes peines sont des amers soirs.
Au-delà de tout ce que je sais,
Le succès ne vit pas à notre ère.
La gloire n'habite pas notre univers.
Ils sont d'un monde où la vie est éphémère.

Je suis un orphelin, une âme inouïe.
Je suis d'un air enfantin, mais démuni.
Si vous me demandez ce qu'est la vie,
Je vous répondrai de mon affamée voix

Que c'est vivre téméraire sans mère

Et austère avec candeur sans père
Dans un univers dépourvu de cœur.

L'enfant de rue vous dira le contraire.
Pour lui, vivre c'est subir la raillerie des nuits froides,
Offrir la chaire toute crue aux nues étoiles,
Et la dissimuler quand s'éclipse leur lueur.
C'est une vie cruelle sous l'ardeur des réverbères.

Je connais qui vous en dira mieux.
C'est l'aveugle qui mendie sans voix.
Selon lui, vivre c'est souffrir des regards
D'un monde qu'on ne peut voir.
Des regards sans cœur et sans âme.

Le sourd-muet vous dira que vivre,
C'est rire des supplices qu'on ne peut entendre.
Parce qu'on ne peut les dire.
Une vie où la douleur décime,
Une vie de pesant châtiment.

La femme vous en dira plus.
Elle vous en dira assez car elle endure plusieurs.
L'être au cœur des supplices.
Elle, elle vit la tristesse et des aigreurs au ton divers.

C'est le cri d'une folie repentie.
Qui avec force et au son d'un sobre cor retentit.
Je suis l'amer fruit d'un regret.
L'espérance d'une mère
Que la douleur supplicie,
La promesse d'un père
Que la ferveur ternit.

L'enfance
Sadlay Fiat-lux Hounyeme

Aux enfances regrettées

Si le rêve était un sentier qui y mène,
J'irai tôt avant l'aurore par les airs houleux.
J'irai seul flanqué d'un cor dans les ères pliées,
Là où sont rangées les douceurs des ans heureux,
Là où sont égarés rire aux éclats et regards envieux.

J'irai palper l'innocence, sourire à la passion,
J'irai avant le matin visiter l'esprit curieux,
Aller vivre près de la gaîté et de la nocivité,
Aller prêter à la crédulité sa chanson.

Que le temps freine ses pas
Et que les ans en fassent autant
Afin que j'aille de ce pas
Offrir tout mûr ce que je suis
Au forgeron qui le mérite le plus.

Que le rebours me fasse volte-face
Et qu'alors trépignant j'attende,
Les âges révolus retombent leurs pas
Pour qu'au portier du début d'infini,
Je scande l'oraison, selon le rite.

Une oraison au ton contrit
Qui ne l'a point vue partir,
Au son d'une affligée lyre
Qui a manqué de l'ensevelir ;

Hommage à mes beaux vieux âges,

Témoignage d'une aphone voix de sage,
Charge avérée du procès contre le temps, pillard d'âge,
Lui qui me prit l'enfance sans aucun gage.

Enfance, instant de pureté, d'innocence,
Enfance, instant de cécité, d'insouciance,
J'aimerais t'avoir au seuil de ma souvenance,
J'aimerais te revoir aux termes des jours de répugnance,

Revoir l'insouciance, me dérober aux difficultés de la vie.
Revoir l'innocence, nourrir et couvrir mon oisiveté
Sans le moindre prix.
Qui y mène, si le rêve était un sentier,
J'irai tôt avant l'aurore par les airs houleux.
J'irai seul flanqué d'un cor dans les ères pliées,
Là, où sont rangées les douceurs des ans heureux,
Là, où sont égarés rire aux éclats et regards envieux.

Amour ingénieux
Arnold Mondo Kobi

Je suis amoureux
Amoureux comme jamais
Jamais comme auparavant
Auparavant vivant comme étranger
Etranger très ignorant
Ignorant l'amour et magie du cœur
Magie du cœur, Magie d'amour
Amour incroyable, je suis tombé
Au moment inattendu, je suis surpris
Eperdument amoureux, je suis tombé
D'un amour si intense, je suis piégé
Affectueusement amoureux, je suis dedans
D'un cœur sincère, mon cœur aime
Qui pensait qu'un jour je dirai ainsi ?
Durant tout ce temps, ignorant l'amour
Venu à l'improvise comme un voleur
Il pénètre mon cœur tout en silence
Soudain il est là, agit dans mon cœur
Contrôlant mon ego et s'imposant tout en silence
De l'intérieur comme de l'extérieur
Un changement inattendu bouscule ma vie
Un changement inattendu mystifie tout mon être
L'étranger pénètre dans mon corps
Tout en silence
Bouleverse mon être et impose la différence
Mort au brave et baveur d'amour
Arrive soudain la désinstallation de l'égo,
Et l'intronisation de l'autre et de nous
Oui, l'amour fort et puissant a triomphé
Oui, l'amour ingénieux et imposant prend le contrôle
Je suis tombé amoureux

Oui, je suis tombé amoureux.

Pourquoi amour ?
Arnold Mondo Kobi

Amour ! Amour ! Amour !
Pourquoi aimer si on sait
Qu'on souffrira un jour ?
Pourquoi aimer si on sait
Qu'on ne sera pas toujours heureux ?
Pourquoi aimer si on sait
Qu'on ne vivra pas toujours le bonheur ?
Amour ! Amour ! Amour !
Comme tu me sembles méchant par moment
Amour ! Amour ! Amour !
Comme tu me sembles égoïste par moment
Amour ! Amour ! Amour !
Comme tu me sembles pénible par moment
Amour ! Amour ! Amour !
Sans prévenir tu brises les cœurs des gens
Amour ! Amour ! Amour !
D'où es-tu sorti vraiment ?
Amour ! Amour ! Amour !
Quel est véritablement ton objectif
Dans une relation de couple ?
Amour ! Amour ! Amour !
Que cherches-tu réellement
Dans la vie des gens amoureux ?
Amour ! Amour ! Amour !
Dévoile-moi ton secret à la hâte !
Amour ! Amour ! Amour !
Apprends-moi ta véritable nature et désir !

Amour ! Amour ! Amour !
Comme ça
Je me conformerai à tes prescrits et désirs
Amour ! Amour ! Amour !
Livre-moi ton secret à la hâte !
Amour ! Amour ! Amour !
Oui, livre-moi ton plan pour l'humanité !
Amour ! Amour ! Amour !
Et sauve mon cœur
De tes souffrances accablantes !
Alors mon âme se réjouira de toi
Et je te vivrai encore jusqu'à la fin du temps.

Je suis tombé amoureux
Arnold Mondo Kobi

Elle a pris mon cœur
Dans la hâte
Elle a pris mon cœur
Avec douceur
Elle a pris mon cœur
Avec amour
Elle m'a dit je t'aime
Au jour du malheur
Elle m'a dit je t'aime
D'une voix douce
Elle m'a dit je t'aime
D'un regard pétillant
Et d'une expression très romantique
Comme dans un conte de fées
Où vivent les personnages merveilleux
Dans un monde imaginaire,
Là où le stress et la peine n'existent pas
Là où seul l'amour fait la loi
Mon cœur emplit de joie
Comme dans un conte de fées
Mon cœur emplit d'amour
Comme dans un rêve
Que des mots doux et tendre
Eblouis ma vie et saisis mon âme
Mon cœur est prisonnier de son amour
Et je suis tombé amoureux d'elle.

Opportuniste reine

Akpao Gninwo Armel

Je grave ton doux nom et ton affreux visage
Sur le front endolori de l'histoire en crise
Comme le signe de la croix au moyen-âge
Sur la première pierre des églises

Je grave ton doux nom et ton affreux visage
Pour que subsistent aux époques lointaines
Les moindres vers de mes sombres pages,
Chères reliques enfouies dans les mémoires humaines !

Sur le front endolori de l'histoire en crise
De ton bras levé qui ébranle le monde, tout le monde,
L'humanité, cet arbre qui perd par milliers ses fruits sous ton emprise,
Te voit sourire au moindre écho de ses pleurs profondes.

Comme le signe de la croix au moyen-âge,
L'univers entier marqué de l'âpre sceau
De ton navrant ouvrage, oh ineffable naufrage !
Se cloître comme dans son terrier où se retranche le blaireau

Sur la première pierre des églises
O Reine virale ! Ubiquiste et opportuniste despote,
Tu trônes dans toute onde émise
Et aux dogmes et aux axiomes, tu escamotes.

Je grave ton doux nom et ton affreux visage
Sur le front endolori d'histoire en crise
Comme le signe de la croix au moyen-âge
Sur la première pierre des églises.

"Le fils d'un homme"

Oh, non !
Sanogo Ousmane

Regarde, ce siècle s'abime !
Oh, non ! Ce siège s'abime.
Attends, La chouette culotte !
Lançons le carnaval de l'intime
Qui veille sur la poésie ? - Le thème !
Que la poésie veille, mon poète !

Le miroir
Sanogo Ousmane

Ce matin, de l'autre côté du miroir
Un monsieur chauve ouvre le tiroir
Dont le fond se trouve un peu noir
J'imagine que c'est mon seul ami
C'est tout mon contraire l'ennemi
Je n'imagine plus, c'est tout moi !

Ce soir
Sanogo Ousmane

Assis dans l'ombre du crépuscule
Je vois des gouttes d'eau tombées
Par une porte solitaire avec peu de
Lueur reflétant l'ombre crétin du soleil
Au fond je sens aussitôt son fumet
La pluie m'a apporté une nuit froide

Lettre à ma dulcinée Charlotte

Diafouka Mabiala Presneil Aimerith

Lorsque je me mets sur mon lit, je vois défiler ton visage

Lorsque je dors, je fais souvent ce rêve étrange de cette femme que j'aime et qui m'aime aussi, elle s'appelle Charlotte.

La distance qui sépare la terre à la lune est celle qui nous sépare, toi à nkoabang et moi à Ekounou

Si j'avais la possibilité de voler ta photo, j'irais la mettre au musée présidentiel. Viens donc te mettre à ma place et m'aimer comme je t'aime tu iras même voler le palais présidentiel d'Etoudi pour te l'offrir à toi-même.

Tu es douce comme une rose, belle comme la fleur de lotus, celle que le roi arrosait lui-même

Si un jour un ange arrivait à tomber malade, je te proposerais à Dieu pour que tu fasses l'intérim de cet ange

Je veux être acteur dans ta vie, car, il est très difficile de donner un autre rôle à celui qui aime déjà.

Je t'aime en hémorragie

Lettre à ma dulcinée Charlotte
Diafouka Mabiala Presneil Aimerith

Viens dans mes bras je t'adore comme un ange
Viens seule que même ton ombre ne te suive pas
À Dolisie, là où je suis né, je te recevrais avec des roses et je mettrai ma plus belle veste comme tapis rouge pour t'accueillir…
Je ferais construire pour toi un musée, on y mettra toutes tes belles photos, je passerai mon temps à regarder tes belles photos parce qu'une belle femme est le paradis des yeux, tu es le paradis de mes yeux, ma joie infinie je suis donc Adam et toi Ève. Allons vivre notre amour loin d'ici.

Dolisie…
Diafouka Mabiala Presneil Aimerith

      Ville de cœur où j'étais enfant de chœur

Tout le monde à une ville de rêve et la mienne c'est Dolisie, Dieu a son paradis et a choisi son paradis, mais, moi par contre je t'ai choisi.

Ô Dolisie, les Français préfèrent Paris à cause de sa tour Eiffel et nous t'aimons à cause de ton grand marché ; ville poussiéreuse et pleine d'amour.

Peut-être que oui peut-être que non je n'irai pas au paradis, mais, s'il y a une autre ville de Dolisie après ma mort c'est là-bas que j'irai vivre.

Chant du tangage
ITOUA L'Okalé

Tangue la voile de nos pas
Et nos silhouettes
Sur l'immense océan de la vie

Pierre !
Regarde venir ton Seigneur en fantôme
Ne pouvons-nous pas comme toi
Jeter un seul pas sur la mer de nos vies
Sans nous noyer

Ces flots mugissant sur nos silhouettes
Et les vagues écumantes
Révélatrices de la rage humaine

Tanguent nos ombres à la tombée de la nuit
Sur le morne océan du désespoir
Que le soleil revienne délivrer nos chemins

Jonas !
Il y a encore des âmes à repêcher à Ninive !

Baleine !
Il n'y a meilleur bateau que toi
Pour atteindre Ninive
Ville salvatrice
Villes aux âmes meurtries

Voici la nuit morne
Dans nos entrailles entaillées,
Descendre immerger
Encore une fois nos âmes cernées

Tangue la vie humaine, tanguent nos ombres
Qui au passage du vent
Comme le sel dans l'eau
Et la fumée dans l'air
Se dissipent

Jonas, pars pour Ninive !

Les larmes de Mars
ITOUA L'Okalé

Que le soleil se lève sur les nuits de mars,
Pour que soient dévoilées les ombres funestes
Et que dansent au clair de lune ces silhouettes
Au rythme du drapeau rouge sang
Planté au cœur de mon peuple mendiant

Je ne mettrai pas mon pied titubant sur Mars,
Car je n'y trouverai rien
Je n'y trouverai que rien
Je n'y trouverai rien du tout
Je n'y trouverai rien en tout cas

Mars,
Une planète sans air ni eau
Une planète sans vie ni mort !

Mars,
Cette scie à dents
Qui mange à petit feu mes baobabs

Mars !
Sangsue, tu suces le sang de mon peuple innocent

Sangsue, tu baignes mon peuple dans le sang chaud

Sangsue, tu essores mon peuple,
Pour recueillir le fleuve de mes veines tendues,
Qui voilà qui coule
Et là flotte l'âme de mon peuple,
Au destin vendu aux enchères
Imbibée du sang infesté du traître poison,

Je sais ce que tu feras de ce sang recueilli
Tu vas le boire
Tu vas boire le vin de mon alliance,
Aujourd'hui, du son funèbre
Demain, cent tombés à mes côtés,
Après demain, sans joie ni paix je pleure,
La paix, mains sur la tête, o malheur !
….. Ton sol boit le sang,
De mon peuple assoiffé
Qui manque cruellement à boire
Tes eaux ont tari, le lit du fleuve a ouvert sa bouche
Pour attendre ces eaux,
Pourtant tu lui donnes du sang,
Et que boira-t-il ?

Dimanche à l'homélie poignardée par le soldat mal vêtu, mal coiffé
Le cheval décoiffé, dégradé aux yeux de tes dignes fils,
Et ces voix qui disent le brouhaha des bombes,
Et ces moutons qui vont à l'abattoir, o volontiers

Moutons de mars !
Aveugles qui voient leur voie rocheuse et qui y vont pour se perdre,
pour ne plus être

O, mars !
Es-tu communiste ?

Nile !
Pourquoi es-tu devenu ainsi ?

O, mars !
Donne-moi la paix
Je refuse de regarder ta nudité
Mais je suis obligé de regarder

Ces moutons invités à l'abattoir
Pour vendre leur sang précieux doré

O, mars ! agneau de la Shoah
Destiné à rougir le ciel la terre la vie la mort....
L'armée décoiffée
Et, ça coule....

La vaine attente
ITOUA L'Okalé

Le soleil s'allume....
Le jour se réveille…
Debout,
Mes yeux fixés sur le chemin sans cligner

Je regarde au loin

J'attends ma bien-aimée
Partie pour l'au-delà
Qui ne vient pas

A chaque froufrou des feuilles mortes
Mes oreilles de lapin debout
Je guette, je regarde, j'examine
Est-ce elle ?

Au moindre mouvement d'une silhouette
D'une ombre
Mes yeux comme des phares
Je guette, je regarde, j'examine
Est-ce elle ?

Quand le vent souffle, comme il me parlait,
Je n'entends plus sa douce voix

Quand le vent marche
Je n'entends plus ses pas
Je ne vois plus sa trace sur le sable blanc

La voix du vent qui jadis
Me caressait, caressait mon âme,

Caressait mes oreilles sourdes au monde,

Sourd, je n'entends plus personne
Aveugle, je ne vois plus rien
Muet, je ne dis plus mot
La salive a refusé d'habiter ma bouche

J'appelle
Au loin
Seule la forêt me répond

L'écho n'est donc pas la voix du diable
C'est elle qui répond

Et je demande : est-ce toi ?
La même question me revient : est-ce toi ?

Si ce n'est pas toi, la forêt parle donc ?

Je m'affaisse
Je n'en peux plus
Reviens !

Une seconde, je regarde
Une minute, j'attends
Une heure, j'espère encore
Un jour, elle ne revient pas

Une semaine, passée
Un mois, écoulé
Une année se meurt
Une décennie, elle ne revient pas

Je perds espoir

Mais,
Mes yeux toujours fixés sur le chemin
Sans même cligner

Je regarde

Mes oreilles de lapin toujours debout
Je guette, je regarde, j'examine
Est-ce elle ?

TSIKA MTITI.
Naida MOUSSA

MAKATI HONI LELA HADO NI REMA.
MAKATI YASAYA HADO NIFOIRIYA.
MDZADZA HANGU YONI TRENDEZA HAMBOUDA
"HENDA CHIYONI BO MOINA".
MIWU GNAMIZA MATSOZI HALELESA.
BO MA YE CHIYONI NA SOME HINDRI .
PVOKO HABADILI WULA MSOMO FUNDI.
MI HANDZA NAMBÉ CHAMI YECHELEYA YIZO FUNDI
YAKO HAMBA
OUTSIPOUWÉ FUNDI WAHO CHEWO DAZA
****
HO KONI MO M'NAZI MI HWENDA TSI KANTSI .
HAMITCHÉ NODJI WUZISA YEBA LEWO AMDJO SOMA
NDAZI .
PVOKO LE PAYA LA CHIYO LE HISA FUNDI NGUNI SOMO
FIKIHI KERI MATSO.
NGUNI WONESO ZINDROIDJI YITSO TSI NDIZO YA SOMA
FATIMA DJANA.
NEDO HANDZA NI RONGOWÉ NGU NAMBIYO" DAZA
OUWO NDO MSOMO AMINA HAPVIRI YAPVO ".
NE MIHONO YAHAHÉ YE TAMBWARIYA YE WAZI YA
HANGU
NE CHEMEZA NGU REDJEZO TSENA "DAZA"
NE HAMBA NGAMDJO ZAMBA YE DJUSA GOGNODÉ.
***
HO KONI MO M'NAZI TSIKA TSI KANTSI
TSIKA MTITI CHAMI HWELEWA OUKA MALEZI TSI
NDAYALA.
***
LEWO TSI KANTSI NILINDÉ YE MOINA YA ROHE CHIYONI
NE LERA YE PVIRA

196

TSI DJUHA NAMTSAHÉ
HO KONI MO M'NAZI TSIMPARISA
MATSOZI HO WUSONI
NA LESO YA DAMOU
HITSOI HAROIWA MIHONOTSI CHEMEZA
TSI DENGE , ZI DENZE PVANOU WOLA FUNDI KADJAKA
WAYETCHÉ.
YILA HADISI YIDJI REDJEZA.
CHA LEWO TSI CHEMEZA KIYO LA MDZADZÉ YA KOZA
NA MAHOZA YA MOINA YA ANGAMIZIWA.
***
MOINA HANGU KADJAKANA HIRIMOU
FUNDI HANANGAMIZA YE MOINA
YE MDOIHUFA .

J'étais petite.
Traduction à Naida MOUSSA

Des fois pour m'apprendre elle me frappait.
D'autres fois, elle me suppliait.
Ma mère avec un bâton me pourchassé " Va à l'école coranique, mon enfant".
Tête larmes coulants
Maman, à l'école coranique je vais apprendre quoi
Puisque, il a changé de d'éducation le maître.
Je voudrais dire mais je le rappelle de ce que le maître me dit.
" Tais toi, ne déshonore pas ton maître".
*** Au tronc du cocotier, je vais m'asseoir.
Seule, me demandant ce que j'allais apprendre aujourd'hui.
Puisque une fois l'école coranique terminée, le maître m'apprend l'art du kamasoutra.
Il m'apprend autre chose que ce qu'il a appris à Fatima hier.
Et quand je veux parler, il me dit " tais toi, c'est l'éducation Amina est passé par là"
Alors que ses mains ne font que violer mon intimité.
Et quand je cris, il me répète encore " tais-toi ".
Et si je dis que je vais le dire il soulève sa longue machette.
*****
Au tronc du cocotier, j'étais assise
J'étais petite mais je comprenais que l'éducation ce n'était pas cela.
***
Aujourd'hui assise, j'attends que mon enfant sorte de l'école coranique alors que le temps passe.
Je me suis levée pour aller la chercher.
Au tronc du cocotier, elle était assise
Larmes au visage,
Avec un châle ensanglanté
Main sur la tête j'ai crié
Je suis abattue, c'est abattant, le maître n'était pas seul .

L'histoire s'est répétée.

Mais aujourd'hui j'ai crié, le cri d'une mère blessé plus la douleur d'un enfant brisé.

***

Mon enfant n'était plus vierge.

Le maître a détruit l'enfant,

Qu'il meurt.

Fraîcheur des vents calmes
Alvie MOUZITA

L'âme vivante dans les palmes ne taira plus nos heures délisses, cette rame vivace des palmes
Épluchera fraîcheur des vents calmes, car vont vers ses cuisses lisses ces pauvres paysans cuire leur repos étale
Les sagaies des paysans vibrent au seuil de leurs lèvres où ait fleuri liberté qui brise fièvres, hisse des vrais fifres

Des vifs murmures sur les courbes murs du fleuve vitupèrent l'oppression mère chargée des bois qui blessent
Et vous mères, qui bercez le sang noir dans les plus grands hivers du soir, lui seriez-vous vigiles au cirque où viennent ses ennemis aux yeux verts?
Amères sur les joues sont les larmes qui coulent. Immense, ô pleure mon cœur pour ce désastre rouge
Ne vous ai-je pas dit mon cœur est un esclave de motte africaine ? Évidemment le ventre anoblit
Les entrailles sont une moule du potier qui vêle génisson, ainsi je ressens l'esprit divin à travers l'amour maternel
Matériels, or, miniers, hormis ces choses pillées
Quand nos mamans sont fusillées dans les villages comme on fusionne vérole au sang dans corps d'enfant noir
Vais-je traîner ma lyre de poète à la mer en fête sur ses délires de marches vers les roches ?

Enfant, je rêvai à mon âge printanier me vêtir des feuilles qui emballent le manioc, sauver du drame les fourmis qu'on piétine comme patine dans gourbis une mauvaise trame
Non, ô foule, mon audience sur ce versant de terre en déclin !
J'ai vu sourire mes aïeux car j'ai gardé fétiche qui à moi révèle science pour guérir mon pays atteint de lèpre
Mères, maintenant je veux que vous pleuriez,

200

Que vous pleurez de joie car ses larmes sont des rosées qui fleurissent
la paix au cœur
Voici les nattes s'étalent dans les paillotes, s'en aillent à l'horizon
remords qui s'évaporent
Dormez, ô vous que rafraîchit fraîcheur des vents calmes au passage
doux et calme d'ondée qui roule roses rosées

MwasiKitoko
Alvie MOUZITA

Tes doux mots laissent sur mes lèvres des ornières d'allégresse et s'épanche un sanglot de cloches sous ma poitrine penchée
Forgeronne, tu modèles des cœurs d'acier, moules et meules, et deviennent sucre d'orge sans feuilles mouillées
Augure ou mage, un grimoire sur tes cuisses ronfle et marche à la sueur des nuits fragiles pour fleurir les flores visqueuses, aqueuses des fleuves où nichent ou nicheront les fruits verts des voluptés

Et puisque tout se fait nocturne sur l'ardoise de nos toits, les alizées mauves qui meuvent soudain le feuillage des mangliers au creux de la mangrove, se greffent en douceur sur le mur de ma peau
Voilà qui est miel fauve des fourmis qui fourmillent si joyeux me rappellent l'hivernage des pâques où tout se vêt régal
Ah Mégane ! Achemine mes pas si froids vers ces chemins qui mènent aux roses cheminées et où roucoulent les fauvettes - ne savant que frissons à livrer
Je m'endors au cirque du lac vaste oubliant mes problèmes couleur d'ombre, si beau de voir surfer laitance des carpes comme une laitière au quartier que bordent des palmiers
Ainsi doucement viennent à mes oreilles, les douces paroles venant des ramiers et chants de ta bouche première
C'est le soir dans une tendresse de mer où me fouillent et me trouvent des liesses qui m'effleurent sans râle
C'est le noir dans une chevelure comme fleuve de cette femme qui tresse les amours sans faire mal

Mégane, ô mwasikitoko, écoute battre mon tam-tam qui va bondissant par-dessus collines galbées d'une pléthore d'euphorie
Je me jette à tes pieds, ô toi svelte rose aux pétales qui fleurent. Verse tes charmes si charmants dans mon cœur comme cabaret où se boivent saudades sous sonate morose

Berce l'enfant qui trouve son sourire dans le rêve marin de tes yeux, senteurs de serre mouillées de rosées

Il est doux le crépuscule qui tombe quand chantent si bas les tourterelles

Ô congolaise, mwasikitoko, créatrice de l'art d'acheminer les mers sans chemin de fer sur les dunes pour une prairie verte

Pour toi j'ai hissé sur les cheveux d'amazone ton étendard qui a su tisser les étoiles sur ma natte bantoue

Incantation du feu
Alvie MOUZITA

Je me connais chiffre trois qui pédale l'os de lumières pour une muraille mussive aux bouches des pyramides
Quand je m'abreuve au lac, sur mon front s'étirent les flammes qui brasillent les perles du cosmos
Et tous les flots du cosinus deviennent orange, ce feu qui me rend fort pour lui je ne dormirai pas
Je réitère, j'appartiens aux légions des panthères noires, dont les yeux sont orange et le front garni du feu rare
Garnies de ce feu, mes paupières font fuir les vipères perfides du fin fond de mon fleuve noir

J'ai dit, je ne dormirai pas dans les nuits profondes, j'ai dans ma gorge un verbe pour invoquer le feu
Mon Afrique, ce tam-tam de moi est paré du collier, corail colorié pour corollaire qui refuse de vieillir
Je ne dois pas dormir mais veiller !
Vêler un feu entre les bois qui n'ont cendres pour filles, feu qui éclaire et fait taire les crépuscules
Feu où s'adossent les âmes de mes aïeux qui deviennent fulgores et volent sans corps dans les cases des peuples émaillées nocturnes

Feu du foyer dans la lune, dans soleil, feu qui fend lumières et file au fil d'étoile filante pour mordre les fiels
Je ne dormirai pas dans les nuits profondes, mon repos aux corps qui travaillent dure j'ai vendu
Ma racine a des sèves qui offrent des chants aux flûtes pour dorloter les fatigues des forgerons
Je dois veiller ! Surveiller ce feu qui saigne à flots bêlés pour expier les âmes mouchetées de sales tâches du guépard
Ce feu qui guette, parle et ne part pas sans panser les plaies des braves, ces bras qui tiennent bravoure pour invoquer feu, protecteur des rêves,

printemps qui reverdit après crève de bruyère ! Feu qui fit Verbe sur terre où parle un nègre

Ce feu, une pharmacopée pour anéantir les monstres

Une femme qui a clopé sur sol pour recevoir semence

Ô vous poètes, faites-vous scribes qu'il vous dicte pulsation de ses flammes pour bouillir vos érables et en faire tisane

SOURDE OUÏE
DJIKOLOUM BIENVENU

Un Etat, une autorité,
Un peuple, une marginalisation,
Un droit, un piétinement.
Une revendication, une sourde-ouïe,
Une grève, une manifestation.
Une jeunesse, une victime,
Un mécontentement, une rage.
Une route, une barricade,
Un pneu, un incendie,
La police, une intervention,
Un gaz lacrymogène, une bastonnade,
Une dispersion, une fureur,
Un jeune, un caillou,
Un policier, un encaissement.
Un édifice, une destruction
Un bien public, un cassage,
Les militaires, un renfort,
Une arrestation, une fuite,
Un tir, une balle,
Un cœur, un percement,
Un saignement, une agonie,
Des morts, une sourde ouïe.

CONSEILS DE NGANA
DJIKOLOUM BIENVENU

Fils, garde-toi de la langue de vipère
À siffler que Mbaibokoum n'est que pour les Mboums
Toi Laka est aussi enfant de cette terre
Ne t'exclue de ses affaires, prends part à ses référendums

Ses oiseaux chantent ton nom
À chaque fois tu pars au champ
Ses chimpanzés, de joie, font des rebonds
Quand tu grimpes ses collines en chantant

Prends ta pioche, ta pelle
Moule les briques, bâtis bbk en une citadelle
N'attende point les autres, mets toi au travail
Force de Mboum plus force de Laka mettra mbaibokoum sur les rails

Africain du Maghreb, africain de la diaspora, africain subsaharien
Toute l'Afrique est aussi ta terre, sois prêt pour elle
Si un de ses Etats est en difficulté, apporte-lui ton soutien
Tous pour une seule Afrique, ce continent sera la référence sous le ciel

Glossaire : NGANA : nom de Dingaonaïmou NGANA, un Laka grandi à baibokoum
mbaibokoum : localité située au Sud du tchad
Mboum, Laka : les principales ethnies, les autochtones de baibokoum
Bbk: abriévation de mbaibokoum

Mon africain
TSOKINI Emmanuelle

Tu es la plus belle des créatures
Dieu t a aimé et créé sans ratures
En toi il a dessiné une belle parure
Tu brilles comme une pomme mûre

Le monde est monde quand tu es là
La nature est belle quand tu l'observes
Le ciel se sent beau quand tu l'observes
La terre rajeunit, rougit quand tu es là

Tu es la forte espérance de ton pays
Mental d'acier tu es notre courage
Tu es le trésor, tu as le trésor

La vie c'est de pleurer, rire,
Être sage, choisi le rire
Tu es toi et tu es adorable

Le monde bavarde sans cesse
Africain, sois un battant confiant
Souris la tête haute et danse

Africain la fille, africain le garçon
Tu as des qualités, tu as la vie
Tu es utile et capable, retiens-le

Ta vie c'est toi rien que toi !

L'unité

TSOKINI Emmanuelle

Au sommet de l'unité
 Règne la solidarité
Qui crée cette amitié
Douce à l'humanité

Elle attendrit les cœurs
Charmés par la rancœur
Elle lie un frère à sa sœur
En cultivant la douceur

L'unité mère de solidarité
Aide à affronter la réalité
Même atroce à supporter
Ensemble jusqu'à l'éternité

L'amour sans LUI
ELEMVA Sarai

À l'amour je dis merci.
LUI, oui à LUI je ne parle plus.
Muette car un cœur plein ne se plaint guère. Il mime ce dont le corps subit.
Je suis libre ET légère.
Je vis non pas pour LUI mais Avec LUI.
ET nos vies sans abris trouvent refuge en LUI.
Car l'amour LUI donne sens à ma vie.

Vingt ans ET plus
ELEMVA Sarai

    Ni jeune, ni vieille,
Pourtant toujours aussi belle.
Indépendante ou pas, l'argent prend son sens.
    Et de pourquoi en comment,
Des questions existentielles.
    On ne découvre plus LA vie,
On se découvre en vie.
    Oppression, et pression verbale du miroir social.
Trente ans égalent, au secours FEMINISME.

L'ainé
ELEMVA Sarai

Il nous parle
Encore ET encore
Sans remords.
On dirait qu'il confesse ses tords
Mais trop fière pour LES assumer
Car dit-il, « je suis bantou. »
Je le regarde parler amèrement face à son miroir.
A QUI LA faute ?
Moi ? Certainement pas !

Hommage à la nature
CHANDRELLE. N. MOUNTOULA

Mon cœur ressent une pulsion
Me donnant ainsi tant d'émotions
En admirant avec une immense joie
La douce nature dans sa splendeur.

Face à cela, je reconnais la grandeur de Dieu
Mon créateur qui avec son amour infini
M'a offert le rire et le bonheur.

Je contemple ce mystère qui est la nature,
Qui me dévoile en miniature le paradis.
Je ne la résiste pas et l'admire sans cesse.

Que des merveilles !
Qui apaisent mon être
En m'offrant la joie
De me sentir plus forte.

Alors moi je n'hésite plus,
Je me laisse transporter par ces images
Qui me montrent la beauté du monde que Dieu créa et que nous devrons protéger
Car il est rempli d'amour.

L'HUMUS DE L'ÉTRANGER

DJELASSEM Ghislain

Elle a été une source d'expérience
Elle a été un objet de mis en évidence
Elle a été chose d'étude pour la science
Elle a été la meilleure des appétences

Elle est symbolisée en opposé divine
Elle est qualifiée d'une race qui abomine
Elle aime même si on lui pointe un couteau tranchant
Elle avance malgré ses blessures éreintantes

Elle est confondue à toute pourriture
Elle est toujours un bac-à-ordures
Elle est destinée pour des travaux durs
Elle est la seule à avoir des actes "aiglures"

Elle est Intéressante, très importante
Elle est magnanime, plus indulgente
Elle est la protectrice, la superbe garante
Elle est la plus docile, une vraie croyante

Elle est recherchée pour son bravoure
Elle est vaillante, on parle d'elle toujours
Elle est l'intelligence, le génie du jour
Elle est celle qui a le vrai sens de l'amour

Elle est délaissée, mais garde son honneur
Elle pardonne avec tout cœur
Elle donne à l'étranger le bonheur
Elle fait rire, elle accueille avec chœur

214

Elle est encore et encore acclamée
Elle est le bouc émissaire recherchée
Elle est aimée de face mais au fond détestée
L'Afrique reste toujours la destinée immuable pour l'éternité.

JE DÉTESTE LE BLANC
DJELASSEM Ghislain

En cette nouvelle aurore mon Blanc frangin
Laisse-moi te déballer les maux de mon cœur,
Ceux que le Blanc m'a tant infligés en douceur
Et qui me rongent. Ça te déplaira, c'est certain

Je déteste le Blanc, tu l'es aussi mais je ne m'attaque pas à ta couleur
Plutôt au système politique de ces hommes au cœur pervers.
Sois mon Messagier, mon porte-parole chez tes frères
Si tu partages vraiment mes peines, mes douleurs.

J'ose croire qu'ils te mettront une balle dans la tête
S'ils savent que tu es des leur et que tu défends ma partie ;
Ça vaut la peine d'essayer. Rends-moi service en leur disant ceci
S'il te plaît dit leur avant à ce qu'ils n'appuient sur la gâchette.

Dit leur qu'on a plus besoin de franc CFA en Afrique,
Qu'on a plus besoin des bases militaires françaises,
Plus besoin de leurs aides qui incarnent la fournaise,
Plus besoin de leur système politique machiavélique.

Dit leur que l'Afrique est capable de se développer sans eux.
Plus besoin de leur présence nous causant des dilemmes,
Plus besoin de leur opinion concernant nos problèmes,
Comme eux, on a grand besoin de vivre heureux.

215

Dit leur que s'ils veulent vraiment le vivre ensemble
Notre relation doit se baser sur le partenariat, le dialogue serein
Et non sur leurs jargon "aide au développement africain"
Ni sur leurs discours paternalistes qui toujours nous accables.

JE TE PARLE
DJELASSEM Ghislain

Jeune d'Afrique je te parle, écoutes moi !
Prend place sous l'arbre à palabres
Ce soir, plus besoin des yeux cinabres
Tu t'en sortiras vainqueur crois-moi.

Comme un bélier égaré qui cherche la bonne direction,
L'homme est un égaré du monde dans un piste incertain,
À lui de forger sa destinée et son bon chemin.
Et pour réaliser ses rêves, il se doit de passer à l'action.

Si l'on abandonne le combat à cause des difficultés,
Si l'on tient compte des propos pessimistes qu'on lui dise
Et qu'à chaque fois il fuit en prenant sa valise
Personne ne sera encore arrivé au sommet.

Réveilles-toi chaque matin avec un objectif à atteindre
La vie ressemble à un champ de bataille
Il faut juste avoir l'audace d'oser et être en taille
Ainsi, tes obstacles tu pourras les pourfendre.

Tu es le maître de ta vie, de ta destinée
Saches que le monde est un hypocrite

Capable de t'anéantir si toi-même, ton histoire tu ne l'as pas écrite.
Crois en toi, bats-toi et ton étoile va briller.

Jeune d'Afrique je te parle, écoutes moi !
Prend place sous l'arbre à palabres
Ce soir, plus besoin des yeux cinabres
Tu t'en sortiras vainqueur crois moi

Mis par-cours
Précieux GOMA

D'où suis-je? Qui suis-je ? Où vais-je ? Au bout du premier round je respire. Oh l'être vert C'est un pugilat sans trêve. À chacun son rythme. Même si je trime. Il faut bien que le nourrisson titube. Car l'équilibre s'acquiert après avoir surmonté la pugnace brise. Je suis la mère, je suis la vie. À tous prix, je vous nourris, je vous béni jour et nuit. De mon échec, j'enfante pour vous la réussite. Mon chemin est une transcendance horizontale mes fils !
Un itinéraire de mère à fils et de mère à père je suis le sein de l'humanité ; Mère illettrés, je t'ai allaité, je t'allaite et je t'allaiterais Et toi tu m'as lettré Mes fils tes frères, tu les as maltraités. Tandis que je t'ai ouvert mon éden En eux tu m'as maltraité. Mais mon cœur de mère refuse pour toi le dédain. Tu n'es pas Cham et je ne suis point mère Noé.

Je suis la mère, le fils et le père. Moi qui seul sur mon Golgotha crapahute. Depuis l'époque des cabanes et des huttes je parachute je ressuscite après mes chutes je bâtis, je me bâtis, du matutinal au crépuscule je suis une hostie blanche le serviteur souffrant qui se donne en pâture. Je peuple le chez-toi du moi dis-moi où en suis-je? Mère verte, fils vert, père vert non ne soit plus pervers car des ténèbres peuvent dorénavant surgir le salut, n'est-ce pas cela fils de David ? La nuit est désormais lumière le noir peut enfin éclairer. Et le sombre peut désormais briller du tartare au barbare je suis maintenant chez moi un cerveau en fuite et chez toi une perle rare comme au football le numéro huit. Moi la mère, le père et le fils vert je suis au réveil.
Finis le huis-clos
Je soupir
Laisser ouvert l'enclos
Place au second round !Après ce mi-parcours,
Je vais bâtir le chez-moi avec mon propre souffle ;

218

vas-y, part et cours
Car de la capacité de nos mains
S'évalue notre niveau de développement humain
Dans un aujourd'hui où le pain se cuit en une seule main.

D'un regard ascardamycte tu scrute mes doigts
Tu tends à mon moi un verre pour qu'elle se pose dans son fond ;
D'écueils en croc en jambe
Je t'enjambe
Moi le père, la mère et le fils.
Oh moi dont Césaire appelait le laminaire
De ma fraiche air
Et de mon air vert
Avec Mveng je célèbre la vie
Mi-parcours c'est la pause
Air vert et air fraiche ravigote toi
Car à ceux qui la veulent, la vie se donne
à ceux qui la peuvent et qui ont pour lutte leur preuve.
Vive l'Afrique.

Résurrection
Précieux GOMA

Enterre moi mille fois je ressuscite
Ton tais-toi m'apprends à faire parler mes doigts
Qui suis-je ?
A ton bigre je réponds sapristi ;
En mon manoir c'est du noir et du vert ; du balle à terre et du terre à
terre ;
Par terre dans le parterre de mon logis, mon rire résonne jusqu'au ciel.
Non je refuse de mourir,
Dans mon univers vert,
car le vert c'est la vie et le solidaire ;
Quand mon frère Mveng joue du balafon ; la petite feuille Chante pour
son pays ;   Non, plus de
chant d'ombre, plus de feu de brousse,
Plus jamais d'hostie noire,
Finis les aventures ambiguës
Basta les pleurs, place aux rires
Non vieux nègre ; plus de cruel
Plus de monde qui s'effondre.
Plus de soleil pour sécher notre liberté,
plus de malaise,
plus d'étrange destin ,
fini la vie de boy ,
plus d'orage sur nos chemins
sèches tes larmes Richard Wright
voici pour toi des goyave ; plus de nausées.
Oh moi, Bouche cousue je ne puis m'exprimer
Car mon ouïe écoutes le tais-toi
Mon œil voit et trembles.
Mais je peux au moins faire parler mes doigts
Pas de droit ;
Que de croix

Mais j'y crois.
La vraie foi c'est celle qui tue en moi l'effroi
Et son seul miracle c'est de mettre l'agir dans mes doigts
Vive la vie,
Je ressuscite.

Grandeur humaine
Précieux GOMA

Qui es-tu homme
sinon qu'une simple poussière inerte
qui retournera si vite dans l'ombre !   Dommage que tu
ne puisses le comprendre sans qu'on ne t'alerte
De nature, la grandeur et le pouvoir sont tes rêves
de hauteur en hauteur tu t'élèves   la grandeur c'est ton oxygène
la basse échelle, te gènes.
L'homme c'est tout un monde
dans lequel le mal et le bien s'inondent
faisant du moi une priorité
et de l'autrui une médiocrité
Quand les nôtres sont bien traités,
les vôtres sont maltraités.
Tel est le cœur de l'homme
peint d'une luminosité sombre
avide du mal
plus apte au sale ;L'enfer est une invention humaine Lucifer c'est tout
humain qui sans gêne
face aux pulsions égoïstes de son cœur ne sait dire que amen.
Les puissants édictent et font appliquer des lois
celles qui abritent leurs chez-eux sous de bons toit
n'en déplaise disent-ils aux sujets à qui elles causent d'alopécies
car ils seront toujours maintenu en sursis.
Ouvre ton cœur
homme, le bien est plein en toi
la vraie grandeur a une senteur, une bonne odeur
ressaisi-toi
la grandeur ne dure qu'un printemps
le prestige qu'un instant
mais la vie est au-delà de la mort, au-dessus de la vie
ça suffit, vas-y vis.

LES RELENTS DE LA DEMOCRATIE AFRICAINE
DJEGUEDEM TRÉSOR

Monsieur le président de la République, chef de l'Etat

Chef du gouvernement, capitaine, général et commandant ;

L'homme d'actualité de tous les débats.

Mea culpa si l'un de tes titres ou attributs est omis ici !

Dis, comment ton peuple vit l'intimité avec la faim après tant de décennies ?

Au 21e S, ton projet social est la pérennité de ton pouvoir

Je me demande s'il y a dans ton palais l'arbre de la victoire.

Tout est bricolé, rafistolé pour assurer ton mandat sur ton peuple, ton auditoire.

Ta révolution est gagnée par le manège des baïonnettes.

Le parlement est infesté par un lobby qui transforme le temple de la république

En un encensoir pour aduler le grand souverain, le monarque de la république.

Le pouvoir aurait certainement la papavérine qui rend les chefs amnésiques.

Cher président, le pouvoir judiciaire est indépendant

Lorsque qu'un forfait est perpétré par les hors clans.

Mais lorsqu'il est frôlé par une tierce, omerta !

Le bâton atterri que sur la tête du poisson chat !

Cher président, chez ton voisin :

Règne l'alternance démocratique éprouvée :

Le peuple vit et le pays a un rang de choix à l'international;

Les dirigeants déménagent sans compte bancaire colossal ;

Les impétrants valent plus que leur diplôme mérité

DANS LES DECOMBRES DE LA DEMOCRATIE
DJEGUEDEM TRÉSOR

Alors que chez toi :
Règne une formalité de multipartisme :
Le peuple périt et la patrie, auréolée des places cadettes sur la scène des nations.
L'unité de mesure de ta fortune est le milliard et se trouve dans des cantons.
Les diplômes ne sont que des cartons, car l'éducation n'est que pour l'obscurantisme.
Encore chez toi :
L'intellectuel bavard caresse son passeport ou simule l'hypoacousie.
Le journal impétueux frelate, dilue son contenue ou se lie pour l'exile ;
L'élection présidentielle accouche des victoires torrentielles
L'opposant prie pour l'asile avec son parti ou se rallie à l'hypocrisie.
Or au début :
Nous te prenons pour un Prométhée
Alors que c'est toi l'inquisiteur pour l'autodafé.
Nous te prenons pour notre projecteur ;
Mais c'est toi les lanternes de nos pleurs.
Ton peuple est épris à l'approche des élections.
Comme un coq derrière la poule, coulent les promesses.
Comme une vierge qu'on le cajole, le peuple cède aux tentations.
Comme sous l'effet d'un sédatif il béni ses données pour des conférences.
Les intellectuels qui prêchent le réveil ne sont pas de rebelles ;
Le peuple qui parle dans la démocratie ne subirait pas de représailles.
Une démocratie sans développement est semblable à une sauce sans sel.
Le pouvoir se garde pas comme une relique, que cette idée se débroussaille !

Le siècle de gloire
EL BASSE

Les vertus ne réjouissent plus le mal
Dans le cerveau de l'homme. L'animal
Sème les graines cruelles
Au pays des barbares et rebelles.

Une partie de leur vie est déjà pourrie.
Les vautours aspirent l'arôme du cadavre fétide
Saignant de funeste et d'acide.
Les mouches murmurent au palais de la barbarie.

Les maçons n'arrivent plus à redresser les tôles tordues.
Dans l'ombre de la gloire, le franc-maçon
Boit le sang au creux de la diablesse ardue.
Ô quelle vie gouvernée par des cochons !

Ô Seigneur, le Clément ! Garde mon âme
Loin du diable qui loue le drame
Dans le tombeau des pauvres et des orphelins !
Ô mon Dieu ! Le ciel se brunit de chagrin.

Elle...
Abdou Rafiou BEREKOU

Ils me trouvent belle
Juste pour leur dose d'adrénaline
Et ils se sont assouvis

Ils me trouvent douce Quand je joue à l'idiote
Et Ils se sentent forts

Ils n'approuvent pas que je fasse de vague
Être sous leur dominance Et ils se sentent fiers

Toute cette éducation reçue de mes parents
 Ne servent plus
Ils veulent me refaire une autre ...

Hélas, me voilà décidée
Et ils me traitent de tous les noms d'oiseau
Ils disent que je suis ...

Souffle

Abdou Rafiou BEREKOU

Mon cœur bat
Au rythme du vent
Qui soulève sa robe

Mes regards s'excitent
Aux vues de ses douces jambes
Tout en espérant un autre geste du vent

Elle a un corps en musique, Mélodie de mon âme
Chant, chant, chantonne
Au rythme de nos reins
La sérénade des anges

Je fige mon esprit sur la douceur de cette   Être Pour qui je m'abandonne telle une ...

Une part d'elles...
Abdou Rafiou BEREKOU

Douceur
Fraîcheur
Dans ces profondes amertumes
Une part de lui me console
Voilà ma plus belle blessure Comme un souffle du diable...

Aigreur Laideur
Dans mes égarements, tu es
L'Astre qui me guide tels les rois nagent
Vers mon renouveau
Par-dessus tout

Douceur Tristesse
À-Dieu-vat
Me rendant plus subtile Me redonnant vie
Par-delà le bien et le mal...

Douceur Sourire

Dans ces instants
Je n'apparais que comme une ...

Tsi zimbi
Balddine Moussa

Tsi-dhulumiwa tsi-tsimbiwa za wutsimbiliwa.
Tsi-hibiwa yehaki hule yisamiziwa.
Tsi-zamba ha haya hawuka ngami wa wutrawa.
Wala ntsi wa wushitaki yesa ngamdji tuhumu nizo.
Hizo nedji fitini, yeba ntsino-hufa ha matchokezo?
Wo mgala wusa yadjuwa, ko wuwade djowu.
Ye wu hukumu ndopvi ye yadji fanyiya upewu?
Tsi dji-kosa ko samaha mahala.
Ntsina wudjirongza yapvo nehisa na-mana.
Tsi dji-zimbiya nedji rongoza ntsino pviya.

Je suis en colère
Traduction a Balddine Moussa

On m'a fait injustice; on m'a fait du tord
On m'a volé mon droit ; on l'a enterré.
Je l'ai dit par honte, car je dois fuir.
Et je ne porterai plainte ; car je me soupçonne !
Je mourrais de honte si je me dénonce !
Quelle maladie ! Se faire attraper par son propre piège !
Comment juger celui qui s'est fait du tord ?
Je me suis fait injustice ; point de jugement !
En colère contre moi-même, suis loin de mes yeux !
Si je me parle, je ne vais pas du tout me répondre !

Portugues poetry

Superiores
Lizete Zitoe

Afinal o que é isto?
Estamos cansados disto!
Pessoas que não sabem que não sabem;
Correm de um lado para outro, como quem vai e vem.

Falam de paz e provocam guerras;
Querem nos amar ou nos amedrontarem?
Se continuarem assim, atiraremos pedras.

Enquanto ainda existirem
A teoria de Freud não poderá funcionar;
Porque ninguém educa ninguém;
Ninguém educa a si mesmo;
Os homens educam-se entre eles
Sabotando a inocência dos menores.

E o que me dizem sobre a teoria do Piaget?
Quando diz que os maiores são o exemplo dos menores?
Se vocês transformaram-nos em um povo sem confiança;
Já não temos palavra nem crença,
Só vamos para onde há comida,
Do momento é o que interessa.

E ainda falam da independência,
Independência?
Mas que independência?
Se vocês transformaram-nos em um povo sem confiança, sem crença.

Eu em particular, se me pagarem "Voto Benjamin";
Se me pagarem melhor "Voto Serafim".
Mas se me pagarem como pagam os vossas deputados,
Faço um poema falando que vocês são bons, são fiéis, são os
melhores e um exemplo para a nação.

Mas como a minha arte não tem preço,
Vocês continuam Superiores desgraçados!

Dormes e eles matam-te

Lizete sitoe

Dormes e eles matam-te
Sonhas e não acordas
Num mundo obscuro, sem horizontes sem paz
Porque te deitas nessa dor?
Suas lágrimas precisam descansar, Roupas húmidas e molhadas de
suor.

Dormes e eles matam-te
Tu nem sabes da cacimba que faz lá fora!
Deitam-te de esperanças e fazes-te de barro;
Tu nem vens, tu nem vais...

Durma, durma bem mas não te chores,
Não te chores das dores da corrupção, do vendaval, da negritude, dos
terremotos, das virgens, dos bárbaros, da burocracia, dos crentes
fanáticos, dos contratualistas, da morte e da vida...

Não te chores, por quê choras?

Queria ser você
Lizete sitoe

Queria ser você que tem um sorriso único,
Que não tem de que se preocupar,
Sua vida vai bem e você anda suave...

Queria ser você que de noite dorme
Enquanto eu choro da minha desgraça,
Que de manhã contempla o sol
E eu repenso no que comer e se alguém poderá me socorrer com
uma migalha.

Queria ser alguém como você
Que tem oque comer,
Contudo, chega final de semana e tem o que fazer.
Queria ser você, oficialmente você!

Que tem mantas fortes e ainda um lugar para dormir,
Que talvez seja feliz!
Com tanta moeda que compra pão
E uma amiga clássica e um colega pintor.

Queria poder estudar e ser um funcionário público,
É tão difícil trabalhar sem saber escrever.
Queria ser você, oficialmente você!

Poder ter um pai que me desse mesada,
Um irmão que tivesse uma bola,
Um vídeo game e tudo oque você gosta.
Sim, aquilo de que você gosta,
Que possivelmente, eu nunca terei.

MONTE PERTO DO CÉU
Maria Manuel Menezes

Um Beija - Flor Malaquite
Tão azul...Será que é verde?
Perto do céu na montanha nevada
Bebe água pura pela alvorada.

Uma girafa come com arte
Frutos da árvore entre finos picos,
Molda os beiços moles em bicos
Dançando um pescoço longo elástico.

Na floresta gelada elefantes,
Búfalos e javalis na erva;
No solo magma expelidos minerais
Do solo frio também dos servias.

Servais às pintas de orelha bicuda
Saltam manhosos na montanha,
Assustam macacos de pelo e cabelos
Que correm ao vento na floresta dos gelos.

Nas savanas capotas e chitas
Campeãs de salto em comprimento -
Zebras, rinocerontes e elefantes,
Procuram água... Como antes!

Não sabem que o Monte sofre,
Não sabem do glaciar que se perde,
Nem sabem do vôo dos abutres necrófagos,

234

Nem da gente secular no sopé dos lagos.

UMA ESTRADA PARA A PAZ
Maria Manuel Menezes

Na fúria dos homens
No recôndito de um segredo
Há uma estrada para a paz.
Na ponta da fúria
No confim dos excessos
No extremo da raiva
Cheirando o ódio no ar,
Há uma estrada para a paz.

No meio de nós
Nas batalhas de dentro para dentro
Em qualquer tempo em qualquer lugar
Há uma estrada para a paz.

Conciliar o cérebro a bom espírito,
Retomar sã emoção, equilíbrio,
Limites sem excessos,
Uma estrada para a paz!

A COR DO MUNDO
Maria Manuel Menezes

Se vejo "o mundo em rosa"
Não quero saber porque vês o mundo sombrio
Ou porque usas óculos escuros,
Tornando - o mais sombrio numa desilusão de óptica.
... "Usas óculos de lentes cor- de rosa..."
Se vejo o mundo em rosa, privilegiada sou!
Sei,
Que no frio da montanha surgirá um fogo solidário onde me abrigar,
Que beberei na folha água da chuva a escorrer pura,
Que um esquilo na mata me observará a colher frutos,
Que o serralheiro não derrubará uma árvore centenária.
Sei,
Que verei nas praias peixes enérgicos sem tóxicos,
Que na cidade o céu não será cinzento de fumos,
Que o olhar do famélico dentro do contentor onde ponho o lixo
Ainda tem um sentimento que não é ódio!
E porque vejo o mundo em rosa,
Acredito em ti que me lês:
Farás a diferença em pequenos actos
Porque amas alguém no mundo,
Para que os que te seguem, não verem o mundo cinzento.

Os Outros Viventes Que Vi

Benedito Carlos Ngome

Vi alguém que achou vida,
Um amor que valia
Todos os seus mundos,
Não importava quantas vezes
Tivesse de se declarar,
Dizia e redizia que sua alma
Transbordava de amores na praia!
Uma parte dos homens sabe
Quanto vale um amor
E a outra é desgraçada,
Vive para remendar o tempo!
Os desgraçados eram os que magoados
Queimavam sozinhos de amores!
Sem correspondência, sem clemência,
Poluíram o mundo com suas lágrimas.
Vi outros ainda mais desgraçados,
Sonham com um lugar onde tenham
De chorar suas saudades reprimidas.
Desejam uma vida onde não lhes seja
Proibido amarem se pelas vielas!
Sem culpa, sem medo e sem intervalos.
Outros ainda havia que produziram cores,
Apaixonados que estavam jovens
Mesmo depois de tanta estrada!
Vieram de vidas passadas e amavam-se
Pelos milénios como eternas crianças,
Eram eles que davam beleza ao sol
No brilho de suas estórias de amor.
Alguns eram chamas sem fogo,

Corpos sem sangue, canetas sem tinta
Passavam vazios de doer penas e pesares.
Não pode maior desventura haver
Do que uma vida sem amor!

Mares de Mim
Benedito Carlos Ngome

Nesta voz florescem
As festas que nesta estação
Remarão os mares de mim!
Naveguem para longe
A sorte da minha alma negra.
Como um segredo sujo
 Que enlouquece os poetas.
Nestes olhos despontam
A vida que em meus amores
Dominarão vaidosas!
Em todas as estações de mim
Confesso-te minha luz.
Como um recesso onde em paz
Amarei os mares de mim.
Mesmo entre os montes
Jorram para o sol
As ondas de mim!
Pinga uma música perpétua
Que os outros
Se assentaram felizes no muro!
Não desejo que o meu coração
Venha doer em ti
Enquanto eu
Escolho sorrisos na praia!
Nestas ilhas amanhecem as aventuras
Que curam me até ficar curado.
Abençoados mares de mim,
Um minuto vale uma flor!
Nas ruas da nossa cidade,

Somos os outros!
Por onde cantamos felizes
Caiu um pouco de nós.
Desaguam nos teus olhos
Todos os mares de mim.
Para que a minha alma em ti faça pátria.
Quando na tua voz florescerem
As festas que os mares de mim
Dançarão nesta estação
E em todas as próximas

.

O amor é uma criança

Benedito Carlos Ngome

Se ela voltar,
Mesmo depois de tê-la magoado
Tantas vezes
Se os seus olhos arderem
Envergonhados quando o vê,
Se ela ficar
Vulneravelmente exposta
Se o coração dela o obedece
Mesmo depois de tê-la ferido,
Se ela emagrece de saudades
Quando ele está longe,
Então: O amor é uma criança!
Se ele for embora
Para nunca mais voltar,
Se jamais esteve
Disposto a perdoar,
E por apenas um erro dela
Decidiu partir,
Então: ele nunca a amou de verdade!
Estava com ela,
Mas é a si mesmo que amava!
Porque neste mundo de mágoas e frustrações:
Importa que o amor seja uma criança!
Se eles não fizerem nada
Quando o mar de seus amores
Despejar-se no amanhecer de espinhos no seu quintal,
Se um ao outro não puderem suportar no dia da tempestade
E deixarem ruir as paredes do seu grande salão
E dos seus olhos não jorrar mais vida
Para fazer brilhar de novo a história deles

Se somente uma mazela
Os fizer dar as costas um ao outro
Para não haver mais regresso
Então a paciência significa menos que vento
E a verdade é de vento, fria numa estação sem fundo e sem coragem
Porque o verdadeiro amor tem a pureza das crianças

O miúdo da rua
Larson Da Piedade Bento Fernando

Acolhido pelas ruas
Abraçado pela solidão
Faço do relento o meu teto
Conservando a pureza do coração

Deambulo pelas ruas da cidade
Estendendo as mãos
As vezes recebo pão
Outras, só a indiferença

Sou discriminado por viver na rua
Maltratado por andar maltrapilho
Fedorento
Mas ninguém se importa
Ninguém me acolhe
Uns fingem não me ver
Outros dão-me uma moedinha
Quando na verdade
Tudo que eu quero é um abraço

Exposto a todo perigo
Faço da solidão o meu amigo
E da esperança moribunda o meu baluarte
De algum dia vingar os meus sonhos

Este sou eu!

Há sempre um caminho
Larson Da Piedade Bento Fernando

Se não podes ser a luz da sabedoria
Sê uma pequena fagulha de conhecimento
Se não podes ser a alegria
Sê ao menos o solo fértil sobre o qual brotará

Se não poderes chegar ao destino
Curta ao menos a viagem
Contemplando o caminho
Não deixe de saborear cada paragem
Suas lições
Contradições
Angústias
Esperanças

Se não houver mais oportunidades
Revista-se de intrepidez
E crie-as com tua inventividade

Há sempre um caminho
Que se vislumbra no horizonte da esperança
Ainda que fores sozinho
Vale a pena continuar.

Eu sou o amor
Larson Da Piedade Bento Fernando

Sem me aperceber
Chegou de mansinho
Me conquistou devagarinho
E sussurrou nos meus ouvidos
Eu sou o amor!

Amarra capulana mulher
Osório Herno Feliciano Vilanculos

Amarra capulana mulher
Embala o seu belíssimo corpo
Que se torna ascendente
Nos sublimes olhos esplêndidos
Os corações se apaixonam fingidos
Nos sentimentos que ardem
E debruçam as singelas palavras
Silenciadas nas dispersas trevas
Oh! E embala as ancas extraordinárias
Misturadas nas noites imaginárias
Ao exibir das missangas nas madrugadas
Despertam sentimentos
Adormecidos agrestes sofrimentos
Nas cerimónias fúnebres
Sem se despertarem luares
 Amarra capulana mulher
Admiradas são as viúvas ao relento
Que prevalecem mergulhadas nas angústias
E enxugam lágrimas nas astúcias
Dos semblantes que se encontram em desalento
No silêncio
Os homens contemplam a beleza nas passarelas
Exibidas nos campos das estrelas
Ao balançar a catedral do seu corpo
Que permanece no vaguear das noites prazerosas
Onde nem se quer recebe rosas
Amarra capulana mulher
Exibe a sua moçambicanidade
Que contemplada é a belezura da sua africanidade

E enxuga as súplicas das angústias
Decaídas em lágrimas nas astúcias.

Doença do século
Osório Herno Feliciano Vilanculos

Doença do século
Não tens gestos e nem raça
E causas a desgraça
E sopras como o vento
E deixas o mundo deserto
Rios derramam pétalas
Na penumbra germina a planta
Da árvore que não dá fruto
E deixas a terra trajada de luto
Doença do século
Inofensivos são estigmatizados no abismo
Na estrema ignorância do altíssimo
E descriminadas as almas repletas pela ânsia
Doença do século
Causas tormento e sufocos
Na surdina dos ecos
As famílias são perturbadas ao relento
E dízimas semblantes
De pétalas inexistentes
E vidas se transformam óbitos
Num século de desastres catastróficas
As lágrimas caem em lamentações
Como fortes chuvas em inundações
Doença do século
Abates em massa
E nos cemitérios sangras corações

Sem distinguir semelhança
Nas noites rupestres
Nos jardins as pálpebras caem em desastre.

No meu tempo
Dalton Alfândega

O dinheiro era só um papel
A nota era apenas um número
O valor não se média
E o respeito não tinha número

A boca falava menos
No adulto não se apontava o dedo
Aquém se lembra!
Ninguém apontava ao cemitério
Era tudo perfeito

Saco no corpo
Agitava os gritos ao pôr-do-sol
Correrias e gritarias ao redor
Na família havia amor

Era uma moeda uma festa
A escola era um lugar de consolo

É bom ter um avô
As noites viravam histórias
Histórias que se perdia no sono

Hum!

A união tinha força
Era *mbava-mbva* sem demora
Rodeávamos as brincadeiras em encantos
Ninguém faltava a escola.

I'm soldier
Dalton Alfândega

Já nasci soldado formado no ventre da minha mãe.
Assim como toda essa gente
Sempre escolhemos a boa arma pra tirar a vida,
Boa arma pra tirar a tristeza,
Uma boa bomba para espalhar fofoca,
Um silenciador para espalhar mentiras.

I'm soldier
Nasci soldado como toda essa gente.
Que acredita numa paz que guerrilha nos olhos e na alma.
Acredita na mentira que na verdade,
Que aceita perder pra todos e puxar a sua parte

I'm Soldier
Deus conhece melhor minhas batalhas
As pessoas estão sempre atentos nas minhas falhas
Vida de batota, cada soldado com sua zona de batalha

Luto igual a eles, atrás de riquezas que empobrece,
Atrás da vitória que ninguém vence,
Soldados formados no ventre
Com todas artes mortíferas que finge que não entende.
Sou um soldado verdadeiro, que só a boca pode-me tirar a farda.

O desamor
Dalton Alfândega

As lágrimas falam o que o coração sente
Ouvi dizer que quem ama luta.
Mas eles não viram as minhas cicatrizes,
Infelizmente!

O que congela dentro do meu corpo não é o coração.
É a própria confiança,
Voltei a amar mas sem esperança.

Mulher!
Teu som sempre é fundo
Tudo que fazes, entrego o meu mundo
Surdo até sou, para não estragar tudo
Mudo me torno para os gestos falarem por mim

Como poderia amar?
O espelho chinês tem sempre o mesmo reflexo
Não vejo a originalidade do amor

Luto, sonho e corro, mas tu não vê o esforço
Somente posso crescer de novo.

E valorizar o meu amor
Por ti,
Valeu o esforço, mas já não posso.

Mulher do defensor da paz
Niurka da Orla

Amado meu
Homem que abraçou a guerra com a vida
Que ouviu os lamentos das vozes silenciadas
Homem que dançou o som dos vultos da guerra
Que mergulhou na guerra clamando por paz
Herói da pátria
Amante da paz
Senhor da paz
Defensor da pátria
A pátria regozija-se das suas lutas
Homenageia-te em cânticos alegres
A pátria me tem como esposa do herói
Sou bendita entre às desgraçadas de África
Como maldizer da pátria que me tem como mãe?
Como amaldiçoa-la se entre muitos sou abençoada?
Como dançar ao som dos lírios com os pés cortados?
Como empacotar-me de vestes alegres estando de luto?
Maldita guerra
Por decorar-me de véus negros
Maldita guerra
Por transforma-lo em vulto sem voz
Maldita guerra
Por leva-lo a sepultura dos heróis
Do que valem meus lamentos?
Se grito e não sou ouvida
Do que valem meus gemidos?
Se clamo e não sou acudida
Do que vale minha angústia?
Se lamento e não sou compreendida
Do que valem às madrugadas solitárias?

Se a pátria festeja lá fora?
Pátria, porque te alegra da minha dor?
Porque nela encontraste um motivo para sorrir?
Pátria, porque dança por cima do meu luto?
Porque nele encontraste uma razão para sonhar?
Sou vento que não sopra
Sou fogo que não queima
Sou água que não molha
Sou a viúva de lágrimas transparentes
Sou a mulher do defensor da paz

Vinte anos
Gerónimo Daniel Mabote

Daqui a vinte anos sonhos transcenderão
Desatinados em palavras estampadas em papel imprenso,
Atiçadas eloquentemente pela força do cupido,
Proclamando aos quatro ventos um amor imenso.

Em vinte anos toda a lágrima se terá afogado
Na fartura das brasas desse amor intenso
Nas cavernosas fragas do nosso já tenro peito

Daqui a vinte anos, sonhos serão a realidade
De uma história esculpida por frementes mãos
Acalentadas pelas encandecestes brasas da idade

Silenciosamente assentadas no vislumbro da ansiedade
Pois hoje é o dia, o dia da nossa herdade
Moldada pela imensurável força de nosso coração.

Guerra

Leide Tila

A maior guerra travada pelo homem é contra ele mesmo
São guerras intrínsecas
Tempestades implícitas
É difícil domar o animal, que lhe faz tão mal.

Nem ele mesmo sabe o que sente, suas acções não se compreendem.
Qualquer coisa é melhor que uma noite escura,
Qualquer coisa é melhor que uma mente impura.

A guerra racial é resultado de todo este mal
Estes furacões e tempestades prejudicam-lhe de verdade
Quando uns acham que ser branco é liberdade
Para outros ser negro representa humanidade

São todos parvos de verdade
Não são conhecedores da verdade
Desviam seus olhos da realidade
E a guerra os torna cegos de verdade

Suas frustrações e depressões
Só lhe envolvem em confusões
Sua cegueira vê o homem em padrões
Que para ele os prefeitos devem se tornar patrões.

Quando não ouvimos mais que ser brancos é uma bênção
E ser negro é maldição
Lá vem a guerra na religião
Uns se defendendo por ser cristão
Outros vão recitando o alcorão
Sem esquecer os que dizem Deus não

E aqueles que carregam uma arma na mão

Estas armas silenciosas
São usadas por pessoas ambiciosas
Para calar pessoas ardilosas
Abre só a boca para dizer que não concorda
Que eles não tardam em enforcar-te com uma corda

A batalha na política
Não é mais pela democracia
Nenhuma destas batalhas se justificam
Não existe mais partido no qual se confia

Lutam pelo poder e pelo dinheiro
E quem sofre as consequências é o pobre mineiro
A depressão do homem cresceu de mais, que nem ele mesmo vive em paz
A morte ele teme demais
Declara guerra e para militar ordena um jovem rapaz
Quando criticado o sangue de um inocente é derramado

O poder político lhe subiu a mente
Quem sofre no meio disto é o inocente
Quando humildemente
Clama por um novo dirigente

O Homem só trava as guerras racial,
Religiosa e política por conta de suas guerras intrínsecas.

Verdades Ocultas
Leide Tila

Nós vemos
Vemos doações que não chegam até nós, só para enganar nossos corações...
Sim nós vemos!
Vemos o índice de crescimento de apoio do governo ao povo tudo isso pela TV...
Sim nós vemos!
Vemos os nossos deputados coleccionando carros em suas garagens, enquanto o povo sofre nas paragens...
Sim nós vemos!
Vemos nossos líderes reunidos falando do desenvolvimento da economia, enquanto isso, o povo nem se quer comia...
Sim nós vemos!
Vemos grandes empréstimos para edificação de escolas e hospitais mas nenhuma destas obras foram vistas nestes locais...
Sim nós vemos!
Vemos gabinete de combate a corrupção entrando em acção mas os verdadeiros corruptos nunca entraram na prisão...
Sim nós vemos!
Vemos departamento de protecção a flora, quando os maiores abatedores   de árvores não são de departamentos de fora...
Sim nós vemos!
Vemos o combate a caça furtiva, mas pra quem tem posses isto se oficializa...
Sim nós vemos!
Vemos o Ministério das Finanças há anos fazendo poupanças dando ao povo um salário magro, enchendo seus bolsos de herança, é nestes que depositamos nossa fé e confiança...

Sim nós vemos!
Vemos nossos líderes dizendo que Cahora Bassa é nossa enquanto
pagamos até pela energia para erguer a bandeira que é nossa...
Sim nós vemos
Não somos cegos
Apenas nos calamos mas vemos.

A pobreza chegou e fez-me sua preza
Leide Tila

Pobre, é assim como me chama o nobre
Em contrapartida, coloco os meus joelhos no chão só para receber
uma migalha de feijão.
Opressão!
País onde camponeses são extorquidos sem ganhar um tostão.
Alimentação!
Com a esperança de na mesa colocar o pão
Muito cedo aprendi a arte da emancipação
Porque o meu país fez uma aliança
Hoje vivo desesperança
Quando ontem a esperança era o sorriso de uma criança
Hoje este sorriso fica somente na lembrança
Enquanto uns vivem bonança
Outros são decapitados aos olhos de suas crianças
Mansas crianças laçam vingança
       Absorvem a esperança libertam a
brutidão
Não dão nenhuma atenção a estas flores
Pela ambição seus governantes colocaram-nas a condenação
De volta a escravidão
Aquela que outrora tinha recebido a libertação
Aquela que meus pais tinham dito não!
Por meu próprio sangue fui traída
Minha pátria amada vendida
Exploram-me o petróleo
Exploram-me o gás
Ainda metem uma bala na cabeça de meus pais
Apesar da independência ainda clamamos por paz
Ergamos uma bandeira branca, ficas ou vais?

259

Amor resiliente
Lorna Telma Zita

Já não te sinto,
Onde foi parar aquele fogo, que incendiava a nossa paixão?
Nem pareces aquele lobo faminto,
Que devorava o meu corpo sem compaixão.

Olho-te nos olhos e na alma,
E por incrível que pareça não perco a calma.
Permaneço intacta embora resfriada,
Apagou-se o fogo e não mais estou viciada.

Se assim o fazes para eu desistir?
Devo dizer-te que vou insistir.
Não te deixarei partir.

Vou desobedecer a sua vontade.
Suportarei os seus gritos e o seu mal humor.
Lutarei contra todos e tudo, acalmarei essa tempestade,
Que apoquenta o nosso amor.
Farei isso! Unicamente em nome do nosso amor!

Mulher
Lorna Telma Zita

Tu és a seiva de toda nação
És a semente que brota a existência humana
Sem ti, o mundo perde o brilho

Mulher és símbolo de luz e esperança
Em ti não brotam só vidas, brotam sonhos

Não importa a sua cor, não importa sua crença
Não importa se estas no campo descalça ou na cidade de salto alto
Mereces ser amada, valorizada, respeitada
Na mesma proporção, pois, tu és fonte de amor e calor

Mulher, tu és guerreira por natureza
Sobrevivente de incansáveis lutas
Que a sua voz nunca se cale.

Que sejas lembrada todos os dias
Não apenas nessas datas, mas pelo valor que representas
Nunca te canses de amar, e educar

Mulher, tu és força da nação
E sempre que te faltarem forças lembre-se
Que tu és mulher, tu és fortaleza, fonte inesgotável do saber
E sem ti o mundo perde brilho.

Há que respeitar
Lorna Telma Zita

Quando tudo der errado
Quando ao invés de amor só traz dor

Há que respeitar o tempo
O silêncio.

Deixar partir o que sufoca o coração
Fechar os ciclos
Desamarrar os laços
E recomeçar
Milésimas vezes que for necessário.

O VERDADEIRO AMOR DA TUA VIDA

João Chico António Santos

Não é aquele que te enche de beijos
Para satisfazer os seus desejos
Nem te enche de adjectivos
Para alcançar os seus objectivos.

Não diz que sem ti não vive
Mas sim à tua alma reavive
Esconde e lima o teu defeito
Para que o mundo te ache perfeito.

É aquele que vela pela tua alma
E te defende mesmo sem arma
É a outra metade da tua vida
Que também sente a dor da tua ferida.

Ama os teus parentes
E os ajuda quando estiverem carentes
Não só contigo se importa
Mas também a tua família suporta

O LIVRO
João Chico António Santos

Podes ter um formato pobre
Seja físico ou electrónico
Com conteúdo sagrado ou platónico
Mas não deixarás de ser nobre.

És amigo do pobre e do rico
Do João-ninguém e do político
Te encontro nos liceus
Mas também estás nos céus.

Ultrapassado ou da actualidade
Tu és mais fiel que a oralidade
Possuis informação e ensinamento
Quem não te ama, lamento.

FACEBOOK

João Chico António Santos

És o rei das redes sociais
Quebraste as fronteiras internacionais
Protocolaste o público às estrelas
Aquelas que só se vê nas telas.

És a sala da liberdade de expressão
Em ti, uns até perdem a educação
Outros tiveram processos judiciais
Mal usadas, as redes sociais podem ser prejudiciais.

Em ti, uns se informam e aprendem
Outros simplesmente se ofendem
Uns fazem as suas publicidades
Outros expõem as suas intimidades.

Também és um meio de transporte
Em ti se passeia
E também se visita a vida alheia
Fazendo-nos perder noite após noite.

Mau dia para ser um bom poeta
Hilton Dany

Hoje eu tentei ser um bom poeta
Ansiei despertar um bom verso
Mas as letras com as quais converso
Segredam-me... Não vale a pena!

Saem-me poemas, mas Sem poesia!
E nesta jornada inglória e vã, fracasso
Mas, tendo-me esgueirado num bagaço
Purifico a frase certa, mas sem melodia

Então escrevo da direita para a esquerda
E sai apenas um verso que me herda
Envergonhando Virgílio e Neruda
Hoje um mau dia pra ser um bom poeta

Palavras ao vento
Hilton Dany

Há ventos e palavras
Na resistência de velhos mármores
Que ventam em estradas já desbotadas
Fazendo dançar ondas e árvores

E as horas esvoaçam num segundo
E as palavras da noite que amiúda
Sopram todos os sonhos do mundo
O vento por entre os fios de chuva
Vindo trazer sempre do Além
Palavras que já foram de alguém

Trá-las como se tivessem sido sempre minhas
Para amanhã as levar a outras vidas
Deixando-me só, com sopros de alento
A escrevinhar palavras ao vento.

Rio

Hilton Dany

No viver – ou ao amar
Ou mesmo quando sono intervala
Quando me salga o rosto um mar
Entre os silêncios do lago
  Sempre rio!

Génesis
Fernando Paciencia Luteiro Palaia

Cânticos de alegria entoavam os teus olhos
 Ao receber-me em teus braços,

Braços que jorravam sangue, suor e dor
Braços cansados.

É dor de parto!

Mãe tu és minha raiz sem fim
Minha primeira pátria és tu .

És minha lei constitucional por isso a ti sem temor me submeto

Obrigado por todos os decretos que ensinastes desde pequeno

Mãe, tu és minha república, um hino incansável de entoar

És a primeira bandeira na qual aprendi a honrar.

Génesis dos meus poemas
Poemas que jamais saberei como terminar.

Pois a medida que me sinto adulto
Mais em teu berço almejo regressar.

Cristalina
Fernando Paciencia Luteiro Palaia

Simplesmente agradeça,
Agradeça pela violência com que o sol rasga os céus em cada aurora

Assista espectáculo gratuito que a natureza lhe oferece
Desde o cantar de uma ave, o germinar de uma flor

Aprenda a contemplar simplicidade,
Com que as crianças dançam a volta da fogueira ao som do tambor

Deixa-te embriagar com o cheiro da terra molhada cada vez que
chover

Ame sem medo de perder
Abrace como se fosses despedir
E aprenda a despedir-se sem ter que partir.

Lágrima na garganta

Fernando Paciência Luteiro Palaia

Alô tristeza ligo te a partir da república da alma
Para lhe informar que este sorriso estampado em meus lábios é uma
apenas falácia.

Pois, estou cansado e queria contar-lhe que há uma lágrima presa na
minha garganta.

Há uma lágrima presa na minha garganta!
Que não quer se calar quando apalpo a madrugada...
Juro mesmo há uma lágrima presa em mim
Se tens dúvida pergunte as almofadas...

E explicar-te-ão as noites em que andei com o vazio de mãos dadas.

Há uma lágrima presa na minha garganta!
Gostaria de oculta-la em um falso sorriso
Para não poder imprimir a resma de tristeza de sinto...

Há uma lágrima oculta em cada promessa
Que nós fazíamos debaixo daquele lençol
Das vezes em que juraste estar comigo cada vez que nascesse o sol

E agora?
Agora só o tempo sabe o paradeiro das nossas juras de amor

Há uma lágrima debaixo da minha garganta
Que de vez em quando me vem visitar a alma

É uma simbiose entre tempestade e calma
Ocultado nos gritos desse silêncio cuja voz é o teu nome que chama.

O CÃO E O PORTÃO
Luciano Canhanga

Levado pelo medo
Da bandidagem em crescimento
Dundão apontou no portão:
Cuidado com o cão!
- Cão mudo, mudo cão!
Gozou a rapaziada de então
Sem comida, sem patrão,
Dundão ficou-se pela placa no portão.
- Cuidado com o cão!
Com vida de cão, é p'ra ter cão?!
Atenciosamente,

Poetics

Collaborations

Polygamy vs Monogamy collaboration
Curated and moderated by Tendai Rinos Mwanaka

Discussion

Mwanaka Media and Publishing: Let's discuss or debate... Just touching on the issues before sending our poems. I have realised when we discuss first we create better collaborations

Mwanaka Media and Publishing: Is Polygamy wrong?

Mwanaka Media and Publishing: Those who support Polygamy, will you also accept Polyandry... Esp men?

Mwanaka Media and Publishing: Those for Monogamy... I have observed a lot of my friends have mistresses, even though they say they are happily married, is Monogamy adequate?

Mwanaka Media and Publishing: Lets attack it whichever way we feel...

Mwanaka Media and Publishing: Ask questions, answer questions

Charles Duncan: I think the question of polygamy or monogamy depends on people's inclinations. I'm a Christian and my whole life is defined by Christian traditions and so I will reply strictly from my point of view, without imposing my beliefs on anyone else. I don't believe in polyandry - it is unnatural to me. I don't believe in Polygamy too. I think polygamy or polyandry are just outward manifestations of greedy and selfishness. If maintaining one partner is that difficult, I think I is almost impossible to create a stable and loving home with multiple partners.

Charles Duncan: Let me stop here for now

Mwanaka Media and Publishing: But isn't polygamy in the Bible in several instances, Charles?

Mwanaka Media and Publishing: You said it's difficult to create a loving and stable home in polygamous relationships... the reason why Monogamy might not be working could be the reason why polygamy might work.

Mwanaka Media and Publishing: Why do married men end up having mistresses?

Mwanaka Media and Publishing: Or women have extramarital affairs

Mwanaka Media and Publishing: Was man created to have only one partner or it's a social construct

Cosmas Shoko: from the onset ,(dating phase) if a man would be honest in a relationship and bring out their cards and say i am polygamous perhaps the issue of relationships outside marriage would be minimized but then people don't want to declare that they are not satisfied with one woman

Charles Duncan: It is and indeed the bible is rich with stories of strife and acrimony in such marriages. Not that the other marriages are free from problems. As you have noted many monogamous couples are having extramarital affairs - but isn't that a problem that can be attributed to other factors other than the marriage itself. I think society in general is suffering from serious moral decay. That the institution of monogamous marriage is still a perfect idea - but the players are inherently morally suspect

Ocean Scott Makwarimbo: Polygamy is Biblically condoned hence justified...it is not Biblically condemned. Direct ancestors of Jesus in Jacob, David, Solomon all practiced it. Again I said direct ancestors of Jesus. If God had found polygamy so despicable then He would have ensured the blood of polygamists would not have passed onto His only begotten Son...personally I do not believe in polygamy but the truth must be said for what it is, the Bible does not condemn polygamy...the demonization of polygamy is the work of the West...

Mwanaka Media and Publishing: Scott, Why don't you believe in polygamy?

Mwanaka Media and Publishing: I think Charles you are defeating your argument... If it's in the bible... That's 2000 plus years ago. It can't be today's society that lacks moral code here.

Ocean Scott: I don't believe in practicing. I feel i can only give myself to one and be committed to that same one... adventure, travel, memories hold a stronger sentimentality between two souls...way i see it

Mwanaka Media and Publishing: Okay Scott, i gather you think happens in Monogamy marriage only?

Charles Duncan: The extend matters. Surely today's society moral decay has broken any record that might have existed

Catherine Bihiirwa: I agree about those two being manifestations of greed and selfishness; which we all naturally are as human beings. We always want something better, dislike discomfort and the likes that come with living with the same person intimately for a long time. This therefore makes polygamy and polyandry inevitable on either sides (if a man isn't cheating, the woman is and vz)

Cosmas Shoko: polygamy by choice for me its okay but polygamy by force because of traditions, cultures etc is not cool

Mwanaka Media and Publishing: Thanks Cathy... But can we please define what is greed and selfish. Greed is taking more than what you can have, consume, use etc... If someone can satisfy 3 wives... How is that greed? If i am not taking someone's wife or husband... How is that selfish?

Mwanaka Media and Publishing: Define the by traditions, culture etc Cosmas... You mean being forced to take another woman or man you don't want to... Like instances of when your brother dies and you are given his wife?

Catherine Bihiirwa: From my point of view, polygamy has never worked in the long run as monogamy might and why it is difficult to create a happy and stable home(making other factors constant) is that the saying that "love is selfish" sets in.

276

Cosmas Shoko: yes that's one example sir, another could be church doctrines like in Zim there is much talk about some apostolic sects forcing young girls to be married to an elderly man who has a chain of women

Charles Duncan: Satisfaction itself is matter of perspective. Satisfaction should not only be sexual. I'm not sure if there are many wives who can say they are satisfied in all material respects.

Mwanaka Media and Publishing: Hahaha you see... If they are not satisfied in material things, it might be because they are greedy too... Materially greed.

Catherine Bihiirwa: Times change and in such times, especially for us Christians, where one wife is the ideal however much you can afford to have three wives, the mere thought of taking a second is greed. There is a reason why the second testament exists(we unconsider the Old Testament polygamous families) sometimes I think if there was a way of writing the third testament, it would be written and it would justify other relationships we do condemn in the African community.

Mwanaka Media and Publishing: Do you have statistics... Because really monogamous marriages are failing badly these days... Check around you, Catherine

Ocean Scott: wait....hold up... you just said you believe a third testament of the Bible would condone and okay same sex-relationships and same sex marriages? Who would be the writer of this third testament...is it not the pope already and similar-minded clergies

Mwanaka Media and Publishing: Does the bible, in the New Testament speaks against taking a second wife? Please quote the verse for us

Mwanaka Media and Publishing: Hahaha Scott stay on the topic. We dealt with same sex relationships before.

Catherine Bihiirwa: Sir, failing compared to happiness and stability are very different things. In this generation we really seek happiness over everything and from people around me, polygamy is never the answer. About statistics I always compare my two family sides (maternal and paternal) the results are so different.

Mwanaka Media and Publishing: Mmm if a marriage fails... How is that still stable and happy?

Catherine Bihiirwa: If it could be written, yes Scott. I believe we are an evolving species as human beings (living judgements aside)

Catherine Bihiirwa: Paul's letter to the Corinthians. The chapter about marriage

Catherine Bihiirwa: Failure comes last. When happiness and stability aren't attained

Ocean Scott: Please Catherine, touch on specific verses...you have my interest here

Mwanaka Media and Publishing: Yes lets have the chapter here.

Mwanaka Media and Publishing: The problem with Christians is they are no longer capable of separating church doctrines like a wedding and bible teaching like marriage

Ocean Scott: humans are animals...we try so hard to deny it...but the evidence of action shows we are simply animals...if not the worst of them...men are dogs... you've heard it...women are what not, if you know, you know...if there had never been a West to demonize polygamy the Bantus would be firm in its practices...your leaders in Jacob Zuma and Mswati are examples of the Africa away from the scrutiny of the West and her many perceptions, i dare ask: if polygamy had never been demonized and had never suffered from that demonification would men still cheat?

Kudzai Munzira: Why specifically New Testament Mwanaka??

Charles Duncan: 1 Corinthians 7:2

Catherine Bihiirwa: Thank you, I was so looking and looking

Mwanaka Media and Publishing: I am following up on the position Catherine had taken in saying the NT says something different on Polygamy.

Mwanaka Media and Publishing: Guys put the verse here... So we can read it

Charles Duncan: 1 Corinthians 7 says, "Now for the matters you wrote about: It is good for a man not to marry, but since there is so much immorality, each man should have his own wife, and each woman her own husband.

Ocean Scott: Nowhere in the Bible in either testament does that arise. I wait to be surprised. 2 Timothy 3:16 is clear as to how all Scripture is to be used: if it was not *EXPRESSLY SAID* it was not *EXPRESSLY MEANT* the fact that Hannah, mother of prophet Samuel was also in a polygamous marriage tells you that is not the business of a whole deity to legislate on the numbers of wives you can have...His is to demand that you be faithful and to committed to the one(s) you choose

Archie Swanson: How would everyone feel about a woman with four husbands?

Catherine Bihiirwa: If one says wife not wives, is it expressly said?

Mwanaka Media and Publishing: but Paul here was talking about marrying... There is no forbidding of Polygamy on the above verse.

Mwanaka Media and Publishing: Yes Archie, we need to hit it both ways... If men can have 4wives, why not women having 4 husbands *kkkk(laughing)*

Cosmas Shoko: she will always be tired but provided for *kikiki (laughing)*

Mwanaka Media and Publishing: No, the verse is for Bishops kkkk

Ocean Scott: 1Cor.7.2 - Nevertheless, to avoid fornication, let every man have his own wife, and let every woman have her own husband. The reading of the King James Version. A whole different insight. The phrase *to avoid fornication* is key.

Mwanaka Media and Publishing: Hahaha

Mhondera Chenjerai: If individuals decide to go polygamy, let them go. If again they decide to go polygyny let them again do so. This

279

thing of labeling polygamy as greedy or selfish, creates the holier-tha-thou of some of us, here and elsewhere. If again someone decides to go polygyny, let them not find monogamy as a sign of deficiency

Archie Swanson: But the Bible doesn't say that a wife can't have more than one husband.... maybe just an oversight??

Mwanaka Media and Publishing: Yes Scott, that verse is for avoiding adultery

Mwanaka Media and Publishing: It doesn't Archie.

Ocean Scott Makwarimbo: Precisely. It does not make polygamy a shut and closed case

Archie Swanson: A good rule may be to say that a wife can have as many husbands as her husbands can have wives

Mwanaka Media and Publishing: Hahaha yes Archie....

Catherine Bihiirwa: Don't you think there is a reason why in this chapter about marriage he answesr with singulars: wife husband. Paul was answering questions from believers. You ought to read this chapter

Catherine Bihiirwa: hahaha, definitely if she can. Why not Archie...

Charles Duncan: What is adultery then?

Archie Swanson: For example if she has two husbands with 2 wives each then she is allowed 4 husbands and if those 4 husbands have 8 wives then she gets to have 8 husbands and if those 8 husbands have 16 wives she gets to have.... etc etc

Mwanaka Media and Publishing: Taking someone's wife or husband, Charles.

Mwanaka Media and Publishing: Kkkkk i see where you are going Archie

Archie Swanson: Maybe this polygamy thing works better for the dudes when only the dudes are allowed ???

Archie Swanson: Feels a bit like patriarchy

Mwanaka Media and Publishing: Kkkk yes its patriarchy... But isn't Monogamy matriarchy too?

Archie Swanson: ... then again what exactly is patriarchy??

Archie Swanson: Is monogamy maybe something like joint ownership?

Catherine Bihiirwa: Quite, Like the Karamojong society in northeastern Uganda. Polygamy was actually a way of family planning. So when a wife gave birth, the husband would marry (no sex with the first wife until the baby starts walking), total patriarchy

Mwanaka Media and Publishing: Kkkk i think Monogamy benefits the woman more.

Mwanaka Media and Publishing: Would the women who has just given birth be ready to fulfill a man's sexual needs?

Catherine Bihiirwa: They have had the child together, why not be patient together

Mwanaka Media and Publishing: How is he going to deal with his sexual needs here. Musturbate? Kkk

Catherine Bihiirwa: Am leaving that for die hard feminists

Charles Duncan: The woman has feelings too. As the man deals with his, she is dealing with both pain and same

Archie Swanson: This might be the solution: Female praying mantises are famous for attacking and cannibalising their mates during or after a sexual encounter

Mwanaka Media and Publishing: Kkkk

Charles Duncan: Hahahaha

Mwanaka Media and Publishing: I am just trying to make you see this might have nothing to do with patriarchy. This is when you see in monogamous relationship, men taking in mistresses. Fulfilling a need.

Charles Duncan: and the male drone bee dies quickly after mating, his abdomen rips open when his endophallus is removed.

Archie Swanson: Yes and In the majority of cases a female spider kills and eats a male before, during, or after copulation.

Archie Swanson: This thing could get out of hand!!!

Charles Duncan: Kkkkkkkkk

Archie Swanson: I mean after sex is bad enough but even during ... that's in VERY bad taste!

Mwanaka Media and Publishing: Kkkkk

Charles Duncan: Mwanaka I have to ask, what is your own stand vis a vis polygamy and polyandry

Mwanaka Media and Publishing: Kkkk you are trying to tie me down.

Charles Duncan: Just trying to get you to support us the fundentalits

Mwanaka Media and Publishing: I am a free soul... In its truest sense. Those who want polygamy should do so freely... Those who want to stick to one partner should do so freely. As long as it makes them happy.

Archie Swanson: ... unless you're a male

Mwanaka Media and Publishing: Even women who can pull up Polyandry Kkkk but i would love to be a fly on the house walls of a Polyandry relationship

Mwanaka Media and Publishing: I really want to hear from feminist women on polyandry

Andrea Matambo: Surely a social construct; man is naturally polygamous. Religion pretends too much -no wonder the many mistresses, extramarital affairs, and women, in the heart of night, throwing foetuses on landfills, in toilets and drainages for fear of condemnation from other 'holy' people if they try to openly abort ...

Andrea Matambo: Often you find, like in most societies here in Zambia, it is the monogamy gang, especially the religious ones, who go about shooting insults and bible quotes at polygamous folks. It's like some have a religious right to attack others on the same. I reckon, sadly, all thanks to the bible or misinterpretation of it. Kayaa.

Prince Kamaazengi: I agree with you Andrea Matambo. I think humans are polygamous naturally or curious if you like. And the same instinct that is responsible for all the discoveries and/creativities that we've known, is the same instinct that makes us discover different bedrooms or to want to have many wives. Monogamy is evil- that is, it devalues truth!

Charles Duncan: You guys make it sound as if everyone on earth is either publicly or privately polygamous... There are many truly monogamous people out there

Prince Kamaazengi: I'm sure. They've "settled down".

Lisa Jaison: Often we look at Polyandry and Polygamy from a moral lens, while totally neglecting the historical factors that have necessitated it to begin with. We avoid a holistic approach that looks at the economic, social, psychological benefits of these unions. We neglect to assess the benefits, particularly in farming communities, where these are economic, in that there is shared labor, a larger workforce, better food security, and that women get to share child rearing duties, and gain a sisterhood.. Reducing the burden of patriarchy. Research has shown that women in polygamous households tend to have better food security, less chores and generally are well off and likely to suffer less abuse than women in monogamous households. The same was found to apply to Polyandry house holds in research conducted in Tibet and parts of Asia.

Lisa Jaison: For me, the question is not one about religion and marriage but more about the actual practicalities that come with love and creating a life with someone, and the feasibility that one person's needs can get met by "only" one person for their entire lifetime.. When I ponder this, the feminist in me views Polyandry and Polygamy as a necessity,

Mhondera C: Great, Jaison...thanks for the contribution

Mwanaka Media and Publishing: I think this is well researched input.

Mwanaka Media and Publishing: Yes the danger is in making love and marriage seem like a prison sentence. 'You can only be free/happy if you only love/marry me, me, me'

Tanaka Chidora: Dangerous!

Mwanaka Media and Publishing: I am sure a lot of African men are saying Polyandry isn't happening in Africa... It is.. In all sorts of ways. The thing with human nature is if you try to block it one way, it comes out in all sorts of ways

Tanaka Chidora: True. It has always been happening. Also, look at all these entanglements kkkk

Charles Duncan: It is. Except it is one sided, I want to hear the other side too

Mwanaka Media and Publishing: Kkkk yes *Pinkett entanglements*

Mwanaka Media and Publishing: Give us the other side Charles

Lisa Jaison: Sometimes it happens more openly, I know for one Polyandry is more often practiced in some parts of West Africa. Locally I know a woman who has been married to her first husband for more than 30 years, but he was involved in an accident 20 years ago and is a paraplegic, So they live with a male "nurse" who is now her partner and father of her last born child. Initially the first husband's family was livid, but have made peace with it because the first husband is really well taken care of by the wife and "nurse". And because the "nurse" has been nothing short of a brilliant stepfather and good care giver to the first husband.

Mwanaka Media and Publishing: I want to hear from women. What is the most important reason you marry? What do you need?

Lisa Jaison: We often marry, for companionship, social status (trust me when I say the social benefits can far outweigh everything else) , economic stability, and sometimes for "love"

Mwanaka Media and Publishing: Kkk i always trust you to say the truth

Mwanaka Media and Publishing: The other women... Let's weigh in. Why would you marry... What do you need?

Charles Duncan: brutal truth... *Sometimes for love*, which polygamy is not really a big issue

Mwanaka Media and Publishing: Hahaha

Mwanaka Media and Publishing: Since women are shy to say what they need... Let's give the chance to men. As a man why do you get married, what do you need in a marriage?

Charles Duncan: In that order: Companionship, To start a family, To share financial burdens

Mwanaka Media and Publishing: Kkk still no love Charles?

Aleck Kaposa: 1. GOD instituted marriage, so i fulfill His wish to have a helper 2. Conjugal rights 3. Children (where possible)

Charles Duncan: I don't know what love ...hahaha

Mwanaka Media and Publishing: Can you please tell us more about God Instituted Marriage Aleck... What's in it?

Mwanaka Media and Publishing: The idea for this social experiment is to narrow down on what is important to each sex... Then see if it doesn't work in any type of marriage.

Lisa Jaison: My personal opinion is that love is intrinsically entertwined with, economic well-being, it's easier to love on a full stomach, and from a socially comfortable position. Meaning that love is a consequence of all these rather than the cause. Hence l believe love is a fickle thing that has a short shelf life in a relationship in comparison to all the other aspects that create longevity..

Mwanaka Media and Publishing: Kkk okay. So in brutal terms no money no love

Charles Duncan: Amen to this. Love is like mist, it rises when the whole atmosphere is settled and stable

Archie Swanson: What ever happened to 'love at first sight' hahaha No more Walt Disney movies then!!

Lisa Jaison: Kikiki, I am sure we all know that one couple that is clearly not in love, but are still together because the social benefits of being married in the community, at church and at work far outweigh the romance of love..

Mwanaka Media and Publishing: Kkkkk what moves things is *Walt Dollars Movies*

Aleck Kaposa: He created one man for one woman (one Adam for one Eve) He said they should create a family ie have children. Somewhere in the Bible it says a man shall leave his parents and cleave to his wife.

Chrispine Juwa: That's why a man will leave his own father and mother. He marries a woman, and the two of them become like one person. (Genesis 2:24)

Mwanaka Media and Publishing: Kkk hai... in actual fact He created one man... Later he realised the man is lonely, and created a companion for him... Its adaptation to the needs of his creation that makes sense here...

Archie Swanson: Now that I come to think of it Prince Charming always seemed to be riding an expensive white horse plus he was a prince after all and his princess seemed to only wear expensive designer gowns!

Mwanaka Media and Publishing: Kkkk yes... You see... Money has always been the driving force behind it all

Archie Swanson: But true love can't just be for the wealthy, surely??!!

Mwanaka Media and Publishing: What is true love

Archie Swanson: Tendai, I am becoming disillusioned ..... please help! Is there no-one out there that has experienced true, selfless, non-materialistic love?!!

Aleck Kaposa: I don't think TRUE LOVE is possible

Archie Swanson: True love must be real! So many book titles, magazines, websites surely somewhere amongst our 7 billion co-inhabitants there is just one couple.. and if there is could they please be put on an endangered species list and kept in a special protected garden

Mwanaka Media and Publishing: Hahahaha

Mwanaka Media and Publishing: Our societies are too material to sustain a non-material relationship

Archie Swanson: .... and by the way could we please just exclude all snakes from the garden this time please!!

Oscar Gwiriri: Love is just a feeling, your own feeling which you put forward to somebody else who then accepts it, per chance, exchanges his/her illusion with yours. There after, you deposit your hopes in one hole through romantic voices and gestures, then, boom, an explosion of ambitions scatter your fears, and your hearts settle in another illusion of union we call marriage.

Mwanaka Media and Publishing: Kkkk surely you are not writing the poem, Oscar?

Archie Swanson: plus can I please point out that certain fruits can cause major upset and should maybe not be allowed in the garden or if they must be there, eating then should be forbidden at the very least

Amani Nsemwa: Can you please elaborate Archie?

Amani N: I think I will marry for

1. Companionship
2. Obligation (Social status)
3. Having children
4. Love

Amani N: I can get all these in polygamy or monogamy, but I prefer monogamy.

Amani N: I'd also go for polyandry at some extent. Cos I have been in love with some of married women, and the fact that they are in monogamy makes my moves a failure

Archie Swanson: Well Amani, the first time around things didn't seem to go all that well according to Adam or was it Eve???? .... not sure

Lisa Jaison: Kikikiki..

Charles Duncan: Thats a myth

Mwanaka Media and Publishing: Yes kkk Adam failed to live alone. And even Eve failed too... God was adapting from the first version all the way to us.

Charles Duncan: So God solved Adam's problem by giving one woman

Lisa Jaison: Kikikiki men marry for economic reasons too. Imagine trying to job hunt whilst child minding too. It's easier to job hunt when you have someone to iron your shirts and cook for you when you get home. When you have a wife who does this for you, it means you have more energy to place towards your economic emancipation.

Charles Duncan: A maid can do most of that. Though a wife still helps to organize things in the house

Lisa Jaison: Given that you can afford a maid. And this works on the assumption that the wife's house hold, overseeing management, organization and coordination roles are of no monetary and social value to her husband.

Lisa Jaison: My reasoning is that marriages are value adding partnerships rather than unions based on the notion of the butterflies we get from the illusion of love. Both for men and women.

Tanaka Chidora: If you want to see that finance is at number 1, lose your job, car and house, or go bankrupt

Mwanaka Media and Publishing: Yes, at the heart marriages are business decisions kkk and polygamy is more lucrative than Monogamy

Mwanaka Media and Publishing: I think what drives man more to marriage is regular sex and having kids more than anything else, and then social/economic status is the next

Mhondera C: Hahahaha. Silence maintained lol

Mwanaka Media and Publishing: Kkk i can only imagine how much its costing you to remain silent Tsano Chenjerai.

Tanaka Chidora: Tendai, then when they have had these, they discover it's not as easy as that. When I was young, the thought of sleeping every night on the same bed with a naked woman always brought a smile on my face. I couldn't wait to grow up and get married. But these days, there are nights when I just want to be alone *(sad emojis)*

Mwanaka Media and Publishing: Hahahaha next time you are paying for this therapy Tanaka!

Mhondera C: My love, take notes from Jaison lol. *So don't insist on asking me, whether I still love you?* It's *sometimes* for love...lolest

Mwanaka Media and Publishing: Kkkkkiest

Mhondera C: Don't start on me my in-law Tendai... Jaison is my advocate in this relation ...sometimes love, and so you are left with combining these sometimes love (through polyandry or polygamy or 'extra') until these *sometimes love, make a wholesome love for you*...so this love is like combined science in Zimbabwe lol kkkkk hahaha. Just my love, will think I'm cheating on her....I will be just adding these fractions until I come with at least a whole number...

Lisa Jaison: hahahaha

Mwanaka Media and Publishing: Kkkkk

Gwiriri: Materiality, yes, it has an effect on marriage. But if we are looking at it from a village point of view, why does a village woman fall in love and get married to a pauper?

Charles Duncan: Societal pressure might be one point. Desperate to get married

Lisa Jaison: Social benefits, as well as the reality that they have a stronger chance of getting out of poverty together than apart..

Lisa Jaison: In some rural communities, once a man gets married, he gets a piece of land to work on and provide for him and his family. Young women do not get the same. So you are better off marrying the pauper than becoming a "spinster" because in any case as a woman you are less likely to inherit the family property if your parents die. You have a better chance of inheriting your pauper husbands land if he dies, particularly if you have children.

Charles Duncan: The inheriting part is only true in patrilineal societies, in some societies in Africa, they have a matrilineal system. Where inheritance normally passes to the women from their family line

289

Gwiriri: Love issues confuse me. Have you ever experienced a situation whereby you get into an affair whilst experiencing heartbreak? Is it that you would have loved the next person within a short time or you are just in a console? I consider that as a mere replacement of the ex with another, then moving on. Is it love that you choose someone with the qualities which you want? I think love is a feeling in an individual, (being in love with love), then you get someone to collaborate that feeling (someone fitting in your frame). My research on love revealed more than seven types of love; Love by familiarity, Love by similarity, Compassionate love, Passionate love, e.t c. Other books talk about Eros, Storge, Pragma, Mania, Agape, etc. This love subject, I surrender!

Mwanaka Media and Publishing: But its attraction (not love) that starts the nonsensical journey... In actual fact Love is the suffering that happens after attraction has dulled a bit. Whatever we might call love is familiarity with what you have... That's why biologist contend love is just a habit... The rest happens in your fantasies. Put two people together for a long time, they develop feelings (familiarity) with each other...

Poetry

Charles Duncan:

In the beginning there was loneliness.
Amongst the swarms, herds and hordes of wildlife;
Loneliness still reigned vast and large.
Before a single rib was rose to life to give breath to love.
Amongst the myriad, He plucked one, the finest of the lot,
Moulded into one fabulous partner fit for man.
There, His will for mankind was made manifest.
For God ordains order, perfection, bliss, love,

Purity and cleanness; not the lust and moral decay - an infestation
that has gripped earth like a viceroy.
For this promiscuity, this plurality of wives or husbands -
The plan conceived by mankind, a breeding ground for strife and
disease,
Will spell final doom on the remnants of mankind.

Mhondera Chenjerai:

My grandfather being the oldest, of my only surviving inheritance,
Treasured in me the secret behind polygamy
"Never ever marry a
second wife who is older
and uglier than your first wife!
Never, ever repeat such with your third or fourth marriage!"
So in this marry for sometimes love, trend, I never wanted
My love to be a single record
But an album, decorated with different
Colours, flowers and nuances,
Like the plumale of parrot.
The rich farmer boasts of having one bull and several cows,
So did the poor, little peasant, when he mentioned in pride, having a
cock
And several hens among his stock.
The chickens and cattle,
Came to remind me,
"What a shame if I don't play poly in this game!"
As they cackled, roosted, mooed, and bellowed in pleasure

Emmanuel Tumwesige:

Many souls wander about
In the jungles and the lonely paths

But there is one I can take- yes one
It is where I can find peace and scrutinize harmony.
My forefathers said a home is sweet when warm and
If in all corners of my compound stands a hut
From which delighted screams diverge to fill my ears with joy
In which per night I enter one or two on God's command for joy
And at day break all, with paunches, hips and tamed bossoms raised
And watered black lips parted to say with no rapture good morrow to each,
The best way to rescind pitiable breeding and
Bringing all worlds close to speak one tongue of love.
Then to fill my Eden with Eves feels best.

Issac Kalibwa:

Take me back to belief in a world of make believe
When nerves bloomed under fingertips
And blood chanted in my ears.

Now life's retreated from the blossoms
Into the fort of seed.
No matter the soul searching I cannot be found, I will not be found.
Benign adolescence, farewell, it's sad
That the multitude of my sin is uncovered,
Contentment's been robbed, I'm ever seeking places in people.

Take me back to wonder at romance with the wild eyes of an infant,
Stoke the flames of faith, I've lost my soulmate
And forever's a scary place!

Lisa Jaison:

You will find this well is the deep kind, that calls for a brotherhood to help you quench.
In its overflow of complexities of quenching waters,
It beckons a myrad of parched brotherhoods to a place of rogue purposeful completion,
Like any colony the center is honey sweet, and moistened by the clarity of organised chaos,
Chaos of brotherhoods creating a killer swam under the positioning eye of the queen bee.
All this, while the sanctimonious lick their parched souls in righteous indignation,
As they pass time, by secretly coveting other men's wives in unholy confessionals.
Grievously muttering vile emasculation at a brotherhood they are certain they have never wanted to be a part off, but are annoyed to have been excluded from.
The Judas position for those that have never been afforded choice.

Oscar Gwiriri:

What is love that has no destination?
After all, who said marriage is the destination?
Destination to where and from where?
Is love a unit or event?
Is love really divisible amongst lovers?

I am yet to understand
The instrument used by poly partners
To equalise love to their spouses,
Maybe I may properly advise a cheating friend.
Anyway, is the cheating not like polygamy or polyandry?

I'm so eager to understand

The weight of a cheater's love.
Confirm if cheating spouses,
Feel the same as their cheating spouses?
Are they not the same as poly...sts,
Just that their affairs are not publicised?

Why do society ban polyandry?
Yet, since time immemorial women cheated?
Why do society condemn polygamy,
While married men cheat left, right and centre?

Why do spouses do things society loathe?
Why does society misunderstand human rights?
Why do human rights violate socio-cultures?
Why did the legislature discriminate poly-marriages?
What do courts understand about love?
...?

Gwiriri:

Mary was cheating with her neighbour's husband,
Yet she was also straying with hers,
On discovery of their collaborating deceit,
Mary negotiated for a give and take settlement,
The spouses swapped partners for good.
The neighbourhood scorned their bargain,
I for one, acknowledged their maturity.

El Basse MANSALY THE YOUNGER:

 Nowadays the woman is like the rainy season,
At the start of the relationship she behaves like the storm,
She laughs like an angel

At the moment the stars lower her beauty at midnight,
So much she falls for the flavor of the kiss.
On the day of the engagement, she charms you as if the verb to love,
Conjugate only in the present.
Alas, she forgets that love also has teeth.
At the start of the marriage, she strokes your beard.
 She walks like a crab.
A few months later his lips turn bitter.
She forgets, that she is a future mother,
Who should take care of her husband
Unfortunately, she ignores you like rotten fruit.
O women, marriage is not a game!
It's an eternal union sooner
Where feelings will never be old.
O woman alone the marriage which can give you a beautiful life!

Gwiriri:

What is love that has no destination?
After all, who said marriage is the destination?
Destination to where and from where?
Is love a unit or event?
Is love really divisible amongst lovers and animals?

I am yet to understand
The trick of those with multiple affairs
On equalising love with their spouses,
Maybe I may properly advise a cheating friend.

Anyway, cheating seems to be a modern culture,
Alongside polygamism, polyandrism and zoophiliaism,
Accelarating us to the sweet grave.

Who are cheaters?

I'm so eager to understand
The weight of a cheater's love.
Confirm if cheating spouses,
Feel the same as their cheating spouses?
Are they not the same as polygamist and polyandrists,
Just that their affairs are not publicised?

Why does society ban polyandry?
Yet, since time immemorial women cheated?
Why does society condemn polygamy,
While married men cheat left, right and centre?

Why do spouses do things society loathe?
Why does society misunderstand human rights?
Why do human rights violate socio-cultures?
Why does legislature discriminate poly-marriages?
What do courts understand about love anyway?

Gwiriri:
Love

Give me the definition of love
And i can prove to you otherwise
To justify why I can't marry.
Is love a steam which vanishes
Or just a droplet in it?
Is love from the heart which doesn't think
Or the mind which doesn't see?
Is it from the sight which doesn't feel
Or the hand which doesn't hear?
Tell me where love comes from

Which defines it as love.
Anyway, who said love is love?
Without convincing answers,
I swear, I won't marry again.

Nouhr-Dine Akondo:

I live in a heaven
A flowerbed of maidens
Because I loved and hopped
From a wrinkling thigh to poking breasts

I came out
Out of the one-man-one-wife clot
From a lecher blame here
To the trampled household hegemony there

I went out
All blind and Blown out
Mine was a thirst for the next Eve to quench,
The next she-hero of my Sodom meant for a clinch
But I met many and stamped four
I wasted genuine souls, all of them four.

The first she-hero had a forked tongue
And she brought in her throng,
Yes, she wrought the crowd of lies
That set out of the house.

With my melancholy injected eye

I went on, and pride on shoulders, I pried
Yet to find fault with two household souls
One after the other, soul after soul

Then came the third she-he-row
Whose peace is that of a piranha feeding row
She had to fight two
But started with a peace treaty with all, to woo.

Anguish and jumpy heart in my mind
I left the household and fights of three behind
To seek peace in a fourth she-peace maker
And she came with the gall and rant trident not a save all.

At the cost of my respect and peace of heart
She was an anthill of magnan ants
She lavished my days and nights with kindred
And save affection and love my eye grew red.

The blame is mine, when with the devil I dined
Seeking to quench my heart desires
While my spirit fled and starved for peace
Amidst a thigh poly-game, my heart waned amiss

Ah, polygamy, who that help?
When made bellow the belt?
Who that help, when built on desires,
With no values nor rules?

Cosmas Mairosi:

My little panga (Infidelity)

My little panga is for Masibanda
 To lovingly palm and cradle at her own leisure
 She lays it on the kitchen table
Feeds it
Folds it under a bedroom sheet to keep it warm
Hides it well in the nooks and crevices of her body
Keeps it under lock and key
And watches over it with a hawk-eye
It's hers for keeps after all.
She loves the pain when I stab her
She has told me so a hundred times.
One day she visited the moon
I snuck into the vlei to sharpen her panga
Had some brief rabid illicit fun
With a bare-breastfed lady of the night
I have since regretted the incident
My little panga is only for Masibanda
It's for her, and hers alone!

Post-poem discussion

Mhondera C: Hahaha. Cos, is getting coarse here hahaha
Cosmas M: Hahaha
Sebastian Jalameso: The coarser it is, the sweeter is the sting.
Sebastian Jalameso: Before the lessons, readers are not given the reason for introducing another character. Something probably should happen to the persona's panga while using it elsewhere.
Cosmas M: Thanks. Was worried I had gone overboard. I toyed around with the idea of returning home with a poisoned panga but thought it would make the poem too long. Since this is a collab, maybe someone else can play around with that part and fill it in.

Sebastian Jalameso: The idea of "a poisoned panga" sounds great. I wish you could do that then someone can pick from there. It would look complete with that idea so that if another person is going to develop it further, it would be easier and the flow uninterrupted.

Cosmas M: Many thanks. Let me see how I can fit it in 2-3 lines tops.

Mwanaka Media and Publishing: Why does it have to be poisoned?

Usman Danjuma: And panga is a bit an unfamiliar expression to me in particular. May I be educated on that briefly, as Tindo pleases.

Sebastian Jalameso: I think it gives a wider scope of interpretation: from moral corruption to a metaphorical death that may transcend generations.

Sebastian Jalameso: I see your argument. The imagery is incongruous. A spear, arrow would do

Mwanaka Media and Publishing: Kkk penis, Usman.

Mwanaka Media and Publishing: The danger is over-moralizing...it becomes preachy like a gospel parable. Already the narrator is regretful for his actions... piling up punishments on him feels like a cliché to me...that's what you expect from every infidelity story.

Mwanaka Media and Publishing: use of Panga is fine by me... This already shows it's an interesting metaphor... Usman wants to know what it is... Sorry i translated the meaning... Panga is a long knife... But as i noted it's a metaphor for a penis(meaning)... I feel readers need to be challenged, pushed or pulled. Also arrow won't fit in as well as panga... Because arrow is thrown to a thing far away... It leaves your hand, or body... Whereas panga stays on your body and the idea that you can insert it into someone's flesh and remove it whilst holding it. works with a penis. It stays attached to your body...

Cosmas M: You explained it (panga) so well Tendai. I have nothing to add or subtract.

Cosmas M: My intention in using the names "panga" and "Masibanda" was to ground the poem to a local setting . In Zim there are three main linguistic groupings: Shona, Ndebele and English - and I thought 'panga' would be recognisable by all three.

Cosmas M: Great question. I also wanted the reader to fill in that part with their own individual retributive experiences which may vary from ' poisoned panga' (STDs), to complications like fights, extra-marital pregnancies, divorce, abortion, morality issues viz a viz religious and social principles. (I once went to a church that believed if you commit adultery you remain unclean for seven years. During that time you can't serve any duty in church or wear church regalia)....

Intergalactic Beings collaboration
Curated and moderated by Tendai Rinos Mwanaka

Oscar Gwiriri:

We are the lively dead
You chose to call ghosts.
We once lived on Earth,
Were buried in sweet earth.
We're an invisible society
Mutually living amongst you,
Enjoying our peace and harmony,
Availed by good governance
In the midst of the dead community,
Resting our souls in eternal peace.

How good would it be
If we take over mother Earth,
And relocate you to St Elsewhere?
We could restore order and nature,
To an intergalactic order, once for a change.

Mandhla Mavolwane:

What will happen to mankind's scars
A step closer to the stars
Stargazing at the shining moon
I need to hear the werewolf at the top mountain of Mars.
 St Elsewhere is brewing anxiety
Where else will the saints create a new society?

Obinna Chilekezi:

We dream of going to mars
When we are miles away from villages
We want to build spacecrafts
When millions are dying of hunger

All basketful of waste
Let first build hospitals for our sick
Before the moonride oh moonraker

Nica Cornell:

I cannot swim into outer space -
it's a girl in a pufferfish suit
keeping the inner space oxygenated
her, alive.

But the Border suffocates,
and I don't know if we deserve seconds
when we swallow the breath from these seas
and silently watch the pufferfish drown.

Joseph Sukali:

Chocked by our own hands
Suffocated by the malicious choices we made
We raped mother earth
We were intoxicated by a gnawing hunger for money
Now we freeze in the cold next to the stars
Our eschatological path has turned tragic
We are strangers far from home
Welcome to the beginning of the end of humanity

Tanaka Chidora:

earth

divine figure 1:
let's find a place for
lunatics,
rapists,
murderers,
liars...
a place for the vilest pieces of vemin ever seen!

a place for satan
and floods
and earthquakes
and corona...

a place where the denizens spend their days
running
dying
wailing

a place where death's scythe is indiscriminate,
where creatures that strut around its dust forget their irrelevance
and hide behind the thinking that something big is going on,
a place where they lie to each other that there is meaning
purpose
love...

a place, in short,
that's so down there
that when we look at it
it's just a small dot that doesn't matter to the eye.

divine figure 2:
and what shall we, I pray thee, call it?

divine figure 3
earth.

Bolaji Tola:

Made a fallow of our fertile...
Now barren what was once fruitful.
So we seek solace in place
We never farmed,
To turn to desert,
What was never a vegetation.
In the first space.

Gwiriri Oscar:

Bravo! Bravo! Bravo!
Here comes the spaceships
To ferry you all now
To a novel nice location.
Earth is scheduled for renovations.
Worry not, I exstinguised Hell's fire,
You' ll all be lodged in it,
It's a place where tribulations
Burned to ashes
And fertigated the base for your farming.

Emmanuel Tumwesige:

Whizzing through the galaxy

An idea afore;
How shall it be transcending the region so odd
Kissing planets and touching new soil
Klinking places an order
Upon the heavens the twinkles be

Mwanaka Media and Publishing:
Hai i love this... Let's keep it going, let's assume we are now in outer space...
Let's imagine the life there. Let's imagine love there, lets imagine living in enclosed
environments like in Mars, lets imagine a better planet than earth with better
environment, we are the first Adams and Eves, what world do we propose or want
for our progenies, Lets imagine God, or gods.., Lets imagine social networks, Lets
imagine, if it a desert like Mars, living with little greens and flowers, growing new
greens, lets imagine the race wars on earth... Are they going to continue beyond,
Gender issues, boundaries and borders, governments, etc

Bolaji Tola:

Lost, was all we held,
In days wasted on earth,
Where rivalries were gems,
Worn across our necks...
A river now of gemstones,
More and more...
For here we only live,
With arms open
To calls far and near....
Now we speak,
One language,
In one singing voice.
A beat, a rhythm.
Now we have,
No race or clan,

No religion of hate,
Nothing but healing,
As we attend to this Earth,
Or Mars I can,
In farming tell...
Azure, alas.
Or is this what they call...
Heaven?

Mhondera Chenjerai:

As we chill down,
Clocks counting down
to the Maskian Mass Exodus,
To Mars,
Earth, subject to renovations,
The ruins are remnants,
Of a life, where we shall be perceived the first aliens
On earth,
Hope is the fuel and lubrication to this secular illusion.
You cannot erect structures, to the effect of industrialization
Maybe in my uninformed illusion,
love making, is the only industry to erect,
In the capital of void,
connecting us with departure,
Away from the hype of Armageddon.
Tonight, I wait to muse
my moron as the last of this episodic act,
On orgasm,
Maybe I'll pick on you! Don't refuse!
Maybe that will be our last most fashionable intimacy,
To star on history of pornography
To be played about a people in haste,

Round up, to evacuation
What comes to be the most convincing reality,
When children to be born in Mars,
Are born astronomers in space exile
and interestingly made to study earth, new curriculum structure, a caricature,
In aghast, refusing the science
Of existence of earth and everything else associated with it
Our most convincing experience of once, as a whole,
Being the resident population of earth,
Equal to a subtle super science fiction
Of all times.
I stand to be informed by my reservations,
If you and I, and all of us,
Are indeed on a terminus to Mars!

Denis Barasa:

They say Satan drooled
And dropped away from Saturn
Plummetting past Pluto
Jettisoning life off Jupiter
Veering very near Venus
Because Mars wasn't massed enough
And so the end was Earth

And from Earth we burn with hellish fire
From Earth we lift our sights towards the heavens
The milky way is but a harbinger
The atmosphere
We long to land on the distant stars
Cause we dimming our own stars on the star we lie on.

Issac Kalibwa:

to seek a star

I'll find her dead and floating in the night of space
maybe fizzling in hail as un-heavy as flakes, maybe

hissing in the pain of rain, maybe whinny-ing in acceptance.
maybe stone quiet and frigid, used to her lonesomeness.
but I'll come upon her and warm her with my feet, I'll stump heaving
into her breast with my hooves

I'll mount her in the hiding of the sun and rub a fire off her skin.
and she will glow in mine own life, cup the rain,
melt the ice in patient ages,
be the foundation for a city of iron.

we'll seek and make light
in the desert of night.

*Mwanaka Media and Publishing: And what if we go to a new planet that is
occupied by intelligent life already... How are we going to negotiate for our agency?
And will we visit earth to connect with those we would have left behind?*

Emmanuel Mtema:

Just when we got there
The black core in our eyes got wider
Like we have been bewitched
Or was this earth part two
But then their faces are not human like
Yet more civilized than ever we have been
Those alien invaders we read About

Were they self-fulfilling prophecies?
We became what we feared would happen to us

Gwiriri:

Of what raison d'etre is man still on Earth,
Other than deforestation, pollution, global warming and species
extermination?
They demolished
Ozone layer and wrecked Wetlands.
Our sentry shamefully slips into Earth.

I wasn't minding their business at all,
Until they slaughtered Mars,
Intending to massacre and
sabotage it like Earth.
Can we just fold our hands and watch, Giant?
It's high time we trounce,
Seize and robotise everyone on Earth,
Efficiently and un-corruptly utilise resources,
Once again, restore virgin Earth.

Bolaji Tola:

Let me stay with what I know,
For in my clan they often say,
The devil you know,
Dance better than angels unknown.
Let me scavenge the remnants of Earth
Even if it's Hades...
Than long for an heaven,
I have no clue,
Of what kind of hell,

310

It carries....

Not a fan of Mars...

Mwanaka Media and Publishing: Okay.... And yet you are a fan of a heaven you don't know? Literally
Joseph Sukali: what a question!
Mwanaka Media and Publishing: Mars might just be a stop gap measure for humans... As long as the humans have inquisitive minds, whether staying on earth or mars, or moon they will continue seeking a way to get out of earth... Even if it is paradise regained. I think even the bible acknowledged some humans, over 2000years ago trying to build Babel Tower to heaven or God or skies
Mwanaka Media and Publishing: Kkkk not question. Its provocation kkkk that's where i work
Okay Ifeachor: Did the humans succeed?
Mwanaka Media and Publishing: Kkkk do you expect an answer or its rhetorical? Humans have been to the Moon, deep space... Robots have been to outer space

Okey Ifeachor:

The earth is for my habitation
Outer space is not my abode
Though the fauna and flora are endangered
I love my earth yet
Trips beyond my sphere in search of the invisible...
Exhibition of human futility
Regenerate the earth for harmonious life
This sphere is for man
The Great Architect made it so
Stop the adventure of no glory
You are not God
The earth is for our habitation.

EL BASSE MANSALY:

La_solitude

The fear of the soul settles here
Like a feeling of loneliness
Almost eliminating my desires
Here i don't feel good
Over there i feel good
Here i think a lot
Over there i don't think about anything

Want to return
Want to go
Want to see my friends from the village
Here i don't see anybody
There I live with everyone
Here I am not smiling
There I laugh every day
Here i am locked
There i'm free
Like a butterfly that greets all women

That live in my heart
Here I do not see the sun
Over there I see everything
Here I don't breathe well
Over there I breathe clean air

Here I sleep alone in my bed
There I sleep with my brothers

Here I don't drink water
There I bathe in the water
Here I do not know the entertainment
There I am in the four corners of the village

Aleck Kaposa:

Everything is just so different

When the Martians speak
You think they gibber and squeak

And when they cast a look on you
It's piercing and fiery,
Makes your heart skip a bit

What goes for bread
Is just dry rocks
Served in ice
Nothing else

And the terrain
Just vast hamadas
Full of flying things

Oh how i miss my earth 😭 😭

Just how everything is so different here

(Abandoned, unfinished)

The Sun's rays are red

Emmanuel Tumwesige:

Oh how it will be flying through the bright stars.
Glad tidings mingling with new friends.
Will they be friends?
Who knows? We shall meet on the __beautiful_ land.

El Basse:

In my prison if there were autumn leaves, spring flowers and summer
flowers.
I'll tell the judge to sentence me to death in this nature
Even though the moon only visits me once a month and the sun
consoles me every night.
I prefer the prison where the flowers smile at me than that of the
animals who want to see me die.

Lisa Jaison:

Go
This is how you treat those that have loved you,
Birthed and fed generations for you
Lost my youth and luster for you
Let you mine my bosom and core to feed off,
All for you to turnaround and declare it's not enough,
You need more, you need adventure,
Risking it all for treacherous hopes of finding her that shines so
bright from the reflection of the stars,
She who shimmers so voluptuously closer to God and the sun,

The mystery vixen with virgin thighs unscared by raising your off spring,
She holds exotic names like Mars and Jupiter,
I relent, very well, go then,
But when the cards crumble , and she burns your soul, denies you gravity and sends her alien lovers to attack you.
Understand if l ask the universe to fold my arms, shut my doors and keep you out
Traitors never deserved mother earth anyway

INTERVIEWS

Best New African Poets Interview with South African Poet, Archie Swanson
Moderated by Tendai Rinos Mwanaka

Archie Swanson's poetry was first published in 1973 in English Alive, an anthology of South African High School creative writing. Poems have regularly been published in the South African poetry magazines – Stanzas and New Contrast. They also appear in the Best New African Poetry Anthologies (2015 through 2020), Experimental Writing: Africa vs Latin America (2017), Experimental Writing: Africa vs Asia in 2018 (two poems in Japanese), Vol. 1 & 2 of Africa vs North America (2018; 2019) and Writing Robotics: Africa vs Asia Vol 2 (2020). Poems were translated by the Spanish poet López-Vega and published in the Spanish National Newspaper, El Mundo (2016) as well as the Bolivian newspaper Correo Del Sur (2016). In 2017 two poems were long listed for the Sol Plaatje Award and the poem flashback was shortlisted for the UK Bridport Prize. His poetry has also been anthologized in Absolute Africa! (2018) and Naturally Africa! (2020) curated by Patricia Schonstein. The poem 'my geurnica' was chosen as runner-up in the English category of the AVBOB Poetry Competition in 2019 and seven poems have been shortlisted for the 2020 prize. Poems have appeared in the Poetry in McGregor Anthologies (2014 through 2020). In August 2020, the poem 'afourer' was selected for the Clemengold Poetry Writing. The poem 'déjà vu' was the inspiration for a Grant McLachlan composition for clarinet, violin and piano performed in the Baxter Concert Hall in May 2019. In July 2020, two poems were translated into Spanish and published in the South American literary journal Libero America. He has published two collections of poems — the stretching of my sky under the editorship of Tendai Mwanaka (2018) and the shores of years with Emeritus Prof Geoff Haresnape as editor (2019) and his third collection, beyond a distant edge, will be published in 2021. He has been a regular guest poet at Off the Wall Poetry, the Cape Town Central Library Poetry Circle, the McGregor Poetry Festival, and the Prince Albert Lees Fees (2018 and 2019). Archie Swanson serves on the Board of the SA Literary Journal. He is an avid surfer who lives in George. www.instagram.com/poetarchie

Mhondera Chenjerai: Quite great and appreciated. Really a prolific writer

Ocean Scott Makwarimbo: Accomplished. I'm inspired. You've left your footprint in ink.

Archie Swanson: I guess when one writes it's just something within you which you do over years. Some poems find their way and have resonance with the reader or hearer. Some don't! I like your comparison between ink and footprints. I guess both fade away in the end!

Archie Swanson: Thanks for the kind words, Chenjerai!

Mwanaka Media and Publishing: Okay i read the bio, but i want to know who Archie is on a personal level. What kind of person he is

Prince Kamaazengi: My questions to Archie. 1. What is your role as a writer? 2. And how do you envision the future of work as far as writing is concerned? 3. Many writers are oftentimes misunderstood especially by the immediate family and people who live close to them. If this rings true, why do you think it is so?

Charles Duncan: My question to Archie. What advice can you give to upcoming writers who dream of being able to earn money from their work? What can they do to get from here to that level?

Archie Swanson: Hi Tendai. I think that on a personal level I am incurably inquisitive. I put great value on friendship and of course my family. I have four fantastic daughters and five grandchildren who are all a great joy to me. I live in a very beautiful part of South Africa called the Garden Route. It's a place of mountains, lakes, long beaches and good surf. I grew up in South Africa during the Apartheid era. My parents were liberal and I went to a liberal non-government school. I became politically conscious at a fairly young age writing my first anti-apartheid poem when I was 16.

Archie Swanson: My role as a writer? To be honest I don't see myself first and foremost as someone on a mission. I always write first to explain things to myself..... to clear my thoughts and reduce my understanding to words. Sometimes just to capture a moment. I do write, though, with the idea that someone may want to read my poem later. I try not to make my poems difficult to understand. I do not write to demonstrate my prowess as a writer. In other words I don't write just for the sake of writing. How do I envisage the future of my work? For me everyday is a new adventure. I'm not sure what I am going to write about next. The poems I write take on many forms and styles and cover a wide range of subjects. I am fairly experimental so not every poem I write works. I will publish my third collection this year. Poets being misunderstood: I think that poets do have a special eye that sees often in a different way. There is some sort of an image of poets - that you have to be a certain kind of person to be a poet, but that's no true - you just have to have that original spark and talent and then work very hard at understanding your own voice and perfecting your craft. I have to say that until maybe 10 years ago I didn't even call myself a poet. I was just someone who wrote down poems (most of which were not published). It was only when I started to submit more poems for publishing that I started to be referred to as a poet and then sort of admitted to myself that I qualified to be called a poet. As far as misunderstanding of poems is concerned, I believe that once you write a poem and put it out there, it develops a life of its own and the truth is that readers are free to apply their own interpretation and get moved whatever way they are moved

Archie Swanson: To upcoming poets: I once attended a poetry reading by James Matthews, a famous anti-apartheid poet who grew up in District 6, Cape Town and who is in his 90's now. After his reading he was asked more-or-less the same question by a young poet and gave a very direct answer. The reality is that there are very few poets who make a complete living out of poetry. My advice would be for you to focus on your craft. There is the saying that you need to spend at least 10,000 hours before you become good at something. It is easy to write a poem but it is VERY difficult to write a poem of consequence that will be read long after you have passed on. That requires the mixture of inspiration, talent and understanding your craft. Read poetry. Write and write. Go to open-mics. Discuss your poetry with other poets. Submit to competitions. Get published in anthologies. Save up and buy the poetry of other poets to support them. Remember that the cream always floats to the top and if your poems have merit, they will eventually be recognized.

Mbuthia Richard: Very beautiful response. Thank you

Beaton Galafa: You say you just clear your thoughts, that you don't see yourself as someone on a mission. I would assume, therefore, that if you were to be categorized as a writer in the strict binary sense of those that do art for art's sake and those that take art as a form of activism, you would belong to the earlier. That makes me curious to know what then ignites the thoughts you aim to clear in your mind. Again, from that 1972 poem you take us back to the miserable conditions of life for blacks under the terror of the Mapolisa in apartheid South Africa, how have your thoughts as brought to life through your poetry evolved in post-apartheid South Africa?

Prince Kamaazengi: "if you want to make money, you must work"? I've heard this many times. Poetry and writing, according to our available reality as "slaves"/workers is not seen as work but in actual actuality, poetry is work and poets are earning a living out of it. Can you respond to this? And how can we as creatives using pen, words and paper makes the industry "work" for us... maximize on profit...

Archie Swanson: Hi Beaton. I do believe that poetry has the power to move people and as a poet I cannot stay separate from society so I do not stand back from writing what are activist poems but I don't want to be limited just to one voice. That's not me. I wrote a poem about a visit to Malawi, maybe 5 years ago. What a beautiful place, but there was also terrible poverty. To your second point, Beaton: My thoughts on post-apartheid society? In South Africa we have majority rule but the nature of human beings has not changed. We still have prejudice, and we have the powerful dominating the poor. There is much still to write about.

Mwanaka Media and Publishing: Still on that issue of post-apartheid South Africa, what is your take on the hot topic of race? And land reform.

Archie Swanson: To Prince Kamaazengi Marenga: There is an unbelievable explosion of poetry around the world, especially among under 30-year-olds. You just have to go to the many Instagram poetry pages to see this or attend many of the open-mic's with a very young demographic. The problem is that publishers are not making any money out of publishing poetry. In South Africa, for instance, I don't believe that there is a single publisher making a profit from published collections. Book stores are not making money either. The harsh reality is also that poets often can't afford to buy poetry collections. I think we are entering an era where new ways have to be found. I like the idea of mixed artistic events with music, poetry and painting incorporated together where entrance fees can be charged. Also if your Instagram page or YouTube site gets enough hits there are ways of monetising things. James Matthews is not saying that poetry is not work, he is just saying that from his perspective it's a lot easier to have a 9 to 5 job if you lucky enough to find one, than to try and live off poetry.

Archie Swanson: Hi Tendai: Yes, there are deep-rooted issues of race. The land reform is still very much with us and is complicated as farming has become a capital intensive industry. It's no use just giving someone land without giving them the necessary capital resources to optimally farm it and right now most governments just don't have that kind of cash. In South Africa we have the added problem of funds committed to transferring farming capital to the poorest of the poor is syphoned off by the politically connected. In the Estena Dairy Project, R244M was stolen by the Gupta Brothers and their associates, some of which went to pay for a lavish Gupta wedding in Sun City. Last week a number of associates were arrested, and Interpol was requested to assist with the repatriation of the Gupta Brothers and their wives from the UAE to stand trial in SA

Beaton Galafa: Impressive. I also like your tailored response, with an example of poverty antagonising the beautiful tourist experiences in the context of Malawi.

Prince Kamaazengi: warm handshake...

Archie Swanson: Thanks to all for the interaction so far. I'm heading out now and will be back at 7pm CAT if any of you want to continue the chat further. Please send questions and comments if you like, in the meantime. Ciao Archie

Amani Nsemwa: Thanks a lot Archie. See you then. I really liked your responses

Mwanaka Media and Publishing: As board member of SA literary journal, you are well knowledged about South African writing. Give us an overview of SA literary landscape. Who are the most interesting artists to read? What are the challenges artists in SA are facing?

Archie Swanson: Some of the best known poets are Wally Serote, Keorapetse Kgositsile, Breyten Breytenbach, André Brink, Dennis Brutus, Chris Mann, Finuala Dowling, Ingrid Jonker, Antjie Krog, Sipho Sepamla, Douglas Reid Skinner, Jonty Driver, Adam Small and Athol Williams. There is great quality in the writing with many very talented poets not really receiving the recognition they deserve. I think the biggest challenge is to get a hard copy collection published. There's no shortage of material to write about! The SA Literary Journal publishes New Contrast *www.newcontrast.net* which is an

321

excellent quarterly literary journal. Another excellent poetry magazine is Stanzas https://stanzaspoetry.org/

Prince Kamaazengi: I enjoyed André Brink's The Praying Mantis....and there is Lesego Rampolokeng, ..who is likened to Dambudzo Marechera. This is just by way of comment.

Mwanaka Media and Publishing: Yes New Contrast is a really great magazine. I was published in the March 2007 issue when Hugh Hodge was editor. Are the arts magazines influential in SA, what do you think they help inculcate. Readership reach. How are they staying afloat?

Archie Swanson: How do we get by at New Contrast? We have the hard copy mag and electronic as well. The subs don't cover the costs so well, but we do at least one university edition a year and the contribution from the universities gets us through. We also launched the National Poetry Prize which is a modest source of income which will hopefully grow in future years. We are very excited to have Masande Ntshanga as our new editor who took over when Michele Betty stood down after an excellent stint as editor. There aren't that many arts magazines and so New Contrast which celebrated 60 years of publication this year's, fills and important gap. As you know the magazine is an amalgamation of works of art, prose, poetry, and book reviews. Tendai, I didn't realise you had been published in new Contrast. Hugh Hodge is of course also a very influential Cape Town poet who has written many wonderful pieces. He is slightly less active now.

Obinna Chilekezi: You take writings from east and west Africa

Archie Swanson: An electronic subscription to new Contrast costs R160 for four editions per year. http://www.newcontrast.net/subscribe/

Aleck Kaposa: Great, am reminded of a poignant magazine _The Staffrider_ from SA, sad it fell by the wayside

Archie Swanson: Hi Obinna. I don't believe there is a country restriction on submissions. I think submissions are handled via

Submittable. www.submittable.com. Aleck, Many publications have fallen.

Mwanaka Media and Publishing: Yes i did... When i was barely beginning on the publishing journey, and it gave me a lot of courage to push my work a lot harder. Hugh was an encouraging influence to me...

Archie Swanson: Right at the start of this chat Ocean Scott said, "You've left your footprint in ink ." which got me thinking of a tracker like our bushmen trackers in Southern Africa that can follow a spoor and tell you everything about the animal of person they are following just by looking at the track. I started fiddling around with a poem this morning. It might not be finished as I usually give a poem a couple of weeks before I wrap it up.

Mwanaka Media and Publishing: Moving to spoken word/readings. I know you are involved in Off the wall, and you have been broadening into southern Africa, i think you have featured is it 3 Zimbabwe poets... Is this the new direction? What importance can be derived from poets reading their poems in spoken word events like off the wall

Archie Swanson: At Off the Wall it is very important to spread the net wide. It's important to get outside influence otherwise we all just start sounding like one-another! During lockdown we have a Zoom meeting with guest poet every Monday at 7.30pm and the second half is open mic with all welcome to read in two rounds of one poem each. The Zoom link for each Monday is on the website

Mwanaka Media and Publishing: Your other interest is surfing, why did you take up surfing? Kkkk it looks dangerous. Aren't you scared of injuring yourself... I am saying that because i shy away from any sport that look too dangerous.

Archie Swanson: From the moment I got on a surfboard when I was 14 I was hooked ... it's hard to explain. I guess the attraction of the waves overrides the fear. Back in the day it was a sort of rebel/hippie sport. We got no support from our parents and just borrowed boards to get going. My 8-year-old grandson, Josh, is starting now. I spoke to him earlier. He was surfing down at Muizenberg in Cape Town today.

Mwanaka Media and Publishing: Thanks Archie... We will focus on your poetry from *Best New African Poets* tomorrow. By the way Archie has appeared in every Bnap anthology since we began in 2015

Poem 1:
bag lady
archie swanson

cold september cape town day
icy southwester rushing down kloof street
she's maybe 50
protruding head-scarfed hair dishevelled
out of place at trendy knead bakery
unwilling to join the pizza oven warmed crowd inside
she seats herself at a table in the walkway
and sliding her bulky bag beneath, orders tea
i step inside and order her the soup special
hoping to remain anonymous but the waiter points me out
our eyes meet
i suggest she sits inside
the waiter shows her to a table
i leave
a month later i'm back again at knead
and there she is
inside this time

extracted from Best New African Poets 2017 Anthology

Mwanaka Media and Publishing: Why are almost all of your poems always in short caps?

Archie Swanson: Hi Tendai. I try to make the page look as uncomplicated as possible. I have shifted a bit from no caps though, spelling proper nouns in caps because I have written quite a few historical poems in the last year and it gets a bit confusing when using names like Egyptian names. I am also writing "i" as "I" now

Amani N: Archie Swanson, What were your thoughts behind naming this poem as "Yesterday's Poem"

Archie Swanson: That's an excellent question..... the honest answer is that I don't really know, for sure. The whole poem is a sort of consciousness stream of the contradictions of the human condition. The title came to me and it stuck. I guess in a way that the thoughts in the poem may stay true for every yesterday. In other words when you wake up tomorrow the truths of yesterday remain relevant for today.

Archie Swanson: "... the place where all appears to fall in line
yet falls apart again on time..."

Tanaka Chidora: Like me, you seem to favour the lower case for your poems even where, according to punctuation conventions, you are supposed to capitalize. Any special reason for that?

Amani N: Brilliant

Archie Swanson: I think the idea is to keep the page as uncluttered as possible, but of course with the hope that one does not confuse the reader

Mwanaka Media and Publishing: Are you the narrator/protagonist in your poems. You use I... Is this I as in yourself...

Archie Swanson: In most cases the "I" in my poems is me but there are times that this is not the case. There's a poem on my instagram page @poetarchie called Amenhotep where the pharoah is speaking. The poem ends with the words ... " ..I am Amenhotep III — 9th Pharaoh of the 18th Dynasty" By the way Amenhotep was a Nubian, ruler of Egypt from the upper Nile .... present day Sudan. Another example of using the "I" as a narrator is my poem 'I Wahtye' about

325

an Egyptian priest who lived about 4,500 years ago and whose tomb was recently found.

Poem 2:
I WAHTYE
Archie Swanson

"Wahtye — purified priest to the king — overseer of the royal estate —

inspector of the sacred boat — revered with god the great — Wahtye"

above the rows of lush palm groves
in the desert hills of Saqqara
I made my tomb

I spared no cost on the statues that line the room —
the walls adorned with praises to my name

the work went on for many years
my passport to the life beyond
the portal to my fame

I had imagined
that my wife and children would attend a great event
with music and with song
but I was wrong
for all before me went

so find me here — alone
in the chamber at the bottom of the deepest shaft
placed in this withered box
no linen bandages for me

no charms or amulets upon my arms
no one to wish me on my way

I lavishly adorned these walls
spent income earned as Pharaoh's priest
but should you ask was all this ostentation worth a jot
my long-still mandible and muted tongue would stir to say
that it was not

Archie Swanson: All of the poems in my two collections of poems can be accessed on my indtagram page @poetarchie. There are IGTV clips on two trilogies of poems - the first trilogy on antiquity (on Egypt) and the second on the bombing of civilians. You can acess a free audio book of my second collection "the shores of years" "on Soundcloud by using the follwing URL or altenatively scanning the QR code in the pic. You can access an audio book of my second collection ("the shores of years"), on Soundcloud, by typing in the URL in the pic or scanning the QR code

Aleck Kaposa: Good one @Archie, i think it's a cool poem

Wafula K'phisa: What inspired you to write this poem, Archie?

Archie Swanson: I was at a place in Kloof Street Cape Town called Knead sitting outside when I noticed the woman. There are tables outside in the walkway outside the bakery/coffee shop/burger place. It was winter time and cold outside and she just had enough for tea. I don't really like inserting myself into poems too much but I had to tell the story. The message of the poem is about acceptance and alienation. The woman had no money and so she felt as though she didn't belong, so even though she'd paid for her tea and had every right to be inside where it was warm (there's a pizza oven), she did not feel comfortable to go inside. I guess once she had been invited in, the next time she felt she could be inside. I feel a little uncomfortable about the poem as the idea was not to present me as the 'good guy' benefactor but rather the barrier to entry that poverty causes.

Kudzai Munzira: This is so touching

Archie Swanson: Thanks Kudzie

Wafula K'phisa: Great Archie. So to what extent can we classify your writings as "the writing of self" rather than "the writing of others"?

Archie Swanson: As a writer, I write from where I stand. It is my perspective whether I am right or wrong. It is up to the reader to eat the fish and spit out the bones as it were. One may write in different voices though – in the first person or in the third person. Sometimes I have tried to give voice to those who have no voice. In my poem 'tell me i lived' about the Sharpeville Massacre I speak with the voice of one of the slain, speaking from their coffin at the funeral. When you talk about 'the writing of self' that could also mean the introverted focus on matters and emotions of the soul and spirit ... feelings within towards oneself and towards those around us. The overwhelming majority of poetry on Instagram, for instance tends to fall into this category. I personally prefer to set my eyes on the things around me in this world - those things that move me. It is perhaps a more extroverted view with my interpretation attached. The great thing about poems is that sometimes they grow wings and fly. Other people reading a poem may relate to it in a different way. They may put a different interpretation on things ... and that's fine.

Poem 3:

non

Archie Swanson

i've never been called a non anything
never a nonafrican
a nonindian
or a noncoloured

but tonight in bandar lampung
this sprawling teaming
cheek by jowl
scooter hooting
clogged south sumatran port city
i may well be the only nonindonesian in town

its karaoke night at the amalia hotel
and as these happy people take the stage one after the other
to sing their swelling bahasa ballads
i am lifted
and drawn by their warm welcome
and I really don't feel like a non anything at all

forgive me
forgive me child of majapahit
for from here so many of you were taken
with your hearts of love
with music and crafts at your finger tips
with songs on your lips
and dancing feet
and we shackled you and called you non
non
non
non
we called you
non

Extracted from Best New African Poets 2015 Anthology

Archie Swanson: My poem 'non – ' is probably the poem I have written that has travelled furthest. I wrote it sitting in the lounge of the Amalia Hotel in South Sumatra, Indonesia after staying at a surf camp in Sumatra. I had an early flight out of Bandar Lampung so I booked in at the hotel to get an early start in the morning. It's a large city of 1.2 M people. The only people I saw coming into the city and at the hotel were Indonesians. It was karaoke night and they were singing ballads in their Bahasa language. They even asked me to join in which I declined as singing is not my strongpoint. As I sat I started writing a poem …. a poem that I thought was going to be a happy poem, but suddenly a sorrow came over me as I realised that this area (Java and Sumatra) was the place where so many of the Malay people were brought to Cape Town by the Dutch East India Company to work as labourers and to later under Apartheid laws, be classified as 'non-white'. The poem was first published in BNAP and then Spanish poet, Lopez-Vega, translated it and it was published in the Spanish National Newspaper El Mundo and the Bolivian newspaper, Correo Del Sur. I never imagined that the poem which really was just quite a personal observation could achieve such a wide reach and that it was relatable to people so far afield

Aleck Kaposa: You draw so much from real life hey

Archie Swanson: Yes, my way of doing things is to mostly observe the life around me and to convey the experience accurately... obviously putting my interpretation onto things. Having said this, I have done quite a few historical pieces where I was obviously not present

Aleck Kaposa: Infusing creativity with reality and even stretching imagination to reimagine this from history

Archie Swanson: Yes because poetry always should add new insights and possibilities

Wafula K'phisa: Thank you for shedding more light on this.

Archie Swanson: I'ts always good to shed one's thoughts!

Mbuthia R: Archie, do you ever get 'writer's block' and how do you deal with it?

Ocean Scott: and is writer's block a bad thing? …also is it possible to tell from reading a writer's work that this is the result and work of a writer merely forcing their pen through a writer's block?

Archie Swanson: WRITER'S BLOCK: I have to say that for me there is no such thing as writer's block as I never put any pressure on myself to write another poem. I simply go about my life and when the inspiration for a poem arrives, I write. I may go for weeks without writing a poem and then start 3 in a day. I always allow probably at least a month before finalising a poem so I always have various poems in various stages of completion to work on. Very often when you come back two weeks later and read a poem in progress you see it with different eyes and can make improvements. FORCED WRITING: When I read a poem I either like it or I don't. I might like a poem that actually was forced and not like a poem that wasn't. For me poems are about the subject matter and then how they are written. What I do know that forcing a poem does not work for me. That does not mean you cannot get a good result from writing in a workshop or deliberately sitting down to write on a subject. My poems that touch on history often take weeks of research with very often only a fraction of the info used in the poem. In those cases I assimilate the information and when I feel in the mood then I commit pen to paper. For me I have to be in a sort of altered state of mind. I can recognize it in myself. I never write when I am hassled or have a whole lot of deadlines to meet.

Charles Duncan: Thank you for your time Sir

Amani N: Thanks Archie

Best New African Poets Group Interview of Tanzanian poet Amani Nsemwa

Moderated by Tendai Rinos Mwanaka

Amani Nsemwa is a farmer, a lazy one. Nevertheless, he likes making love as much as he does like coffee, the lords haven't yet blessed him with a kid nor a wife. It all started ten years back with letters to beautiful chicks at numerous schools, then to poetry, when there was no one to write to. He's tricked by good romance, and to a great deal when there's PlayStation. When he isn't reading or holding a smartphone, he's probably listening to the Ladysmith Black Mambazo, watching Coming to America, Playing Scrabble or dreaming of Keri Hilson. You can connect with him on Instagram @papaamojamoja.

Mwanaka Media and Publishing: Kkkk yes let's engage Mr Loverman

Oscar Gwiriri: What effect does music have on your writing?

Amani Nsemwa: Music has a great impact on my writings especially for the messages conveyed by different songs. Also the history of several musicians such as South African Male Choral family group the Ladysmith Black Mambazo or Congolese Fally Ipupa aspire my writings a lot. Therefore I cannot deny that my writing is to some extent influenced by music. Also songs such as Neria by Oliver Mtukudzi were usually played during our childhood in our families. Therefore the messages and stories they carried always live in use and they can be spotted on my writings

Mwanaka Media and Publishing: You are a playboy?

Amani N: No I am not. I tend to stick with one woman. Even though my previous relationships hasn't worked into marriage

Mwanaka Media and Publishing: And you love to make love?

Amani N: Ah of course. I love this chore!

Ocean Scott Makwarimbo: Nationality? Your poetry; what issues, societal or otherwise, does it normally address? Are you from the Mwanaka school of thought: that without rhyme a work cannot be said to be poetry...i.e, message over rhyme or the Makwarimbo school of thought: that rhyme is putting a poet's mind in a box and asking them to think in a box not outside it for message which can be obtained by stylistic approach, motif, technique outside the rhyme box...i.e, message over technique. What do you hope to achieve through poetry? Is the poet to be taken to be their work or should a poet be divorced from their work...in other words is a poet what is spoken for by their poetry? What should be a writer's ultimate aspiration: to simply be published or to also be collected?

Mwanaka Media and Publishing: Hahaha really? Mwanaka school, that i am not aware of? Mwanaka school is not about rhyme over message... It's about poetic language over message... Just to correct Ocean Scott's misunderstanding of my poetic standpoint.

Amani N: I'm Tanzanian. My poetry normally addresses societal & political issues. I am into both school of thoughts. But mostly I rely on Makwarimbo's school of thought. And this has been highly due to the poems I used to read at school. Most of them were in form of free verse. for example Summons collection by Richard Mabala and Song of Lawino by Okot P'Bitek. So in 10 poems only 1 can follow the rhymes rule. I hope to be able to publish more works and expand my network. I want to reach an extent whereby my works will be influential in building our society. No, a poet should be divorced from their work. I think the writer's aspiration should be more than getting published. He or she should strive to make an impact and influence changes in a society. While building other young talents in the society

Mwanaka Media and Publishing: Kkkk and you have decided to join Ocean scott... Putting words into my mouth

Amani N: Hahaha. I couldn't understand the concept at first. But now I got it and I have clarified, I'll focus on this on my coming works. And strive to come out with the best poetic language

Mwanaka Media and Publishing: If it is to be poetry it has to have poetic language... If it's only a message... it is not poetry. Poetic language can be employed in both free verse and fixed verse... Scott thinks it only works with fixed verse that's why he zeroed on rhyme scale. Its poetic language like for examples, similes, metaphors, images etc... that makes poetry, poetry... Poetry is beautified thought... Not just messages

Amani N: Yess yess.. I get it

Ocean Scott: poetic language is subjective...and the devices have been expanded to accommodate the creative...hence the thinking outside the box i argue for, they are not the traditional student's companion kind of ish... I can't be using the very same similes my grand ma and her great grandma were using...slow as a snail...fast as a hare that's all our new school argues...let us be us and expressive in that is our clarion call... metaphors, similes will always we remain...what we are argue is that their content not their form/purpose ought to change...and poetic language especially in our day and age is subjective...what I've put across as a metaphor you'll probably believe it does not rise to the level of affording that status

Mwanaka Media and Publishing: Baseless ranting

Emmanuel Tumwesige: In my view anything poetic should have the basics of poetry. We wish to be understood in the best way possible when communicating, it is therefore important to sustain the attention of the audience in a beautiful way whether free or fixed verse. At a funeral we condole while encouraging not condoling while amounting sorrow. Language can be twisted to beautify the delivery of the serious message.

Ocean Scott: We're talking

Amani N: Well said

Mwanaka Media and Publishing: Scott, I thought what Emmanuel said is exactly what i have been saying. You understand when you talk about *we young people*... You are speaking for a generation... The same generation i am writing, reading and publishing in? If i am finding poetic language in the same generation you seem to be speaking for, and you want to peddle your messages as poetry, when they are just bare messages, then it's just meaningless and baseless pontification.

Joseph Sukali: In your bio, you said "The lords haven't yet blessed him with a kid nor wife". I am interested to know your religious perspective and how that has impacted your art... Highlight if your art is a product of your academic background and let us know more about what has built you up to this far... Which schools of thought do you subscribe to in general?

Amani N: My religious perspective is that there is God, our creator and that we should strive to build each other and live in a peaceful society regardless of our differences in beliefs. Art is not only a product of the academic. For me the more I got exposed into art and fellows artists I tend to get this urge to create more and more, and to understand my fellow artists works better and better. Up to this point works from other fellow artists are what has built me to a better position. Surely I tend to come up with my thoughts and creativity, but I am always inspired by the works of other artists. My school of thought is generally that poetry should be creative, and appealing. Therefore we should always strive to strengthen our poetic language. That is what makes poetry, poetry.

Emmanuel Mtema: I like the last paragraph, In this world where not more people are interested to read, a poet's success has shifted from impacting the community to just getting published in a celebrated anthology that only other poets will read not for the impact even but just learn the styles and poetic devices used... How do you ensure that your poetry is bringing an impact??

Amani N: Thanks. As for now, Positive feedback from the people who are not poets or writers is what makes me think my poetry has a certain impact to the readers. Again getting featured in Anthologies like this, that is read widely has always given me an assurance that there will be a time whereby the BNAP will be longed for by readers across nations. Then, I will be happy that my pen has made a long-lasting impact

Mwanaka Media and Publishing: What of negative comments from poets that are readers?

Amani N: Negative comments from poets readers always weigh me down. It normally takes a long time for me to understand their point of view. I like to be criticized yes, but in a positive way.

Mwanaka Media and Publishing: Can you clarify between negative and positive criticism?

Amani N: A poet who is learning or emerging can come up with a certain piece that does not have a poetic language, but it has a great idea. A negative critic will just crash the work, that it is not a poem or that a poem cannot be just like that, without taking into consideration the idea behind it or the amount of energy and effort that was put before it. On the other hand positive critic will be open that the piece lacks poetic language/flow, and elaborate what could be done to make it presentable, even giving some suggestions. In this way the writer will always come up with something better in the next time.

Mwanaka Media and Publishing: Mmm i wish i could share with you the negative/positive criticism i received for my first book... And it is exactly that which made me a better writer than any praise i got. It was brutal... And the publisher, Van Schaik Pub, South Africa... Gave me a chance to reply... And petulantly i went for the critic. The publisher knew enough to know i was just being reactionary to criticism. That report, after i had sorted myself, helped me to rewrite, pushed me to become the writer i am. So unless the critic is abusive like calling you names, there is no negative or positive criticism.

Amani N: Anhaa.. Now I understand Tendai. Thanks for the tips. I have got to make myself ready for them criticisms

Emmanuel Tumwesige: Exactly, critics always push us high above. As long as my head is not put off there's positivity in the negative

Amani N: Well noted. I will be on it..

Emmanuel Tumwesige: Sawa, but don't think I'm among the best writers. I'm almost a step off the beginning.

Mwanaka Media and Publishing: I don't know many writers from Tanzania... Can you please give us an overview of Tanzanian writing and literary landscape?

Amani N: There is a quite number of writers in Tanzania, writing across different genres, from Poetry, Novels, Academics, Research and Political Reforms; but few have not managed to make fortune from it and to reach international levels. Notably is Eric Shigongo, who emerged as a story-writer then later came up with his publishing company and newspapers. He later went on to become a member of parliament. There are also so many emerging young and talented writers who have not yet reached the international levels but are well known in the Tanzanian context of writing. On the other context, political reforms writers have recently been facing unwelcoming environment, whereby many have gone missing or being attacked with unknown groups of people. So generally, I would say Tanzanian writing is still emerging and it would take huge amount of efforts and devotion from this generation and the coming ones.

Emmanuel Tumwesige: I think Tanzania is Uganda's twin.

Mhondera Chenjerai: you being a lazy type of a farmer, and a passionate/enthusiastic love maker, how do you earn a living? Do you make it from love making or from farming? How does farming and or your love making escapades support or help boost your writing? My regular brief appearances in Tanzania, presented me with difficulties, especially when I was faced with Kiswahili speaking lovemaking prospects at the hotels. Literally, I suffered communication breakdown. And my question is, how do you manage communication with international love makers, especially those that do not speak your native language or English

Amani N: I earn living through the little farming products I get. I call myself lazy because I have not utilized farming into its full capacities. But there's plenty of farm products from avocados, beans and eggs which always suffice for food and a little amount of gin to make me sleep well after tiresome works. I make love whenever it happens to be possible, but It's not what gives me income to sustain life. Farming has always been satisfying to my soul since the very first days of my life. My father used to grow mushrooms and he kept cows, doves, pigs and ducks. So even if I am not making fortunes from farming, the feeling of cultivating and keeping livestock always gives me peace. I'd say I write in calmness when the farming produce is at their finest. And this is what I wish, that my fellow writers will engage into farming however small it is; then inspire the rest of our societies. I have not yet came across anybody who does not speak Swahili or English. If I come across one, I suppose I'd ask for assistance from my fellow writers who speak their language, as I have always felt home when I come across my fellow writer

Mhondera C: It really feels great, learning much from this clarity

Amani N: I appreciate

Mhondera C: Hahaha. Lol. It was really quite a light moment off from the busy and serious mic, Ansemwa. I love the free spirit you are as you apply yourself to demands of interview

Great one. Don't you want space in Zimbabwe, lest I be your neighbour and your regular visitor every morning, who changes the adage 'an apple a day keeps the doctor away' to 'an egg a day, makes Cecil the Great your regular visitor!' lol

Amani N: Haha. I appreciate. BNAP is always a great platform. Hahaha, surely. I'd love that. I promise one day I'll be there. I have read a lot about Zimbabwe from post-independence days up to the latter days of Mugabe, the Shona & Ndebele lifestyles back then when I was at school, all left me in awe. So, as long as I live, I'd like to visit Zimbabwe

Mhondera C: Consider me, your host

Amani N: I really appreciate.

Poem 1:

INNOCENT SOULS

Amani Nsemwa

The wilderness of *Ubena Zomozi* bestows me with peace.
I am tired of the city
pretending to be pregnant so that she could ask for money.
Yet we're a middle-income country.
I am pleased of a decent rural life
Melodies of *The Ladysmith Black Mambazo* bestowing me with peace.
I am tired of not being able to sing like them.
And so I love them.
I crave and I am grateful
That columnists either disappear
with no cause
or turn out to be praising everything that is done and yet to be done.
With their toothy smiles.
Whilst the activists are gifted with bullets.
I urge you women of Africa,
Feed us well.
Feed us well that we might not forget to hurt the innocent souls.

Extracted from Best New African Poets 2020 Anthology

Beaton Galafa: Amani, Reading *Innocent Souls*, I notice melancholy underlying the experience in the poem from two possible themes, urban-induced resignation (through an economically

339

demanding society in a middle-income country - signifying economic pressure among others) and tyranny in a contemporary African society (seen through images of the activists gifted with bullets), what triggered these powerful images?

Amani N: You are right. I was triggered by the conditions of majorities in the country I am from. We were told that the World Bank has announced we have moved in middle income economy, but the same cannot be reflected by individual lives of the majority population.

I was also triggered by the increase of disappearances of some writers and activists, and some politicians who happened to get shot by unknown mob gangs

Mwanaka Media and Publishing: On disappearances of writers... Was Mugufuli a bad leader?

Amani N: I think he was just a good leader, maybe using extra measures and lacking some good advice on some matters like that.

Beaton Galafa: Great. So, doesn't it scare you that what you try to address in your work (as evidenced in this particular poem) can be unsettling to the powers that be, and that you would someday encounter a fate not so different from those that have been gifted with bullets? Because post-independence Africa is replete with examples of writers who have suffered at the hands of governments they became critical of - especially in the immediate post-independence.

Amani N: Basically I am not afraid, because I just basically ask questions. These leaders of ours cannot just be left out without being criticized whenever they do something wrong or something that isn't for the benefits of majority. And art is partly supposed to point out evils of the society. What I strive for is to write deeper poems that will not just have, like this one, straight meaning but a multitude of meanings to criticize and point out the evils in leadership & society.

Beaton Galafa: What other themes does your poetry explore? And, how do such themes resonate with your audience's experiences in

340

contemporary Tanzania? Also, in what languages do you usually write? What prompts you to write in the particular language/s? I am asking because I know Tanzania as predominantly Swahili speaking, yet your poem in the BNAP anthology appears in English, any reason/s for that? I also notice that this specific poem contains elements of a love letter, and ironic to the resignation we discussed earlier- some element of hope in a Christian realm. How do you manage to have these themes appear side by side in a work as relatively short as this one, yet managing, in my own view, to present the experiences so well and uniquely clear to the reader?

Amani N: I also write about love (relationships), humor and culture. These themes are somehow most readers will concentrate on in contemporary Tanzania. In the few events I attended concerning poetry, majority of poets concentrate in social & cultural aspects, very few poets cover politics but the audiences have always been in need of it. I usually write in English & Swahili. But most of my poems are in English. This is majorly due to the fact that my Swahili lacks some good vocabulary. We usually speak Swahili but few people can write Swahili in its correctness like poets from Zanzibar..: I tend to choose a character to speak to whenever I write some of these pieces. I think that helps me to speak to other people who may fall to the character I chose

Poem 2:
MY ZIMBABWEAN BUNNY
Amani Nsemwa

Dear Sue,
My Zimbabwean bunny.
How's it going? Are the banks vaults not yet full out there?
Cos I hear you guys carry a basket of money just to purchase a bread.
But I feel that y'all safe and nothing goes wrong.

I am amazed by how sweet it is to see your beautiful eyes,
I am astonished by your cheerful heart,
And the tone of your skin makes me contemplate on why the term
natural always sound like African.
How do I get to meet you?
I have got no passport to travel up there, nor a reputation to make
you at least think of me.
But I pray for your sweet dreams,
And that your charm might not be decisive but rather the peace.
I am out of words for now.
Until then.
I remain,
Your distant relative,
Tanzanian bloke.

Ps. Sleeping is sweet,
So as coffee.

Extracted from Best New African Poets 2019 Anthology

Mwanaka Media and Publishing: I have also observed that in most of your poems you will be addressing someone... What's the idea behind it

Amani N: The idea behind this is that I be thinking if I choose to address someone I can be able to convey different kind of messages as we always have of talking different topics to different people

Mwanaka Media and Publishing: Haha i hadn't figured its Susan Muchirahondo you were addressing above. Sue, please come here

Amani N: Haha I was addressing her. I tried to portray the picture I got about Zimbabwe, and relating to the circumstances we face in Tanzania.

Beaton Galafa: Great tactic, I should say.

Amani N: Thank you

Mwanaka Media and Publishing: ...so is it you addressing your fantasies or it's the character

Amani N: It is the character

Mwanaka Media and Publishing: Kkkk its safe that way!

Susan Muchirahondo: Lol present!

Mwanaka Media and Publishing: Sue, how do you feel being addressed?

Susan Muchirah: I felt really special and like the incredible creation I am...a gift to mankind lol

Mwanaka Media and Publishing: Haha

Best New African Poets Interview with Kenyan poet, Richard Mbuthia

Moderated by Tendai Rinos Mwanaka

Richard Mbuthia is a teacher, a poet, an editor and a motivational speaker. He has great passion for poetry. His is passionate about helping to inculcate and developing the poetic craft
in children. He is a published poet. Some of his books are: The Setting Noon and Other Poems (2017), Letters of Gold (2017), Bounding for Light (2018) and Sparks in the Dark (2019). The last three are children's poetry anthologies he has compiled and edited. He is also published
in a variety of local and international poetry anthologies, magazines and in different forums online.

Archie Swanson: Hi Richard. Which country are you from and what was your childhood experience growing up?
Beaton Galafa: Hello Richard. How does the social and political terrain in Kenya affect your poetry? We have seen how first generation writers of Kenya (e.g. Ngugi wa Thiong'o) resorted to using Literature as a form of political activism in the early years of Kenyan independence, does your writing reflect such heritage?
Obinna Chilekezi: Hello Richard what should be the role of a poet in this crisis ridden Africa
Mbuthia R: A creative writer is very important in this time of the pandemic. Such a writer speaks to the tattered spirits of the readers and mollifies the psychological effects of the pandemic. Different genres can be used to explore varied facets of the pandemic and help in the propagation of information on the same in a more entertaining way. Thank you Tendai for this introduction. In addition: "So far, since 2017, I have compiled and edited four children's poetry anthologies. My aim has always been to arrest the sparks of poetic expression that emanate from the recesses of the children's hearts.

344

The titles are: _Letters of Gold (2017)_; _Bounding for Light (2018)_ - Published by Mwanaka Media and Publishing; _Sparks in the Dark (2019)_; _Echoes of the Sun (2020)_ Thank you Archie. I am from Kenya in East Africa.

Precious Ifeoma Benjamin: Nice to know you Richard

Mbuthia R: I started reading at a very early age. I was introduced to the magic that books carry at a tender age. The twenty six letters of the alphabet have always held me in awe. How those letters can be arranged on a page to communicate different messages. The power they wield has always astounded me. I would describe myself as an introvert. I communicate better through writing rather than through speaking. I started writing poems when I was in Grade 7 in 1991.

Amani N: what do you consider you best ever achievements since you have started to write?

Precious Ifeoma Benjamin: Have you ever been discouraged in your writing life by anyone or circumstances. Has challenges ever wanted to make you give up. If yes, how did you solve those challenges In your writing experience for years?

Mbuthia R: I think the fact that I have been able to tutor kids in the art of writing poems for the last four years and producing a poetry anthology each of those years since 2017 is a great achievement to me. This in itself keeps me going. I see the seeds sprout and grow into glorious plants. Thank you Beaton, Well, I am not a revolutionary as such. I also endeavour not to delve or embroil myself in political activism. I am more of a social activist - a dyed-in-the-wool didactic poet. I love the results I get with the poetry I put out. Each and every poet (and writer) has a journey they have travelled - a journey fraught with varied experiences. These experiences and lessons shape and hone the kinds of poets we become.

Mwanaka Media and Publishing: Do you mind sharing with us some of the personal experiences you experienced that you think shaped who you became?

Mbuthia R: Yes, I have been discouraged countless times in my writing journey - by both people and circumstances! But I have learnt to take everything in my stride especially after ascertaining that I would be doing myself a disservice if I ever gave up my heart's passion: Some of the challenges I have faced include: i) It has not been easy to tap the children's poetic talent - in a bid to determine those to whom poetry comes naturally and those that have no interest in the same. ii) I have self-published all these anthologies. The costs of effecting the same have not been easy on my pocket. iii) it has not been easy to market the anthologies outside the school setting. iv) some people cast aspersions on the whole idea of children writing poetry. They feel that I write the poems for the children. There couldn't be anything farther from the truth!

Mbuthia R: Okay, Tendai. I grew up seeing my dad hauling my mum over the coals countless times. I was usually woken up by my parents' spirited and incessant arguments and aggression towards each other. This usually filled my heart with great sadness and I would find it very hard to go back to bed. I grew up wetting my bed up to the time I was 14 years! It was a shameful experience. The cause of this was the kind of environment I was growing up in. An environment of anxiety! Slowly, but surely, I started fighting the feeling and its attendant 'causes'. My detest for strife and quarrels has known no respite since my teens. When the writing bug 'bit' me, I realised that I had finally found a weapon with which to counter my fears and gory realities. I have since used my writing to speak up for the 'voiceless' and to talk about topics that are disconcerting and 'uncomfortable' to talk about.

Amani Nsemwa: So great and wonderful exchanges to build us up. Thanks, and well received Rich.

Mwanaka Media and Publishing: This is heart rending... we share the same background.

Mbuthia R: Yes, sure Tendai. And it shaped me big time.

Mwanaka Media and Publishing: Thanks for sharing.

Mbuthia R: Let me also add this, my experience as a child is part of the reason I am passionate about having kids write their own poetic pieces. This is because I believe that they too have their story (just as I too had when I was a kid). Writing has a cathartic effect and this is the kick I get from it!

Poem 1:
Empty Yourself
Richard Mbuthia

At the toll of the last bell
As it decisively does knell
Punctuating the timeline's finality
With such crude equity
Desires of old come dashing
Those that had gone hoarse
Screaming for attention
Attention that had long gone stale
Clamoring for yesterday's bread
To grace the king's table tomorrow
The morrow whose sun set yesterday
With fiery rays in the gloaming.
At the toll of the last bell
As it decisively does knell
With ruptured pride of youth
Breaking hymens of yesteryear
Slivers of grandeur bespeak
Sodden memories hanging loosely
On a broken twig in a gust.
The sages of old quietly scream
That before time goes beyond itself
And the clock can't be unwound
Before the veins slump, arteries solidify

Before your time stops
With clocks still ticking
Before blood grows cold
Reach right inside the vault
And yank the doors open
Speak all you have ever wanted
Act. Fast. Time waits not anymore.
Release your dreams to the four winds
Empty the closet that held you captive
Enjoy the breeze, soar
Take in the sights, smile, laugh
Enjoy the camaraderie of family
Strike intense rapport with friends
Before the clock stops ticking
Before rigor mortis sets off from lands yonder
To say this let it suffice
Before the long trek comes a-calling
Empty yourself.

Extracted from Best New African Poets 2017 Anthology

Mwanaka Media and Publishing: When you say 'Release your dreams to the four winds', what are the 4 winds? What inspired you to write this poem?

Amani N: Do you also leave what you have portrayed in a poem in one way or another?

Mwanaka Media and Publishing: Also on your bio you say you are a motivational speaker... The poem reads like a motivational poem... Was that your intention. How do you stay poetic whilst writing motivation as well?

Mbuthia R: Wow! The questions are real boilers... interesting. I meant give yourself up to every possibility and opportunity that may arise. I was inspired by the transient nature of life...and that life is tied up in time. Time itself is limited and hazily 'dries' up before it has properly been handled. Sometimes I let a poem create itself as I write. The end product comes as a surprise when I 'pen off'.... Exactly Tendai. The poem is partly motivational and partly didactic.

Archie Swanson: It's a challenging poem.... in a way, terrifying. Well written. Intense. Descriptions are focused and well-honed. A great write!

Mbuthia R: Thank you very much.

Mwanaka Media and Publishing: Why Empty yourself as title

Ntensibe Joseph: What was the intention of making it a mono stanzaic piece

Mbuthia R: Human beings have so much tied up in them. They have so many talents and gifts that should be used to better the lives of other humans. So, when life 'comes to a close' these talents and gifts should have been expended. Thus the title 'Empty Yourself'

Mbuthia R: Joseph, That is how the piece looks like here but it has stanzas. Let me see if I can repost it.

Mwanaka Media and Publishing: Other than the last line... You seem to have kept most of the lines in pentameter? I have read your other work... Mostly sonnets. You seem to stay within formal structures/strictures?

Mbuthia R: That's an insightful observation. Sometimes, I just find myself taking the pieces down that route...

Mwanaka Media and Publishing: Academic influence?

Mbuthia R: I guess also the kinds of poems that inform(ed) my poetic reality from the outset.

William Blake, Ernest Henley, Shakespeare etc

Poem 2:
Bangui: Oozing Drops of Red
Richard Mbuthia

The smoking embers of a unity defied
sting the hollowed hearts of selves defiled –
lacerated…serrated…defeated, wounded, forlorn…
women, children – Muslim – slink in the shadows of fate
in the shadows of a dark reality – annihilation!

Boots on the ground, in the streets
bang on doors, pounding obdurate wrestlers
   laughingly pulling the triggers
               of their restless AKs.

The crimson hue of Ubangi -
the Bloody Mary of a peace broken;
welling, swirling, swelling in Bangui
lining throats of bloodthirsty Séléka!

Immobilism's squirting pleasures
of hope denied, Freedom deferred,
         and Humanity interred -
at the nation's cemented cemetery,
are the noble meal of the pauper at the helm.

Extracted from Best New African Poets 2020 Anthology

Mwanaka Media and Publishing: Was this written in response to Wanjohi wa Makokha's Bangui poetry project... I will go back to Beaton's question... You said you are not interested in politics... But this is a political poem. Also don't you feel restricted by formalism?
Mbuthia R: Yes, this was in response to Dr Wanjohi's call: I found myself experimenting with political jive. It is also a social activism piece.
Mwanaka Media and Publishing: Okay i see that too

Amani N: In your writings, have you ever felt that if you will write to a certain extent you might become a public enemy, that you might get attacked physically due to what you have written? Does this atmosphere also influence your writings? Or you are just a free soul and never scared of the physical attacks that might arise from the writings you do.

Ntensibe Joseph: Not the structure makes sense-to me. I hope the variations of lines in the subsequent stanzas was equally intentional

Mbuthia R: Yes, it is purely intentional and strategic. You will also notice that in this piece I use enjambment with reckless abandon. Nsemwa, I must admit that every time I write I do so with the fear that physical and emotional backlash might arise from my writing. I remember that I lost my first job straight out of school in 1998. I used to be the patron of the writing club of a certain school in central Kenya. As the patron, I used to write different pieces and post them on the school notice board. On this particular day, the owner of the school stopped by the notice board, read the piece, tore it from the board and angrily bounded to her office. The title was "Struggle is the Purpose of Life." She sent for me and said that she felt that I wanted to invite the workers against the administration (for workers were being shortchanged!). I was dismissed. My writing had led to my dismissal!

Amani N: Well. I get it Rich. I'm sorry that you went through all that, but thanks for sharing. It's always huge

Mbuthia R: I appreciate. The one thing I learnt from that is that writing is a potent tool.

Amani N: Surely..

Ntensibe Joseph: Well thought display of words... Keep the pen rolling: So, would she have opted for the lie of "comfort is the purpose of life." I trust she was also struggling to express her fury and ill placed reasoning.

Mwanaka Media and Publishing: As a writer are there issues or things you can write about?

Mbuthia R: As a writer, I try to avoid writing on issues religion.

Mwanaka Media and Publishing: Haha why

Mbuthia R: Issues of religion are as abstract as abstract itself. I have a firm belief and faith in God. So, unless I am trying to share my belief with others, I avoid engaging in religious discussions and writing about them (for any other reason other than the one I have written above).

Grace Elegba O: As a creative, are there days you feel like giving writing up? If yes, what do you do on such days

Joy Odewumi: Just calm down Grace. Relax on your bed, reflect ,think only good thought and remember only the good times and not the years. Do have a good evening. Aiye o si rush.

Emmanuel Mtema: Richard, do you at some point find yourself wanting to write something that you think will conflict with how people perceive your character? If yes, then do you proceed with writing or its pens down for you?

Mbuthia R: Yes, there are days I have felt like giving up...but my heart of hearts refuses to let go. Sometimes writing is just a labour of love but I keep writing for my own sanity's sake! Very interesting question Emmanuel. I have written some sexually explicit poems and I find it hard to share them. Some of them are heavily clothed in metaphors to remove the edge from their bite.

But all in all, if it is something worth writing, I write and worry about sharing later!!

Andrea Matambo: Dear Richard, whenever you are sharing your works, don't you sometimes fear that, a). No one will READ and really APPRECIATE my works, I will touch no life? b). I will not get any pecuniary benefits from my literary works? c). If and when faced with any of such fears, how do you address them deep within you, how do you carry on and keep on writing?

Emmanuel Mtema: Do you think there should be a distinction between the writer's character and the personality of the writer when he is not writing? For example we differentiate an actor's or comedian's character in action from the person's actual personality

Mbuthia R: With the Advent of social media, some of these fears are almost done away with. With proper use of social media, the work is sure to reach far and wide and chances are that many more people will actually interact with the work of art. To receive pecuniary benefits one must intend so from the outset. Sharing on social media will not necessarily bring cash to the writer. This creates awareness of the kind of work written by the writer (exposure).

But if the writing is meant to fetch money, then it will be packaged differently. (There are different models to choose from for this to be effected): I guess many are the times that a writer's personality and the 'personality of his work' cannot sit cheek in jowl because of their incongruity! I think it is important for a writer to be true to self and churn out work that resonates truthfully and dutifully to his/her heart's pinings.

Mwanaka Media and Publishing: any parting words?

Mbuthia R: I wish to thank all of the poets who engaged me with questions during this interview. Thank you Tendai for featuring me and my work here. In closing, I say: Words are your possession and they work the way you treat them. If you decide to make them shudder, cower and cringe, they will fear you. They will hide in crevices and crannies – far from reach. But if you let them gambol and frisk like calves at the sight of green pasture, then the milk and honey of creativity will be your portion. Choicest words inhabit the recesses of a mind that honours them! Treat words well and they will make your writing healthy.

Best New African Poets Interview with Malawian poet Joseph Sukali
Moderated by Tendai Rinos Mwanaka

Joseph Daniel Sukali is a Mzuzu University graduate with multiple publications to his name. He is the author of *Dealing with a Heartbreak: Therapy for the Broken* and has co-authored a love poetry anthology, *Whispers of Beating Hearts*. Sukali has managed to get his works published in *Best "New" African Poets 2020 Anthology* and *An Anthology of African and Eastern European Languages*. The author is also a columnist and editor of a number of magazines including; Love Feast Magazine, Malawi Talents Magazine and Writers Global Movement just to mention a few. The 27 years old is an award winning spoken word poet with two albums to his name that's far.

Mwanaka Media and Publishing: Thank you. Tell us a bit about your childhood and why you are interested in mental health issues?
Amani Nsemwa: You wrote about dealing with heartbreak. What were the main motives behind this? What was the inspiration behind?
Sharon Kagoya: Is he married?
Zozo Chandilanga: You have achieved a lot, proud of you Joseph... Who are you? What's something you believe in, that sets you apart?
[13/06, 6:04 pm] Mwanaka Media and Publishing: Hahah i like this one. The girls have come to party!
Charles Duncan: I am in Malawi and I should say I haven't yet heard of some of the writing related initiatives that you are involved in. Which I believe mirrors a trend elsewhere where writers really need to push hard to get their voice out there. What are you doing currently to make sure these initiatives you are involved in get out there and have an even wider following?
Joseph Sukali: I was born in Thyolo, I have spent most of my childhood in Zomba where I did my preschool and junior school... I have always had a closer relationship with my parents... I lost my dad

354

when I was 16,... I got depression and after recovering while in my first year of college, it's when I got interest in mental health...i currently focus on relationships and loss related depression. The inspiration was nothing but experience and social observation of my environment

Lisa Jaison: What's your take on how mental health is dealt with in the African context?

Joseph Sukali: I am a nobody who knows he is a nobody. What sets me apart is that I am a free soul. I don't conform to social constructions... I have chosen to live life by my rules. Am currently just writing and not putting out the work... I am building a fan base, getting small works published in different outlets...but I'm holding my major works... I have three books already done... Just waiting to build enough connections Internationally and locally...am not rushing like I did with my first book

Joseph Sukali: Am not married

Sharon Kagoya: Seeing someone?

Joseph Sukali: Free agent

Tanaka Chidora: I see a bottle of whisky on your table. I would love to host you one of these days, that is, if you happen to find yourself in our teapot-shaped country called Zimbabwe. My question: many artists I have interacted with are unashamed alcoholics, using the wise waters to retrieve hard-to-find creative juices. Do you also imbibe to create? I should say my relationship with beer has reached that level where I no longer know whether my creativity is fired by it

Joseph Sukali: I must admit, I get frustrated a lot regarding how much we play mental health down in Africa. I think most people have not understood that mental health is just like physical health... It affects an individual and their general performance... If we treated depression, anxiety, PTSD and all other mental disorders, the way we fight malaria or TB we would be having a different conversation. Africans are still stuck on stereotypes that hinder people from admitting when they have mental illnesses... This affects men a lot...

For example in Malawi the issue of suicide has gotten worse at the moment... Mostly young men and men who grew up on the social teaching that men are supposed to be strong... It's very detrimental.... All in all, i don't think we are doing enough as Africans in addressing the issue

Joseph Sukali: I mostly write when sober... I have pieces that I have written under the influence and they are insane.... but all in all I don't use liquor for my creative juices... I will probably visit Zim soon... I have friends there.

Tanaka Chidora: I usually drink after writing, but sometimes during the process of drinking, I see vistas opening up and I gladly indulge

Joseph Sukali: You write with the ancestors when you drink. It's magical

Lisa Jaison: Interesting, what roles do you think traditional beliefs and religion play in this dynamic?

Joseph Sukali: I think due to the patriarchal nature of most religious beliefs and African traditions, it all goes to the stereotypes where a man is expected to be the bigger guy...that's where the root is... That belief is what we need to uproot first

Beaton Galafa: You've introduced yourself as a spoken word artist as well as a contributor to various literary outlets. How does your spoken word poetry differ from your written poetry in terms of language and style? What informs such differences if any? Is your audience the same in both poetry types?

Joseph Sukali: The difference only lies in the fact that when I am writing a piece intended for spoken word, I write with a picture of myself speaking the lines to an audience... While when writing ordinary poetry I write to a reader not a listener... I hope you get what you mean... Often times spoken word pieces are written longer in my style... I think an example of the pieces would be ideal... One for spoken word, one just a reading piece

Joseph Sukali: I don't know if you notice the small difference

Beaton Galafa: I have gotten an idea of the nuances, from these two pieces yes. I notice in both you rely on the use of simple language, if this is recurring in all of your poetry, how do you manage to produce images in the reader/listener's mind, to keep them hooked from the start to the end?

Joseph Sukali: As for readers... I usually use emotions that most people can relate to... Imagery is not the only one to hook people with... There are a lot of devices one can use... My favorite is emotions

Mwanaka Media and Publishing: I have always wondered about artists who drink to write. What inhabits them to be less creative when they are not drunk? My own creativity doesn't need the waters to flow

Tanaka Chidora: It's a myth that writers drink to write, although there are some who do. I drink after writing. Heavily

Aleck Kaposa: Personally i am the Christian type, i have never touched alcohol before or after writing and will never attempt to drink

Gwiriri Oscar: There are people who seem to be doing good, not only in writing, but other things too, under the influence. As for me I'm a sober character, though.

Precious Ifeoma Benjamin: I don't even take any at all. Not in the league

Amani Nsemwa: Sure. I have met many artists who works better when they hit a drink

Emmanuel Tumwesige: Joseph I appreciate that you keep your work in simple language. I think it easily uproots the insight of a surface reader. Thank you.

Joseph Sukali: We write to communicate after all...thank you for the encomium

Emmanuel Tumwesige: As for this poem I think you crucified the fruit than the pollinator. Do ever believe that some writers are

357

absorbed in their writings? If so, have you ever been eaten up by your creation?

Mwanaka Media and Publishing: I think it is passed down from our fathers generation of writers like Marechera, Hove, Mungoshi, Ginsberg etc who seemed to find inspiration when drunk or drugged.

Joseph Sukali: I appreciate your thoughts... I am not sure about other people's experience...but I don't believe I have ever been absorbed in my own writing... I only get absorbed in my recitals

Emmanuel Tumwesige: Anyway it is hard to tell, but keep penning to the sun

Mwanaka Media and Publishing: Are you religious? If so isn't that an inhibitions to your creativity. Religion suppresses inquiry, questions, other perspectives etc... And the second question related to this... It seems the *write simple language police* is dictating what a poet should do. Was poetry, in the beginning meant to be consumptive (commercial) art like for ex photography? Why do we allow all these inhibitions (prisons) to limit us?

Joseph Sukali: Am not religious...so I am a free being...I have no limits. Apparently I don't follow any writing rules... I think it's a weakness but I personally consider it as a strength... I don't follow writing rules...especially in poetry... I love breaking the rules... My poetry anthology is basically about breaking rules of poetry... I don't do traditional

Prince Kamaazengi: You spoke for me too....I oftentimes say: don't think outside the box, burn the damn box with your thoughts and think freely!

Emmanuel Tumwesige: It shouldn't be burnt someone needs it. Just by pass and walk on. I also fail to follow rules

Kudzai Munzira: Religious poets like John Donne, George Herbert and William Blake, just to mention a few, actually became prolific Christian poets because they actually had questioning minds and let their Christian thoughts roam free, to the point that some were almost deemed to be bordering on "heresy." Check "Tiger" by

William Blake for example or "Love bade me welcome" by George Hebert. So in the end it is up to the religious poet himself/herself to be shackled by the confines of religious convention or to break free and explore new realms in terms of religious poetry. I always do the latter as a published Christian poet.

Mwanaka Media and Publishing: I do agree... Religious poets of the past were free... It's hard to find good religious poems these days... Just like music. I will give you an example of these songs 'makanaka jesu' 'mutsvene jesu'.... i have heard them repeated on an on... Sometimes just those titles, on and on until the song ends... There is absolutely nothing, no creativity... Oh another one is 'My God is Good'... You find the same happening to poetry.

Aleck Kaposa: As a sinful Adventist myself i don't go over boundaries and crossover to blasphemy or wild sex scenes or other such wild imaginations. I do not see this as being curtailed/inhibited by religion, no. My thoughts roam free but within the accepted Christian boundaries. I believe what i write must not influence people to do evil. I am very free and write about almost anything, i hope i am not seeming to contradict myself. The soon-coming Christ is my King and i am never ashamed of him

Andrea Matambo: Religion, to a great extent, limits Art I feel. Some things I dream to write I cannot in my country because my people (We even have a government ministry to this effect) keep screaming "Nooh, we are a Christian Nation."

Joseph Sukali: This is sad to an artistic mind that yearns to go beyond the scope of limited thought system

Mwanaka Media and Publishing: Kkkkk yes you contradicted yourself to distraction, Aleck

Issac Kalibwa: Hello, Joseph. It was reported in different media that the cases of Gbv and abuse went up during the lockdowns imposed because of the Covid 19 pandemic. I also believe that poets have pieces of their souls, the tales they experience or encounter in their work. This is why, in my experience, poets are much more possessive and jealous with their work than say, writers of fiction. Do you agree? I'd like to know whether you write from experience.

Joseph Sukali: I don't know about being possessive.... I am not sure if I am but I damn love to have my name attached to my work... I don't know if that qualifies as being possessive.

I write from experience, observation, intuition, and imagination.

Mwanaka Media and Publishing: I thought in your intro bio you said you are keeping a lot of work to yourself... Publishing just a few?

Joseph Sukali: I didn't say am keeping to myself... I said I have not published them yet... I want it done professionally and I need funds n fans for that to happen... Am in the process of establishing such... Otherwise it's not like I don't want to put out the works... If a publisher came with an offer to do the publishing, distributing and marketing for free... You would have 3 of my books out by July...

Mwanaka Media and Publishing: Andrea, I hope all the artists in Zambia, whether Christian or not are fighting against this. Jesus from what i read never forced anyone to be Christian

Emmanuel Tumwesige: As if this is a continuation of the spoken one you previously showed. I can read the anger inside. And my question is, have you written any praise poem?

Poem
Am Equally Human
Joseph Daniel Sukali

I body slammed, disturbed horrifically deep within
Every exhale seemed like the last, wrangled in the struggle
My body twisted to his squeeze; muscles tearing apart as bones broke
My soul was pushed into the dark as he pushed in
Cold waves of despair flashed through my nerves
I am screaming but can't be heard! where is the voice of the voiceless??

Help! Help! Help!
The silence gets louder than my cries of rescue
My innocence dies to the taste of the forbidden fruit
So forbidden and abominable is the way of the taste
My dignity drained as he thirstily drunk from my well
My purity gets purely impure leaving me anguish in pain,
His manly manhood steals my pride
Blood gush out as my thoughts commit suicide
The combination of his seeds and my blood drip
The ugliest scene of painted memories of abuse
My body can't move, there's a dark cloud hovering over my head
I can't see, breath or feel a thing, all I can hear is the drum beating in
my chest
I drag my trunk home in silence, brutalized both physically and
psychologically
Traumatized by the inhumanity of some human beings
I feel lost and alone with questions tearing the defense of my mind
Why me? What did I do to deserve this? How would God let this
happen?
My heart burns to his cold soul, I am only thirteen; He is supposed to
be my father!

Can someone please hear me! I am done hiding in dark cold corners!
I have endured the trauma long enough
For my mother would put the blame on me
To my father am dead alive and inexistent
But my voice is inaudibly loud enough for the ear that wishes to
listen
For the pen that dreams to write a story that was never told
Of a morally chocked society and the death of decency in humanity
A generation of social media feminists who speak more than they
listen

To the untold stories of molested timid girls who are broken in and
out
The pain of holding the truth is soul torture and burdening
The pain of watching the abusers walk free is agonizing
I really want to speak out and I really need your help
I want this whole thing to be over once and for all
All the sexual assault, the mutilation from violence against women
The gender bias, male chauvinism
All that the society has internalized in promoting our vulnerability
Remember, our sex is not a disability
I'm your mother, aunt, sister, niece: I'm a girl, I'm a woman
Let it stick in your head that I am equally human.

Extracted from Best New African Poets 2020 Anthology

Gwiriri: I understand you are a man: What does it take to place
yourself in the shoes of a raped girl? Is it by imagination, research,
etc.? How do you know that you have replicated the actual emotions
of the victim?
Mwanaka Media and Publishing: Very good question, Oscar.
Joseph Sukali: Yes I have written praise poems.
Joseph Sukali: It's imagination and hearing stories from those with
the experience... I know I can't give the exact emotions but I do my
best to just make it relatable...The goal is not to put out the actual
emotions, it's about delivering the subliminal message with the best
provocative tone and emotions as possible... I have had a chance to
talk to more than 5 people who had been sexually abused in their
childhood...they were all suffering from PTSD so they sought
counselling, I have learned a lot from their stories... That's why I am
able to write from a girls' perspective. FYI... I am not a certified
therapist... I only have online certificates in psychotherapy and
relationship counseling. I help people for free...I am constantly
studying Mental Health and modern psychotherapy approaches just

to be able to be in a position where I am able to contribute to the fight against mental health... Writing only compliments this goal...

Gwiriri: Psycho studies and writing goes hand in hand forsure. Thanks for the frank response

Best New African Poets Interview with Zimbabwean poet, Oscar Gwiriri

Moderated by Tendai Rinos Mwanaka

Oscar Gwiriri is a Certified Forensic Investigations Professional (CFIP) who also holds a *Master of Science Degree in Strategic Management, Bachelor of Business Administration, Associate of Arts in Business Administration Degree, Diploma in Logistics and Transport (CILT, UK)* and a *Diploma in Workplace Safety and Health,* as well as other ten certificates in the fraternity of United Nations Peacekeeping. He was born on 15 June 1975 at Gwiriri Village, Chief Mutasa, Zimbabwe. He attended Manunure Primary School (Honde Valley) and Dangamvura High School (Mutare). He has more than 35 publications both in English and Shona languages. Oscar is both a creative writer and an academic. He was nominated twice in the National Arts Merits Awards (2019) categories for his books *Hatiponi* and *Chitima nditakure.* Oscar is contactable on email: <u>oscar.gwiriri@gmail.com</u>

Amani Nsemwa: How do you manage to make your work reach readers within and outside Zimbabwe? What strategies/methods are you using? Also if you are interested in Shona language (which is good), don't you think it will be hard for readers who aren't speaking Shona to grasp the messages behind your works?

Gwiriri: BNAP is the first port of call for marketing. I reach out to readers through the press reviews of my work, as well as reading/reciting at arts festivals. My initial marketing strategy was to feature at functions as well as on National TV as a guest poet during talk shows. I once did a duet poem with Linda Gabriel in commemoration of a National Hero upon the announcement of his death. Initially I wrote in English with the notion of reaching out to a bigger market, but later shifted course after realising that there were many Shona literal gaps to fill. My academic engagement opened my eyes to see that I should be proud of my indigenous language more than any other. Moreso, there are certain themes which come out well through indigenous languages than otherwise. I like what Mwanaka is doing, publishing an indigenous piece with a translation. That retains true art. In this instance Shona articles may still be translated to other languages as long as the theme is globally topical. I have quite a good command of English, but I will strive to write in Shona so as to leave and restore our traditional legacy, especially through old world books.

Amani N: Well understood. I like this

Aleck Kaposa: You have a busy day time job, how do you find time to write so many books for adults and for children?

Mwanaka Media and Publishing: What's the difference between poems you write in Shona versus those in English?

Gwiriri: Quite true. My schedule is always full, being full time employed, having to write and voluntarily editing some upcoming writers' manuscripts, as well as managing family time is quite a daunting task. I would rather need 36 hours a day. However, I am working distant from my family, hence I write at night during week days. When I have a foreign trip, I spend that spare time I'm away from family through writing. Thank God for the new technology, sometimes a new idea props up or I observe something interesting on my way, I just drive off the road and jot some drafts for a story and save in my phone. If it is poetry, I write when the inspiration is fresh. Sometimes I dream about something to write about, then I wake up and write immediately. For children books, i watch the behaviour of children, especially when they are playing, then draft the stories.

Mwanaka Media and Publishing: How much of your work spills into your poetry

Gwiriri: When I write Shona poems, I feel satisfied that I would have expressed my feelings accurately, using the actual and appropriate language dictum. Shona is richer towards expressing Ubuntu/Hunhuism, which is my major philosophy. It has a sufficient and rich vocabulary, just like Swahili. As for my English poetry, it is more of a translation from Shona thoughts to English scribbling. I have been proof reading my English poetry anthology, but could not finish it because an idea on a Shona novel had cropped up. I seem to be biased towards Shona, unless if I'm writing a textbook. A quarter of my work environment, half family-social interaction, then the other quarter personal feelings. The work environment exposes me to different people's behaviours, hence I write about them, as them and the job as the persona. That is Human Resources principles versus human behaviour conflict.

Mwanaka Media and Publishing: Your daughter is also a poet... Is she following in your footsteps, do you help her with her poetry or influence her writing. I remember one poem i read from her was on police corruption... And i gather you work in the police... Was she inspired by you? How do you feel about it all?

Tanaka Chidora: I read your novel, _Hatiponi_, and was impressed by your effortless use and coinage of Shona terms. During our chat during an awards ceremony, you confessed that some of the words are products of dreams. I was reminded of that today when you mentioned dreams. May you please comment on that?

Gwiriri: My daughter, Natasha is quite a good poet. I discovered it when we were doing oral poetry prompts during a family interaction. My older son, Onashe (18) is rather into music, and the younger one, Onald (10) is also a writer. I'm expecting publication of two children books by Onald soon. I can say I have an arts family. I don't know what influences them, but I think the writing environment I create motivates them. They have the artistic vigour, but it may be obstracted by school studies. They usually pull their writing spirits when I come home with a newly published copy. I help them with positive criticism. Natasha's poem on the police was written when she observed a certain corrupt police officer being arrested whilst she was going to school. I could not censor her poem because it belongs to her. I taught my children to write down anything that fascinates

366

them and share with the World. Quite true, some of my writings are influenced by dreams. There are times when I dream almost a whole length short story or novel. I put that down the moment I wake up. The challenge is that I have to promptly write about it, if I procrastinate, the actual vision fades away and I will not be able to write it exactly as it is supposed to be. When I'm feely tired, I squash the dream into a poem, but won't feel satisfied because I would not have emptied everything. The remnants compels me to write many poems on the same theme based on the dream. On 29/05/29 @ 0135 hours, I dreamt about me dying of Covid 19 then wrote it as a poem entitled *Sudden death*. I foresee some events through dreams and write about them.

Tanaka Chidora: To what do you attribute these dreams? Do you believe in the supernatural?

Aleck Kaposa: Amazing

Gwiriri: Frankly, I'm confused about it. I just take things as they come. From a traditional point of view, when someone is gifted of a certain artistry like hunting, elders say the spirit should be fortified through a beer ceremony, but I have never pursued that. I just listen to the writing spirit and do what it commands. I can openly accept that I have a writing spirit, because there are times when I feel compelled to write about something, if I disobey the urge I get depressed until I write. I remember writing my novel *Honzwa* in one night. When the spirit attacks, I abandon other works and appease by writing on the imminent theme. This has created a situation whereby I have too many draft (40) novels. Fortunately, I try by all means to complete them. If only we could live by writing alone, I could be a full time writer.

Mwanaka Media and Publishing: Interesting. I have the same spiritual haunting too... I think by writing down those dreams you are already giving offering to the spirit that makes you see... You don't necessarily need a beer ceremony or any other offering. From my readings on the Maya civilization (ancient mexican civilization) they believed there are several animal spirits, and the most powerful spirit animal is that of the writer (Scribner) because it outlives everything. So we can only embrace the spirit and let it speak through our creative output. From your explanations, you write a lot. Don't you sometimes feel you have put so many words out there, so much of yourself out there? Harking to Benedette Meyer's provocation. She said writing is like pregnancy to her. She sometimes felt like she should stop writing, she fights against over expressiveness, against giving birth to more words...

Gwiriri: Thank you for this notion. I have no choice, I have to vomit or belch the words out there and relief my spirit. Otherwise, if I don't empty my head, I may go berserk. I write to relief myself and underlined deep socio-bitterness. I don't just write out of interest, but compulsion. Though, I love and enjoy writing. There are times when I wonder if the article is mine when I start proof reading, however I try to preserve my drafts, especially those I would have written out of spiritual impulse. There are times when I laugh at myself as I laugh over an idea when I am writing. Over expressiveness is rather a relieve to me. I don't care much on how many books I would have churned out, but just the relief sets me free. Suppressing over expressiveness drives me crazy. I'm rather a multi-purpose writer with draft books on logistics (reverse), self defence, disaster management, old world books, creative writing, Shona proverbs, poetry anthologies, Quotes, e.t.c,

Mwanaka Media and Publishing: Give us an overview of Zimbabwe writing, especially what's being written now. How well it is being received

Gwiriri: Zimbabwe is a writing country. Despite a low reading culture due to different reasons, writers continue to write. Some have made a publishing break through, but many are still yet to get there. There is however a mistaken notion, not only in Zimbabwe, but across Africa that protest writing sells much due to the reason that the much celebrated authors are those who wrote pre and early independence (1980). However, I have observed that there are many literature gaps which our writers are not pursuing. Politico-protest literature is awash amongst the upcoming writers. We need to cultivate a pre-event or forecasted writing culture rather than the post-event writings. Some writers lack market research mechanisms of course, thereby spending their energy on exhausted themes. The readers are exhausted of old ideas. Fortunately, I have encouraged some to explore on old world novels, and many have taken hid. One of them had his book selected as a school literature setbook. The motivational books frenzy has also dominated the book industry. I have also noted various spoken word activities and competitions. Before the Covid 19 restrictions, book launches were amass. Informal writing (mixed languages and unedited) seems to be taking over on the social media. Generally, writing is well received in Zimbabwe. I have been to prestigious places through writing books.

Poem 1:
Boudoir putsch
Oscar Gwiriri

The centre of power axis politic ravaged,
Scarlet Mercy with a sword in her left hand,
A Delilah sacred scissors in her right hand.
What else can you say to Uncle Roberto
When the whirlpool of power is forced
To sing a rapturous occult quasi-peace song.

She stares and flash blinds his eyes in public,
Her nails savage his legacy and flesh to nullity,
Spits on securocrats' faces, provoking havoc.
She is the master of the Book of Law,
Her wand of power draws our man asunder.
He's gone dumb and deaf to our voices,

Dampened by the Abrahadabra song she sings
In his ears all-night long like an active cricket.

extracted from Best New African Poets 2020 Anthology

Poem 2:
Tribute to Chiwoniso Maraire
Oscar Gwiriri

I still recall you and your sister,
In your green Mutare Girls High blazers,
Passing through the N Section I lived,
Enroute to the P Section you lived,
Beautiful sisters always together,
In our cool Dangamvura suburb.
Born and bred in the USA, you were, but
You still played with us gregariously.

I watched your moves of self-discovery
From *Peace of Ebony* to *Vibe Culture*,
Your Mbira maestro accomplishment
In the cultural music prepotency,
Raised the Zimbabwean flag world over,
Cutting across racial and cultural barriers,
Inspiring and standing in for the girl child,
Aspiring and unifying the music fraternity.
Oh Chiwoniso, you are such a heroine!

Your conspicuous voice stands superiority
In the test of time amongst music genres.
Whenever I listen to your sonorous voice
Always feel the tranquility of your oul

370

Serenading and soothing my lonely soul.
I'm yet to see who can fit in your shoes.
Gone you're, but your music lives for you.
Rest in Peace the Queen of Mbira,
Chiwoniso, the Shining Emblem of Mbira.

extracted from Best New African Poets 2020 Anthology

Beaton Galafa: Hi Oscar. Your reference to a mythical Uncle Roberto and Delilah and the events unfolding in the poem ignites images of a Mugabe's Zimbabwe (especially his last days), when did you actually write the poem?

Mwanaka Media and Publishing: My question is on Tribute to Chiwoniso Maraire... It seems you are interested in African spirituality; i have also a read a few other pieces from you that seemed fascinated by African spirituality. Does your interest in mbira music goes beyond your love of Chiwoniso's music into the spiritual world.

Gwiriri: Thank you for the critical analysis Beaton. I wrote the poem *Boudoir putsch* whilst in my village in year 2019 after observing an altercation between our village head and villagers over a particular burial tradition. The grapevine was that the herdman's wife had taken control over him, and had caused him to stray into a Pentecostal church resulting in him abandoning the roots. I also tackled the conflict in my short story entitled *The crusade*, published in Zimbolicious 4. Mbira music is sacred. When I was growing up I attended some traditional ceremonies whereby the mbira was twung to evoke ancestral spirits. I just recognise it, but I'm not much into it. I listen to mbira music here and there, and also have links to mbira gurus like Mbuya Stella Chiweshe. However, I'm also into Blues music, Rock music and any genre which encompasses extra-ordinary artistry. Interestingly, as an old world books writer, it won't be just not to acknowledge the mbira, as well as traditional song and dance. I was fascinated by the fact that Chiwoniso Maraire, having been born and bred in the USA upto teenage, she embraced mbira and marketed it to international heights, yet some amongst us shunned it. My interest in African spirituality is by observation and not practise. However, I pay enough respect to the practitioners for preserving our ancestral tradition.

Sebastian Jalameso: I gladly absorbed it well into me. Thank you for the great creative deposition.

Reviews

Poetry and Mother Nature: Review of Selected Poems in *Best "New" African Poets 2017 Anthology*

Andrew Nyongesa

Department of Social Science
St Paul's University
KENYA

Book Title: Best "New" African Poets 2017 Anthology
Publisher: Mwanaka Media and Publishing Pvt Ltd
Year of Publication: 2018
Editors: Tendai R Mwanaka and Daniel Purifacacao

"Best" New African Poets 2017 Anthology is a compilation of 338 poems that traverse Africa from English, French, Portuguese speaking to African vernaculars addressing diverse subjects from gender issues, global warming, identity politics, culture, spiritualty, love and politics. This review is an eco-critical reading of *Best "New" African Poets 2017 Anthology* that proceeds through close textual analysis of thought, style, and feelings. According to Lawrence Buell, a text upholds ecocriticism if "the nonhuman environment is present not merely as a framing device, the human interest is not ... the only legitimate interest, human accountability to the environment is part of the text's ethical orientation and finally there is some sense of the environment as a process" (9). It is the contention of this review that selected poems of *Best "New" African Poets 2017 Anthology* adhere to Buell's eco-critical blue print. These poems include among others the collaboration of thirteen poets entitled "As her children fight for her breath" (p. 1-8), Mwanaka's "It Took a Judas" (9), Inya's "Burning", Olenrawaju's "The Rich Garden", Mala's "Human's for or Against Human and Galafa's "The Humming Bird."

To begin with, the thought expressed in the poems in the anthology abide by the tenets of ecocriticism. According to Mugubi (2017), thought refers to themes and the subject of a work of art (45). As Buell asserts, the themes and subjects in selected poems in *Best "New" Poets 2017 Anthology* downgrade human interest and demand human accountability to the natural environment. Inya's "Burning" castigates continued deforestation that feeds the desire to use trees as firewood without knowledge of the role of trees in preventing desertification. The end result is desertification as illustrated in the first two lines, "[t]he sky is a furnace/of angry sun fighting" (p. 10). The last two lines of the first stanza single out deforestation as the major cause of the desertification "for the fallen trees/ crying in the fire" (10). The destruction of trees gives the sun a lee way to vaporize all the moisture from the soil and produce dust that threatens human existence. The persona says "[a]ny tree that comes down /finds the eye of the earth" (stanza 3) and the "eye that stays calm" is that prepared to "gulp dust". In the last stanza, the persona praises trees as sheds against the hot sun and censures humankind's craving for deforestation. The choice of words demonstrates direct denunciation of human activities that eradicate "green" or trees: "say this to haters of the green/ who war against standing trees".

Moreover, several poems in the collaboration, "As her Children Fight for her Breath" raise the curtain over what Buell describes as the lack of human accountability to the natural environment. Abel Sehloho singles out the effects of environmental destruction such as high temperatures (the unforgiving sun burns) and their perilous effects on plants (Flowers wither in shame). Sehloho points out human activity as the major cause of nature's vengeful attitude towards her offspring (trunks are pulled down by the gravity of our punished land). This line suggests that humanity has overexploited the natural environment which results in Mother Nature's vengeance. The side effects have been pronounced in the soil hence the

374

line"[o]ur land is losing the battle". Lisa Jaison takes Sehloho's cue to demonstrate Mother Nature's vengeance through temperature rise. Jaison writes, "[t]rapped in this merciless heatwave/yearning to die fast like the plants and livestock" (p. 3). Jaison refers to odd heat waves that have in recent times visited temperate climates in our world. Indeed Sanderson (2017) avers that the "increases in numbers and lengths of heat waves have previously been identified in global temperature records, including locations within Europe" (p. 191). The persona fears that the melting of glaciers in the North Pole will affect Africa through the rise of sea levels: "[a] cold blast of the arctic/whose glaciers they say are/ melting" (p. 3). The persona in Jaison's piece adopts a forthright stance when he asserts the leaders of super powers have a hand in environmental degradation. The persona says, "[p]lead with him to stop trumping with that pen and place a signature/ calamity is not a myth," (4). This line suggests that some leaders such as Donald Trump refuse to support policies that would otherwise reverse climate change and its destructive effects.

Chenjerai Mhondera turns his attention to humanity's recklessness with regard to poor waste disposal which pollutes waterbodies to affect aquatic life. The persona says, "[t]he smell of bursting raw sewage / rivers of these ugly thick flows of wastes cascading dirty and hurt in/ city" (p. 4). As a result of the pollution, the persona is unable to engage in hobbies such as "swimming, skewing, canoeing" which he suggests are "booed in sense that water is dirty" (p. 4). Kudyahakudadirwe shows the desperation of African communities in the face of the effects of global warming in Africa. With a green Africa, droughts could easily be evaded by performing simple rain-making ceremonies. But currently, arranging such rituals has become an exercise in futility. The persona says, "[t]wo rain making ceremonies after, not a drop/Not a drop to extinguish the fire on our tongues," (p. 5). The subject of global warming is too esoteric to be grasped by Africans that have not had formal education such that some confuse the subject for a person. The persona writes, "[t]hey blame someone called Global Warming who/ no one in the village knows by that name" (6). Antonio Garcia is saddened by the divisions of world powers over the Paris Agreement, blames the American President for portraying the current generation as visionless. Garcia writes, "[t]he Paris treaty is moot/ Trumped by backward thinking and derided" (p. 7). The word "Trumped" is an indirect reference to the American president, Donald Trump who consistently referred to Global warming as a hoax aimed at denying Americans jobs in coal industries. Cosmas Mairosi summarises the collaborative poem by underlining climate change as a tragedy of the human race. The human pollution of the earth has resulted in dreaded cancers and skin diseases that will result in the final destruction of the race by 2280 AD. Mairosi writes, "2280 AD: RIP Human Race/ Earth was yours, a sublime gift to keep/But greed and recklessness was your undoing," (8). It is clear from these poets that unless humankind changes their attitude towards the environment, climate change poses the worst threat to our existence.

Ecological concerns of the poems in *Best "New" African Poets 2017 Anthology* are demonstrated through style. According to Buell, the nonhuman environment does not exist merely as a framing device (p. 9). Most poets employ images from the natural environment for aesthetic purposes and this is what Buell expunges from ecocriticism. The present review therefore differs from Kibutu (2012) in which poets appropriate attributes of Mother Nature to symbolize the human world (1). The poets in the anthology deviate from Kibutu's trajectory to directly address human exploitation of nature by use of free verse mode to evade the temptation of mere reference to nature to restore humanity back to the centre of the cosmos. Literary scholars contend that as much as free verse is not the same as prose, styles such as alliteration, repetition and rhyme are used, but irregularly. According to Litcharts, free verse is unconventional in nature and therefore without "strict meter and rhyme scheme" (para 1). The poets in *Best "New" African Poets 2017 Anthology* adopt this unconventional verse to overturn conventional emphasis on humanity at the expense of the natural environment. In Mwanaka's "It took a Judas" the poem takes a conversational tone with a non-human persona who vows to do something to ensure that humanity experiences the cruelty it has meted out on Mother Nature. Through extravagant use of personification, Mwanaka successfully demonstrates how plants and animals suffer under the merciless treatment of humankind. The persona says, "I will ask humans how it feels to have a body part removed from their bodies or their babies' bodies" (p. 9). The nonhuman in this line complains against the recklessness with which humans chop off its limps and body parts.

Some poets have also employed ambiguity with regard to the role of President Donald Trump in the Paris agreement. The word "trump" is used as a pun in attempt to effect figurative expression of the message. Gracia describes the Paris climate treaty as a brilliant idea, which is "Trumped by backward thinking and derided" (7). The word "trump" has two possible meanings: first, to defeat someone in a highly public way or the persona's feeling that President Trump has taken the world back to the age of ignorance by referring to global warming as a hoax. Considering the setting of this poem when debate on climate change has been raging, the second meaning of the term carries the day. The poet Jaison uses ambiguity in the same word when she writes "[p]lead with him to stop trumping with that pen and place a signature/ calamity is not a myth," (4). The word "trumping" has nothing to do with the first meaning "defeating someone in a public way." The poet urges Trump to append his signature on the Paris Agreement to commit himself like other world powers to expediting measures that curb climate change. As Litcharts suggest, poets irregularly employ alliteration, rhyme and consonance as part of the free verse mode. Chuma Mmeka in the collaboration, "As her Children Fight for her Breath" irregularly employs consonance "bustled and hustled" assonance, "fuming, spitting and smoking" , alliteration, "sand and sooth scourged…skins" (1). As earlier indicated, the irregularity typical of free verse turns the attention of poetry from human concerns to the Mother Nature. Mmeka contends that because humankind has neglected the natural environment, she revenges through "[a] thundering torrent of treacherous rain" (1) and lots of dust. The natural environment oscillates between the two extremes. Jocubus Nieuwoudt employs the same irregularity using rhyme scheme. In the third poem of the collaborative poem, Nieuwoudt uses irregular rhyming pairs such as "forgotten/forsaken", "groans/clouds", "apart/separate", "children/ forsaken". Nieuwoudt uses irregular rhyme to overturn focus on industry and agriculture at the expense of Mother Nature. The neglected tree in his poem symbolises Mother Nature. The persona says after a million years, "the tree stands no longer" and a heavy smog hangs low/ on the graveyard" (2). The death of the trees symbolises total pollution of our natural environment.

Finally, poems in *Best "New" African Poets 2017 Anthology* exhibit ecocriticism through the feelings, particularly mood and attitude. According to Mugubi feelings constitute an essential part of the content in literature (45). Antonio Garcia adopts a forthright attitude with regard to Donald Trump's dismissal of the Paris Treaty on Climate change. By saying "Trumped by backward thinking and derided" Garcia candidly tells off the opponents of the treaty. Mairosi uses a mournful tone and mood to underscore the demerits of ignoring the clarion call to control global warming. He writes, "2280 AD: RIP Human Race" (8). That Earth has been a free gift to humanity, but the "greed and recklessness" exhibited by the majority of the populace will bring humankind to final destruction. Mala employs a macabre tone to show the impact of human greed on Mother Nature and quality of life on the planet. In the poem "Humans For or Against Humans", Mala demonstrates how humanity's excesses have resulted in mass deaths "human skulls shattered" and "blood mixed marrow on roads" (13). The poet suggests that these human excesses have been extended to the destruction of Mother Nature. For example "set car tyres in wild flames that eject gases" (13) to destroy ozone.

In conclusion, selected poems in *Best "New" African Poets 2017 Anthology* abide by the tenets of ecocriticism to remind the audience to shun from human-centricism and shift the focus to conservation of Mother Nature. The ecological features of the poems stand out through the subjects expressed, poetic devices and the feelings depicted.

REFERENCES

Buell, L. (2005). *The Future of Environmental Criticism: environmental Crisis and Literary*

Imagination. Malden. MA: Blackwell Publishing.

Kibutu, J. (2012). The Celebration of Nature in East African Poets: A Focus on Kenya, Uganda

and Tanzania. MA Thesis. University of Nairobi.

Litcharts.   "Free   Verse   Definition." https://www.litcharts.com/literary-devices-and-terms/free-verse.

Mwanaka T. & Purificacao D. (Eds) 2018. *Best "New" African Poets 2017 Anthology.*

Chitugwiza. Mwanaka Media and Publishing. P. 1-25.

Mugubi J. (2017). Style in Literature. Nairobi: Royallite Publishers.

Sanders M. (2017). Historical Trends and Variability in Heat Waves in the United Kingdom.

Atmosphere   8.   10:   191-200. https://www.researchgate.net/publication/320178280_Historical_Trends_and_Variability_in_Heat_Waves_in_the_United_Kingdom.

Review of "beyond a distant edge" by Archie Swanson (Baldarchi Publishing; 2021)

Geoffrey Haresnape

Archie Swanson is issuing a third collection of poems in four years, and this during a time when the Covid pandemic has put a brake on so many things including literary activity. Readers who were impressed by *the stretching of my sky* (2018) and *the shores of years* (2019) will be glad to see this new arrival which displays the same adroit combination of visual and verbal material that characterized the earlier books. If the poet alluded to the elements of air and water in the titles of his earlier volumes, his *beyond a distant edge* now takes a leap beyond mere planetary phenomena into the depths of the multiverse itself: "is there a place beyond/in darkest space/beyond nebulae/beyond energized gases". is the question asked by the eponymous poem. Swanson exhibits a wish to explore "where our expansions have not reached...[a] place that is no place at all". It says much for his insatiable curiosity and helps us to understand how he can be compulsively active in the more knowable areas of history, geography, religion and the physical sciences.

For Swanson geography and history are linked. He seldom visits a place without telling us something of its past. He has moved freely around Southern Africa while at the same time making his roots known in the Karoo, the South Western District and the City of Cape Town. Sometimes his evocation of a locale can be linked to childhood memory. In 'the call box' the "china-hat roof and bright-red door" of a telephone booth suggests a stasis reassuring to a little boy in apartheid middle class Cape Town. A planted bomb totally destroys the booth leaving the message that the "Armed Struggle had come to call on white suburbia". Other poems document Swanson's connections with farming families and the quotidian minutiae of life in the town of George.

When abroad, he seems to gravitate to London, England, where he walks the "charter'd street" and interacts with those who show "Marks of weakness, marks of woe". Although – or perhaps because

– he is a South African, Swanson is no sufferer from the 'cultural cringe.' His independent attitude in the metropole is illustrated by 'chariot of fire,' which is a take on the Royal Airforce Bomber Command Memorial in Green Park and the sculpture of airmen which it contains. His approach to the airmen is ambivalent...he feels for the danger which they faced – "these men that went to war at twenty-two" – but sees them as representative of activities which led to the destruction of 353,000 German civilians during World War II. They are "memorialized in bronze yet cast in shame". Swanson's corrective to unreflecting national pride is the image of "a Dresden mother with her blackened pram / incinerated on the day the bombers came". In Egypt, Swanson transports himself imaginatively into ancient times, interpreting the experiences of hieratic rulers and officials, ('I Wahtye' and 'Amenhotep'). The uncertainty principle is shown to apply to their lives as much as it does to modern humans.

Religion is the provenance of many poems, either directly or implicitly. I choose one example in 'my Guernica,', Swanson's re-telling of the notorious atrocity which took place during the Spanish Civil War. How does one explain unmitigated oppression? With an urgency reminiscent of Uys Krige's 'Lied van die Fascistiese Bomwerpers' Swanson's poem highlights the mutilation and loss of life caused by the attack from the air. Where is true religion here? It may be found only in the selfless act of "Aronategui the priest" who died saving a child and in the bell of Santa Maria warning the town's citizens to flee from the bombing – unnoticed acts at a time when Franco was preaching 'n heilige oorlog' in the name of Spain's official Christianity. Among the other artistic portrayals of Guernica with which Swanson's interacts, is Pablo Picasso's renowned painting. Its austere tonalities are echoed in his wish to make his own depiction "grey on grey and white on black."

Swanson's verse techniques are arresting. A basic element is monologic narrative. The poet will meet someone in the street or describe a walk during a visit to a foreign city. He gives the details of the encounter or of the tour just as they are, but subtly guided by his gift for image-making. Sometimes in moments of heightened emotion the writing will be infused with regular rhythms or rhymes. Less frequently seen is his penchant for intense compression: e.g., 'Kalaghadi water hole' deals with a family relationship, tourism and big-game poaching all within six lines: "in the foreground /   my daughter is playing chess with her husband / in the distance / an elephant is drinking / ivory queen takes pawn / checkmate elephant".

I am particularly interested in Swanson's engagement with Concrete Poetry which Milton Williams describes as a form where "the manipulation of the word on the page...draws a larger picture of the action described" (*Patterns of Poetry*). George Herbert's 'Easter Wings' is the best-known poem of this kind in English but there have been 20th century practitioners like e cummings and Ezra Pound. Swanson's most consistently successful poem of this kind is 'hominid humanoid', the "automaton", with "solvent-fuelled stare" and "shuffling gait". Its shape on the page is established by means of skilful typography, two arms akimbo and legs reaching down to each clumsy "REBOOT". 'hominid humanoid' invites comparison with "one of the last Titanium Quartz Model G Robots" in the poem 'binary love.' This construct indulges in "a sort of clanky mechanical love" with a fellow machine: "I downloading you and you downloading me to the cloud".

Like everything else in these times, this collection bears the marks of Covid 19. The virus makes its presence felt in indirect ways in several poems. 'frog call' deals with its invasion of the planet full frontally. It was as if "the mouth of hell opened and death exhaled".

Responding to the pandemic in rhythm and image is not the least of the achievements in **beyond a distant edge.**

Geoffrey Haresnape
University of Cape Town Emeritus Professor of English and Creative Writing

How Mzinyathi brought the Zimbabwe case to the world: a review of "Under the steel yoke."

Lind Grant-Oyeye

In 1986, the world awakened to the strength of writing from African when Professor Wole Soyinka was awarded the Noble Laureate for literature. The Nobel committee's press release for the award highlighted the sense of urgency and the expression of human contact in his works. Thus, Soyinka communicated to the world the phenomenon of African oratory and storytelling: the wealth of history, struggles, and moments of triumph that color the arts in the African context.

Artists from across the continent have continued this tradition of expressing political, cultural, and economic urgency through art forms such as poetry that speak of history and circumstance. Artists, therefore, do not only speak of their personal truths but serve as media for the collective, telling the stories of communities and nations. The collection of poems "Under the steel yoke" by Jabulani Mzinyathi tells the emotive story of a people through an artist's voice. Published in 2018 by Mwanaka Media and Publishing, it is one of many literary offerings from Mzinyathi. He has contributed to anthologies and literary magazines, such as the Best New African Poets anthologies. He is the author of another full-length poetry book, "Rightful indignation."

The emotional and philosophical setting for the poems is Zimbabwe. The author takes the reader on a journey, moving swiftly through various aspects of political life in the region. It provides vivid imagery of what it means to exist in a place of political reflection and introspection while surrounded by dystopia. Divided into sections with sub-titles such as derailed leadership, fighting, ideals, and hoping, the poet provides a detailed account of political change, a sense of loss, a feeling of hope, and rhetorical questions everyday

385

people may ask at their dinner tables regarding the leadership of their country It also uses relatable metaphors. For example, "*Holding on*" uses a relay race as an analogy for political power transition. The speaker carefully asks what competition is this/ when there is no competitor. The reader is stylishly invited to ponder the political landscape, especially relating to electoral processes in the region.

The tone of the work is mainly urgent in nature, with occasional spurts of apparent resignation to divine intervention associated with Deus ex-Machina situations. This contrast is depicted in words such as "in the floods of terror we drown," which adds a layer of expediency to the poem "This time." . On the other hand, the poem "*Bitterness in my mouth* "calls for divine intervention, which the reader may interpret as resignation to fate. However, in the African context, however, calling on one's god may be deemed as being pro-active in the itself- a way of seeking direction for action. Furthermore, Subversion to the status quo is expressed adeptly in various aspects of the book, in straightforward and almost prose-like language while retaining its poetic characteristics. We refuse to be cannon fodder/ Refuse to be pawns in their games are the last lines of the poem *"The Exorcism,"* The speaker makes some of a call to action through self-declaration of a stance or action, eschewing passivity

This book demonstrates strong knowledge on the author's part of various socio-cultural issues and strengths in African society, such as the Zimbabwean experience. Imagery and metaphors are used, which in subtle ways highlight unique circumstances experienced by various groups, not necessarily directly related to political melancholy. "Once great among nations/ now become a widow." This line from the poem *"Bereaved"* uses the experience of widowhood as a metaphor for changes that can be devastating to a nation. There is a surreal feeling inviting one to question what it means to be a widow in Africa. How does a nation's perceived loss of glory compare with bereavement? The anchor poem "Under the steel yoke" borrows from the experience of farming and the use of yokes- a steel yoke being one that it is impossible to break free from without dire consequences. The writing style invites the reader to muse alongside the narrator on the possible outcomes of an impossible situation of being yoked with steel.

The writer uses several poetry forms and styles in the book. For example, in the poems *"Thoughts"* and *"lesson for the future,* "alliteration and internal rhymes are used effectively. In addition, individual poems appear as either narrative or lyrical, whereas as a collective, the book comes across like an epic poem broken into six sections. Finally, the writer continuously interweaves the story of the Zimbabwean political experience put forward as the past, the present, and the future. Although a few of the poems run the risk of being perceived as diatribes, they are stylishly presented, and the context dares the reader to think of a poetic way to depict real-life experiences of violence.

"Under the steel yoke" is a book of poetry written by an author with varied life experiences, such as working in his country's educational and judicial sectors. It draws from a wealth of mundane encounters and unique experiences of a nation. It questions the leadership styles and political uncertainty while expressing some hope, especially in the younger generation. The lines of the last poem in the book," The sun will set Dawn will sprout/ Birds will twitter /The cocks will crow Each one to their chores /That is how it is/ That is how it should be The children will play/ On the road to the future "is a finale of how hope may exist alongside despair. The book provides a poetic introduction to the political struggles in Zimbabwe, enough to educate the reader on the circumstances while leaving a desire to find out more.

Bibliography

Press release. NobelPrize.org. Nobel Prize Outreach AB 2021. Wed.
29   Sep   2021.
https://www.nobelprize.org/prizes/literature/1986/press-release/

Oliver Schreiner Prize for Poetry 2020 – Review
Prof Rosemary Gray; Prof Ivan Rabinowitz; Ms Claudia Fratini

Reviewing poetry is seldom a task to be taken lightly, nor is it something that can be done hastily without thought or pondering. Poetry is that beast that lives in the realms of literature, colouring the landscape with its metaphors, metres, rhythms, rhymes and forms – a beast that many admire but few dare to approach. What is it about poetry that is simultaneously alienating and alluring? What is it that draws us towards it only to have us resist the connection like two positive poles of a magnet? Could it be that in those strangely arranged words that dance on the page, a choreography transcribed through spaces, dots, lines, swirls… 'silences', we are faced with images of life, lived experience that require of us a deeper connection with ourselves and others. Perhaps this need for a deeper connection with the other and 'Other' is something that has caused the gradual decline of poetry's interrogation in graduate and post-graduate literature programmes[1].

Academia has a great love of interrogating, discussing, pondering, ruminating over the concept of 'Other', as long as the other stays on the page, remains a theory, a 'something' to be analysed, dissected, catalogued through the safe lens of the microscope that is theory. Poetry on the other hand, demands of us an engagement not only of the mind by also of the spirit, the metres, rhythms and rhymes stirring-up something primordial in the reader, a connection, dare one say, to the Jungian manifestation of the Shadow[2] – that part of

---

[1] Although in recent years there has been a move towards promoting Creative Writing programmes that focus on poetry, the question remains, why promote these programmes when there is no active motion to create a platform for their study and promotion?

[2] [That] moral problem that challenges the whole ego-personality, for no one can become conscious of the shadow without considerable moral effort. To become conscious of it involves recognizing the dark

our lived experience that has no place in a fast-paced, rational, clinical existence where time-is-money and emotional rather than e-motional engagement is 'pointless' and 'wasteful'. A double-edged sword some might say, because in the same way that poetry challenges 'ego' in the reader, does it not amplify ego in the poet. A not so innocent question, but a question that needs asking and may in itself reflect the disconnect between today's world of profit and gain, and the appreciation of the artist / wordsmith / creator as prophet, storyteller, observer and interrogator of 'life' and raw 'lived-experience'. It is in this environment of disconnectedness that awards such as the Oliver Schreiner Prize for Poetry, become vital to sustaining the importance of this genre that reflects, in its alienating forms, our need to be reminded of what it means to be human.

This year's selection of anthologies has presented a kaleidoscopic view of 'humanity'. From experiences that touch the personal 'lived-experience', to elegiac journeys through landscapes and emotions – each body of work is testament, to a greater or lesser degree, to the role of the poet / wordsmith as prophet, storyteller, and observer of humanity. That said, as in every adjudication, a result needs to be reached, and as such, certain criteria needed to be met. Our point of departure was that we were looking at anthologies thus, the individual publications needed to reflect the poets ability to comfortably navigate different forms within the genre whilst still maintaining a narrative flow that pushed the boundaries of linguistic mastery and expressive imagery symphonically.

Overall Winner

Allan Kolski Horwitz – *The Colours of Our Flag*

Although recognised as a literary activist among aspirant creative writers, **Allan Kolski Horwitz** has not himself been recognized for his own literary expertise. This is his fourth anthology. It is commendable for its wide range of techniques, poetic timbre,

---

aspects of the personality as present and real. This act is the essential condition for any kind of self-knowledge. Carl Jung, *Aion* (1951)

390

polyphonic, contemporary vision, and historical reach. He experiments with various styles of versification, the mood shifting from tender to angry. The topics are wide ranging. Although somewhat spoilt by not too subtle sexual innuendos, the linguistic mastery and imagery manage to sustain a narrative flow that takes the reader on a guided psychedelic yet grounded journey of lived and living 'Africanness'. The opening poem, 'How Far' serves as both an introduction to the anthology and a challenge to the reader: "How far can I go with you / How far (ll.1-2) … I will show you / Once our horizons meet" (ll. 5-6).

Gritty but tender; aggrieved but optimistic; remote but intimate: from within an oxymoronic aesthetic, Allan Kolski Horwitz finds solace -- and, perhaps, absolution -- in the controlled cadences of poetry. The poems are both boisterous and graceful, quarried from detailed observation of human frailty as well as a yearning for an ever-elusive companionship. 'Bo Tree', for example, is a wonderfully understated meditation on the balm of reciprocity, 'when minerals in deep earth rise slowly' and 'the Bo bends to offer its medicine'. In 'Stoned Over Louis Botha', the imagery is stretched, wrenched, and enlarged in a Dylanesque ballad of urban torment, demonstrating the poet's desire to transcend the limitations of graphemic utterance. And in 'Seven Minutes Past Three' -- perhaps the centrepiece of the volume -- Horwitz dares to confront the unspeakable. There is conflict, fear, outrage, and prophesy, animated by the poet's refusal to yield to superfluities of diction. In poem after poem, the poet chronicles an outlaw space on the edge of civilization -- bullet-riddled, untouchable, lawless, polluted, sullied by craven ideologies. Yet in poem after poem, too, Horwitz allows the Bo tree to offer its vivifying fragrance, giving lyrical authority to experience.

Best Newcomer
Angifi Dladla – *Lament for Kofifi Macu*

Angifi Dladla in his work, *Lament for Kofifi Macu* presents himself as a voice that will certainly warrant attention in the future. His second anthology in English, *Lament for Kofifi Macu* presents images that speak of 'lived-experience', an uncomfortable reconciliation of that which is seen and heard outside with the reality of a fading 'new dawn'. There is an uneasiness in the poems, a resignation of fermented disillusionment with glittering promises and yearning to return to honest simplicity – emotions that come through in the poem, 'When I'm Gone'. Although the expression and flow in the poems is 'raw' and the imagery at times jarring, his work imparts a passionate intensity that render the poems 'real'. We look forward to reading and experiencing more of his works in English in the future.

Highly Commended
Naomi Nkealah – *And they call themselves feminists*
Naomi Nkealah – Similar to Dladla's collection of poems, Naomi Nkealah's poems are awash with unfettered passion – they shout out at the reader asking of him/her to closely question their 'feminist' leanings. Her poems are a 'moral challenge' to the all who read them to re-evaluate what it means to be 'woman'. By presenting this collection, Nkealah lays bare the inconsistencies in feminism's claims of 'liberation' - the poem 'MBA' in which she explores three words so often associated with the women 'unseen': "Molested ... Battered ... Abandoned", concludes with the lines, "MBA – is what we called her / a woman free by law / but chained by marriage" (ll. 16-18) is just one explores these contradictions. Her work comes highly commended as a voice of the unspoken.

Mmap New African Poets Series

If you have enjoyed *Best New African Poets 2021 Anthology* consider these other fine books in **New African Poets Series** from *Mwanaka Media and Publishing:*

I Threw a Star in a Wine Glass by Fethi Sassi
Best New African Poets 2017 Anthology by Tendai R Mwanaka and Daniel Da Purificacao
Logbook Written by a Drifter by Tendai Rinos Mwanaka
Mad Bob Republic: Bloodlines, Bile and a Crying Child by Tendai Rinos Mwanaka
Zimbolicious Poetry Vol 1 by Tendai R Mwanaka and Edward Dzonze
Zimbolicious Poetry Vol 2 by Tendai R Mwanaka and Edward Dzonze
Zimbolicious: An Anthology of Zimbabwean Literature and Arts, Vol 3 by Tendai Mwanaka
Under The Steel Yoke by Jabulani Mzinyathi
Fly in a Beehive by Thato Tshukudu
Bounding for Light by Richard Mbuthia
Sentiments by Jackson Matimba
Best New African Poets 2018 Anthology by Tendai R Mwanaka and Nsah Mala
Words That Matter by Gerry Sikazwe
The Ungendered by Delia Watterson
Ghetto Symphony by Mandla Mavolwane
Sky for a Foreign Bird by Fethi Sassi
A Portrait of Defiance by Tendai Rinos Mwanaka
Zimbolicious: An Anthology of Zimbabwean Literature and Arts, Vol 4 by Tendai Mwanaka and Jabulani Mzinyathi
When Escape Becomes the only Lover by Tendai R Mwanaka
ويَسهَرُ اللّيلُ عَلى شَفَتي...وَالغَمَام by Fethi Sassi
A Letter to the President by Mbizo Chirasha
This is not a poem by Richard Inya

393

Pressed flowers by John Eppel
Righteous Indignation by Jabulani Mzinyathi:
Blooming Cactus By Mikateko Mbambo
Rhythm of Life by Olivia Ngozi Osouha
Travellers Gather Dust and Lust by Gabriel Awuah Mainoo
Chitungwiza Mushamukuru: An Anthology from Zimbabwe's Biggest Ghetto Town by Tendai Rinos Mwanaka
Zimbolicious: An Anthology of Zimbabwean Literature and Arts, Vol 5 by Tendai Mwanaka
Because Sadness is Beautiful? by Tanaka Chidora
Of Fresh Bloom and Smoke by Abigail George
Shades of Black by Edward Dzonze
Best New African Poets 2020 Anthology by Tendai Rinos Mwanaka, Lorna Telma Zita and Balddine Moussa
This Body is an Empty Vessel by Beaton Galafa
Between Places by Tendai Rinos Mwanaka

Soon to be released
Zimbolicious: An Anthology of Zimbabwean Literature and Arts, Vol 6 by Tendai Mwanaka and Chenjerai Mhondera
Denga reshiri yokunze kwenyika by Fethi Sassi

https://facebook.com/MwanakaMediaAndPublishing/